gift

W9-AHC-644

OTHER TITLES BY RICHARD POLLAK

The Creation of Dr. B: A Biography
of Bruno Bettelheim

The Episode

Up Against Apartheid: The Role and the Plight
of the Press in South Africa

Stop the Presses, I Want to Get Off!, *editor*

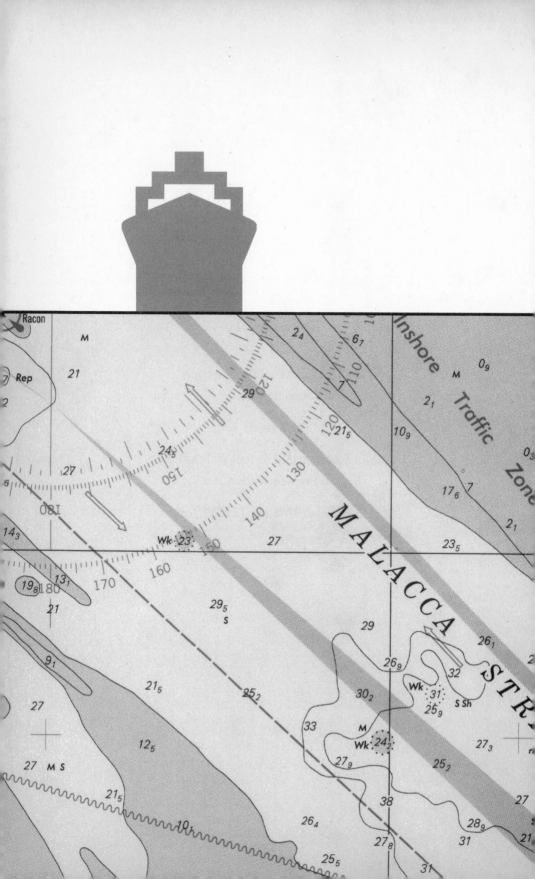

THE
COLOMBO
BAY

Richard Pollak

SIMON & SCHUSTER

New York   London   Toronto   Sydney

SIMON & SCHUSTER
Rockefeller Center
1230 Avenue of the Americas
New York, NY 10020

SIMON & SCHUSTER and colophon are registered trademarks
of Simon & Schuster, Inc.

For information about special discounts for bulk purchases,
please contact Simon & Schuster Special Sales:
1-800-456-6798 or business@simonandschuster.com.

Designed by Jeanette Olender
Map design by Jeffrey L. Ward

9-10

Manufactured in the United States of America

10 9 8 7 6 5 4 3 2 1

Library of Congress Cataloging-in-Publication Data
Pollak, Richard.
The Colombo Bay / Richard Pollak.
p.   cm.
Includes bibliographical references and index.
1. Colombo Bay (Ship).   2. Container ships.   I. Title.
HE566.C6P65 2004
387.2'45—dc22   2003058688

ISBN 0-7432-0073-X

The author and publisher gratefully acknowledge permission to reprint material
from the following work: "Cargoes," in *Poems*, by John Masefield (New York: The
Macmillan Company, 1953). Reprinted with the permission of the Society of Authors,
Literary Representative of the Estate of John Masefield.

FOR DIANE

CARGOES

Quinquireme of Nineveh from distant Ophir,
Rowing home to haven in sunny Palestine,
With a cargo of ivory,
And apes and peacocks,
Sandalwood, cedarwood, and sweet white wine.

Stately Spanish galleon coming from the Isthmus,
Dipping through the Tropics by the palm-green shores,
With a cargo of diamonds,
Emeralds, amethysts,
Topazes, and cinnamon, and gold moidores.

Dirty British coaster with a salt-caked smoke stack,
Butting through the Channel in the mad March days,
With a cargo of Tyne coal,
Road-rails, pig-lead,
Firewood, iron-ware, and cheap tin trays.

—John Masefield

PROLOGUE

I am a landlubber. Though I grew up hard by Lake Michigan, the mighty ore boats on the horizon did not make me yearn to ship out for Duluth. My heroes were not Horatio Hornblower and John Paul Jones but Superman, Batman, and Robin, who dispatched not pirates but the bad guys of Metropolis and Gotham City, gritty urban realms like my own Chicago. As a teenager, I did read *Kon-Tiki, The Cruel Sea,* and *The Caine Mutiny,* and struggled with *Moby-Dick,* all good yarns but not tales that made me wish that I had sailed the Pacific on a homemade balsa-log raft, or dodged U-boat torpedoes in the North Atlantic aboard the *Compass Rose,* or faced a typhoon while the batty Captain Queeg worried his steel balls. Nor did standing on the pitching deck of the *Pequod* in pursuit of a great white whale seem all that much fun. For all their drama and instruction, these stories seemed less exotic than, well, damp. My nautical adventures rarely extended beyond the ditties of *H.M.S. Pinafore* and brief rowboat excursions on the lagoon in Jackson Park, during which at least one oar often floated away, leaving my father to pole in pursuit with the other one like a gondolier possessed. In subsequent decades I went sailing and canoeing a few times, pleasant enough diversions in balmy weather but not pastimes that moved me to share Water Rat's view, as imparted to Toad, that "there is *nothing*—absolutely nothing—half so much worth doing as simply messing about in boats."

When I reached my sixties, however, the Hudson River traffic beneath the windows of our Manhattan apartment began to exert an unexpected pull, especially when vessels paused below. One typical barge was about a city block long, her flat deck broken by several hatches and two or three pieces of spiky machinery. Her anchor line stretched taut toward the George Washington Bridge as the ebb tide pulled at her in vain. A tugboat tended her, handsome in a fresh suit of light gray with white trim, her stern resting on a shimmering golden runner thrown across the river by the setting sun. I got out our opera glasses, knowing that they never enhanced these boats as well as they did Dawn Upshaw; I could not make out the name of either the tug or its charge and vowed once again to buy a telescope and tripod, or at least a proper pair of binoculars.

There appeared to be no activity on either vessel, nothing that would explain why they had lingered. A brisk wind blew from the west, but there was no sign or prediction of a storm from which the tandem might have sought refuge in the river. Perhaps they were just taking a few well-earned hours off, or were making "a schedule adjustment," as the announcers explain when the Number 1 subway train tarries at Times Square. By late the next morning they had left. Had they gone upriver or into the harbor? Was the boat loaded, if so with what? How many men (and women?) were aboard, who were they, what did they do? To my surprise, I was pondering these questions a lot of late, even wondering where the Blue Circle Cement barge went on its frequent trips past our windows and, more tantalizing, what seafaring was like beyond the gentle concourse of the Hudson, past the gateway of the Verrazano-Narrows Bridge, out on Melville's "unhooped oceans of this planet."

This last question may be nothing more than confirmation of Ishmael's conviction that almost all men in their degree will at some time or other cherish the ocean. Or perhaps I had been bobbing too long in the harbor of Social Security and needed to slip anchor for a while. Whatever the reason, I had developed a serious itch, which only intensified after I began talking to a new friend, Jeremy Nixon. As a boy in the south of England, Jeremy did hear the call of the sea and, at eighteen, sailed as an apprentice on a general cargo vessel. Now, at forty, he still had something of the British tar about him, especially when he recalled steering 12,000 deadweight tons into Maputo, Mozambique, on a Christmas Day wrapped in ninety-degree heat and soaking humidity; or fending off thieves and vendors as they tried to throw grappling hooks over the rail when his ship was moored during a passage through the Suez Canal; or watching whales breach in the Pacific and an albatross circle for days over his vessel's wake.

Jeremy was now a senior vice president of P&O Nedlloyd, whose fleet of 146 container ships plies some seventy trade routes connecting more than 250 major ports in 120 countries. He is normally a cheerful bloke, but over lunch one day he suggested in somewhat aggrieved tones that merchant vessels and those who man them deserve a bit more attention and respect than they get, given that they are the lifeline of the globalization that millions of consumers depend on daily for thousands of goods, essential and frivolous.

Certainly I had never given this maritime universe much thought. When I went to Morris Bros. on the Upper West Side, I hoped to emerge with the right size sweat socks; where they came from and how they got to the rack had never seemed pressing matters. Nor when I dug into New Zealand lamb had I ever speculated about its refrigerated transit from those distant islands. I knew vaguely that containerization had revolutionized the transportation of goods beginning in the late sixties and that trucks hauling the modular boxes on the interstates tended to suck imperiously at us four-doors as they passed. At the minor league ballpark in Syracuse, New York, I had watched a Conrail double-stack train rumble beyond the left-field fence in counterpoint to "Take Me Out to the Ball Game," requiring the entire seventh inning to pass. The scores of containers between engine and caboose were headed east, probably to Boston or New York, to be loaded onto a container ship, of which it turns out there are more than 7,000 moving across the oceans every day. These vessels have a nominal capacity of more than 7 million "twenty equivalent units," the standard industry measurement that assigns one TEU to a twenty-foot-long container and two to a forty-footer, most of them eight feet high and eight feet wide. Some 90 percent of the world's cargo by value moves in these boxes, though the U.S. shipping industry no longer plays a significant role in this trade; foreign-built and -owned vessels and foreign officers and crews now deliver the billions of dollars' worth of foreign-made goods that touch every aspect of daily life in North America.

In 2002 some 6 million containers arrived at U.S. ports carrying products ranging from plastic patio furniture and frozen beef to chinos and Game Boys—and sometimes stowaways, who have promised the Chinese Snakeheads and Asia's other criminal gangs thousands of dollars to smuggle them into the West, and who arrive either starving or dead. "Did you know that piracy, too, is a growing menace?" Jeremy asked, inducing visions of hooks and eye patches, and of walking the plank at the point of a cutlass while sharks circled below. I resisted the impulse to say, "Shiver me timbers." Instead, I asked if he would arrange passage on a P&O Nedlloyd container ship; he said, Done.

When I told my wife and daughter of this plan, I expected a few indulgent smiles but not quite so much hilarity. We had just sat down to a restaurant meal, and I already had complained to the waiter that the music was too loud. "Dad," said Amanda, who had been coping with such grousing since her now distant adolescence, "what will you do if the sound of the engine drives you crazy, tell the captain to turn it off?" Diane laughed, her eyebrows signaling that after two decades of marriage she knew a distaste for intrusive music hardly exhausted the catalog of my crotchets. Another, she reminded me, was my tendency when out of town without her to come home a day or two earlier than scheduled; she noted that should this urge come upon me in the middle of the Indian Ocean, evacuation helicopters might be in short supply. There followed some merry observations about "guy things" and the suggestion that perhaps we should construct a widow's walk outside our eleventh-floor windows. Buoyed by these loving endorsements, I presented arms for the jabs Jeremy recommended—against typhoid, tetanus, and hepatitis—and took out a short-term insurance policy that covered up to $100,000 in medical costs and $75,000 for emergency medical evacuation, with an extra $7,500 thrown in should my remains require what the policy termed "repatriation."

Then, for reasons that remain cloudy, I watched a video of *The Perfect Storm*. I had read Sebastian Junger's book but had forgotten the cameo role played by the *Contship Holland,* which just managed to survive the cauldron of winds and water that ultimately sank the swordfish boat *Andrea Gail*. Junger writes that the 10,000-ton vessel "took waves over her decks that peeled land/sea containers open like sardine cans, forty feet above the surface. . . . When [she] finally limped into port several days later, one of her officers stepped off and swore he'd never set foot on another ship again." Thirty-six containers had gone over the side, a scene re-created in the movie with special effects of persuasive verisimilitude. I took comfort in the knowledge that this was, after all, the "storm of the century," the result of a freak confluence of deadly weather systems way back in 1991. Then I recalled Jeremy's descriptions of gales that recently had roughed up two ships bound for Seattle, sending scores of containers overboard and damaging many more. He also had mentioned in a recent email from Taipei, where he had gone on business, that a typhoon was heading his way. He typed no smiley emoticon, but his words seemed to carry a certain bravado, the sort of blithe do-your-worst view of nasty blows that sets mariners apart from us mere mortals. Not long after receiving this communication, I boarded a jet at Newark International Airport and flew to Hong Kong, where two days later I was to join P&O Nedlloyd's *Colombo Bay* for a five-week voyage back to New York via the Suez Canal.

I woke up the next morning at five in the Excelsior Hotel and tried to go back to sleep, but the Manhattan clock behind my eyes read 5:00 PM. I was wide awake, hungry, and full of anticipation for the adventure ahead. Beneath the sixteenth-floor window, vessels of all shapes and sizes crisscrossed Victoria Harbor in the gray light. I knew jet lag would touch down in a few hours, but right now I felt energized, impatient not to be sailing for two days. I ordered breakfast, took a shower, and unpacked my laptop. The local access number worked instantly, and down came half a dozen email messages, two from Diane. "Hi Sweetie!" began the first, written while I was still in the air and telling of her day practicing the Mozart piano concerto she was preparing to perform and of teaching her students, of the fierce thunderstorm that had just blown through New York, of the typhoon near Japan she had worried about until she saw how far it was from Hong Kong. "Love ya, and have a ball," it ended.

"By now you may have heard," the second began, "that the World Trade Center has been attacked again, catastrophically, and both towers have collapsed." Collapsed? The Pentagon had been struck by a plane, too? Diane had never been given to practical jokes, but this had to be one, an ill-considered reminder that in 1995, when I was in Israel without her, Timothy McVeigh had made his statement in Oklahoma City. Room service arrived; the waiter bowed and withdrew before I could fumble for a tip or think to add it to the bill. "This is really bad, there must be thousands dead." Thousands? She assured me that she was safe in the apartment and that Amanda and her boyfriend, Gustav, were at home in Brooklyn unharmed. I turned on CNN and watched in numb disbelief as the planes crashed and the towers imploded again and again, and the TV anchors and correspondents tried in vain to seem less stunned than their viewers. Thousands? Yes.

I muted the sound and, unable to keep my eyes off the screen, mispunched Diane's number twice. I forced my back to the set and tried again: 9 for the outside line, eight digits to access AT&T, ten more for her number—my right hand now trembling so badly that I had to put down the phone so I could steady it with my left—and another fourteen for my calling card. Thirty-three numbers to produce a recorded voice announcing what I had assumed—all circuits were busy. As the tone beeped, I realized Diane's email had not mentioned Merle, my first wife, Amanda's mother; her office was only a few blocks from the towers. I fumbled at the keypad again and again, a half dozen times in the next thirty minutes, then gave up, envisioning overloaded communications satellites popping like balloons.

I sent Diane an email saying I was coming home, though even as I typed the television voices made clear that all planes in the United States had been grounded and all airports locked down. Okay, I would fly from Hong Kong to Canada, to Toronto or Montreal, and take Avis or Amtrak to New York; surely that shouldn't be too difficult. Repeated calls to five airlines produced busy signals as the television continued loud and clear, its smoking pictures less credible with each repetition. I sought refuge in the mundane conventions of journalism, speculating about how the *New York Times* was covering the cataclysm, as if knowing—or just imagining it—would somehow make the "story," so cinematically preposterous on TV, real. How many reporters and editors had the paper assigned? Was my friend Terry Pristin one of them; if so, what "angle" was she chasing? It was still September 11 in Manhattan, 7:00 PM now, plenty of time left to come up with tomorrow's page-one banner. What would it be? How could the paper sum up the day's horror in the haiku of a headline? What photos would they run under it?

The phone's bell pricked this rumination. Hearing Diane's strained voice and description of the carnage in Lower Manhattan only reinforced my determination to return as soon as possible, to hug her and Amanda and be enfolded by them. I also needed to *do* something, volunteer at the site, give blood, try to comfort the families of victims, anything. This was no time to go larking about the high seas on a project that now seemed indulgent and, worse, irrelevant. With typical calm, Diane said that everyone she had talked to was feeling the same way about their work, was suffering the same paralysis. Her own practicing seemed pointless; she could not stay at the keyboard for more than twenty minutes without getting up to have yet another CNN session or to wander from room to room as if some explanation for the havoc might be found in a closet or under the kitchen table.

She assured me this despondency would pass. Besides, the last place I belonged was on an airplane, even one bound for Canada; I would be safe on the ship, should embark as planned. When I finally talked to Amanda (who said Merle, too, was safe), she urged the same course, as did Jeremy in a message to P&O Nedlloyd's Hong Kong office; I could always fly home when the ship reached Singapore, he wrote. Still, I waffled, wallowing in a trough of isolation and helplessness. The next day I reached Diane at Sarabeth's Kitchen, a neighborhood restaurant where she was having lunch with our old friend Irene Patner, whose vital, life-embracing husband recently had dropped dead of a heart attack. As my vacillation poured into Diane's cell phone, this tough new widow got the drift and shouted over the din, "Of course he should go!" Ishmael also gave no quarter. If I had grown grim about the mouth, if it was now a damp, drizzly September in my soul, if I wanted to knock off the terrorists' turbans—and I did—he also recommended shipping out.

CHAPTER ONE

A labyrinth of roads and roundabouts leads to Hong Kong's Stonecutters terminal, where thousands of containers rise up to seven high in a vast canyon land of international commerce. The *Colombo Bay* has just arrived at this sprawling port from Kao-hsiung, Taiwan, after a twelve-day crossing of the Pacific from Seattle. Three giant gantry cranes loom above, yanking boxes from the ship with noisy clanks, pulling them up and across her deck, and dropping them with an echoing clatter onto idling trucks queued up on the quay. From the waterline, the jet-black hull and gleaming white accommodation superstructure near the stern rise fifteen stories to the bridge and monkey island above. She is some 105 feet wide and more than 900 feet long. Writers forever measure such lengths by noting that three football fields could be laid out on the deck. I prefer the less brutal pastime, so imagine Barry Bonds nailing one of Roger Clemens's heaters in Yankee Stadium; the baseball would have to travel over the centerfield scoreboard and well into the Bronx to match the *Colombo Bay*'s length. She weighs 60,000 deadweight tons and can carry a maximum of 4,200 TEUs stacked below and above deck, the boxes on top turning her into an elongated Rubik's Cube. There are larger container ships, and much bigger supertankers; still, moving up the wobbly gangway, I feel like a Lilliputian clambering onto Gulliver.

Matt Mullins, the first officer, greets me at the top, reports that the captain is ashore, and takes me up in the elevator to my quarters on C deck. Speculation about conditions onboard had proved irresistible for several fellow terrestrials, who cheerfully predicted seasickness, rations of hardtack, bouts of scurvy, and that I would be sharing a shoe box with half a dozen snoring seamen, all of us tossing in spine-bending double-decker bunks, if not hammocks. A French friend wondered with some *alarme* if there would be flush toilets. I was not sure what to expect but assumed that the *Colombo Bay* was not the *Love Boat* and was prepared to share quarters and make do with a concavity of springs. What I found was a firm double bed neatly made up with a sheet and pillowcases of pale yellow and a matching duvet. The cabin is mine alone, about sixteen by eighteen feet, with cream-colored walls and beige carpeting. Across from the bed is a desk on which rests an intraship telephone and, to my surprise, a small television set. The desk is of wood covered with a Swedish modern grainy laminate, as is the cabinet above it, a closet to its left, the couch and table to its right, and the night tables flanking the bed, on one of which rest two fresh towels and two bars of Lux soap. A desk chair and an armchair with Stickley pretensions complete the furnishings. Four double-bulb fluorescent ceiling lights and a single fluorescent bulb over the bed promise ample illumination.

All is shipshape clean, including the bathroom, which comes complete with a flowered shower curtain. I might be in a commodious, utilitarian motel room were it not for the seat that hinges down in the shower and the chains hanging beneath the table and chairs ready to be hooked to latches in the floor, hedges against stormy weather. Two large, rectangular portholes look forward, the view blocked by the containers stacked only a few feet away. As consolation, the wall by the bed offers *Veduta del Pantheon di Agrippa oggi Chiesa di S. Maria dei Martiri*, a somber engraving by one Luigi Rossini.

On the desk are three pages about the *Colombo Bay,* one of them listing the names and ranks of the ship's company of eight officers and thirteen crew, which seems a remarkably small number for such a large vessel. I am surprised, too, to see my name at the bottom of the column, along with that of a Mrs. E. Davies, both of us identified as supernumeraries, a term I associate with opera walk-ons; in my case at least, it may mean, as the dictionary puts it, "someone exceeding what is necessary, required or desired." The other sheets advise that the *Colombo Bay* is seven years old, is registered in London, and was built by Ishikawajima-Harima Heavy Industries Co., Ltd., in Aichi, Japan; that the ship's diesel fuel weighs almost 6,000 tons when all bunkers are full; that breakfast is from 0730 to 0755 and from 0830 to 0855, lunch from 1200 to 1230, dinner from 1800 to 1830, and tea and snacks are available in the officers' pantry, presumably at any hour; that the officers' laundry is just down the corridor from my cabin. The emergency signal is at least seven short ring-blasts followed by one prolonged ring-blast. At sea my emergency station is on the lee-side bridge wing, and my lifeboat station is Number 1. "We hope you have an enjoyable voyage," one page concludes. "If you require anything—please ask!" I make a note to ask about the location of lifeboat station Number 1.

If I needed any evidence that containers play a central role in my own life, it now spills into the cabin. One blue Brooks Brothers button-down shirt, made in Thailand; gray dress slacks, from India; blue Helly Hansen rain slicker, Sri Lanka; blue rubber rain pants, Taiwan; red baseball cap, China; Panasonic CD player, Japan; CD pouch, China, Korea, Philippines, or Indonesia, take your choice; Bell and Sony tape recorders, China; Panasonic tapes, Japan; Olympus Infinity 5 camera, assembled in Hong Kong from parts made in Japan; Casio quartz travel clock, assembled in Thailand; Sanford Uni-Ball Onyx micro pens, Japan; IBM ThinkPad AC adapter, China; laptop carrying case, Indonesia; shoulder bag, Korea; garment bag, Taiwan. The red bathing suit, knit gloves, watch cap, Samsonite toilet kit, socks, yellow highlighter pens, and swimming goggles bear no indication of their provenance, but odds are that at least half these items were made in Asia, too. "What most North Americans don't understand," Jeremy had said in one of our first talks about this voyage, "is how reliant they have become on Asian products." And on imports from elsewhere: ThinkPad and its power cord and mouse, and Gillette razors, Mexico; khaki shorts, El Salvador; gray shorts, Guatemala; Van Heusen button-down shirt and Jockey shorts, Costa Rica; blue dress jacket and blue denim shirt, Canada; Sanita clogs, Denmark; blue woolen Lands' End sweater, Scotland. I made no effort to categorize items I didn't bring with me, but for the record the aforementioned Lux soap was made in Indonesia and the *Colombo Bay* herself, as noted, was made in Japan. Full disclosure: my Kodak film, Duracell batteries, Lands' End warm-up jacket, New Balance running shoes, black sweatpants, two belts, large brown suitcase, and Penguin paperback of *Moby-Dick* were Made in the USA.

I have brought along the book in part as penance. When Miss Drell assigned it at Hyde Park High School in 1951, its bulk seemed bigger and meaning more elusive than Ahab's quarry itself, leading me to harpoon the Classics Illustrated version to haul in the gist. I managed to get through college without taking another crack at the novel, though the 1956 film version gave a boost to my fledgling journalistic career. I was tapped to be the movie reviewer of the Amherst *Student* when my predecessor lost the post after praising Gregory Peck's performance in the title role. Now I am discovering this literary marvel for the first time, mesmerized by the yarn, yes, but more by Melville's astonishing ambition, his depth of insight, and his muscular prose, which famously reaches biblical and Shakespearean heights. "Merchant ships are but extension bridges," he writes, amplifying this scorn when Ishmael tries to impress one of the two principal owners of the *Pequod,* the good Quaker Captain Peleg.

Dost know nothing at all about whaling, I dare say—eh?

Nothing, Sir; but I have no doubt I shall soon learn. I've been several voyages in the merchant service, and I think that—

Marchant service be damned. Talk not that lingo to me. Dost see that leg?—I'll take that leg away from thy stern, if ever thou talkest of the marchant service to me again. Marchant service indeed!

The other *vade mecum* I have unpacked is an edition of *A Personal Record* and *The Mirror of the Sea,* which brim with the clear-eyed affection for the merchant service of Józef Teodor Konrad Korzeniowski, who ran away from the Polish Ukraine at seventeen and served on merchant ships for two decades before settling in London to become Joseph Conrad. Unlike *Heart of Darkness* and his other fiction, which dwell on man in extreme situations struggling between good and evil, these memoirs are full of wry charm and a contagious enthusiasm for the seafarer's life. He writes of "the magic ring of the horizon," the "white fillet of tumbling foam under the bow," the tall masts that support the balanced planes that, "motionless and silent, catch from the air the ship's motive power, as if it were a gift from Heaven vouchsafed to the audacity of man." Sailing is an art, ships courageous before the wind gods that would do them in. Not so the infernal steamship, which he views with disdain. "The machinery, the steel, the fire, the steam have stepped in between the man and the sea. A modern fleet of ships does not so much make use of the sea as exploit a highway." So, Melville dismisses the *Colombo Bay*'s merchant calling, Conrad the vessel herself; still, I welcome these crusty cabinmates.

I have just placed the two books on the night table when Shakeel Azim knocks on the door and offers a quick tour. He is the second officer, boyish looking despite his forty-eight years and thick, black mustache, and smart in his summer uniform of black trousers and short-sleeved, open-necked white shirt with the two gold bars of his rank on the epaulets. He asks where I am from, and when I say New York he shakes his head and asks if my family is all right. "Terrible, terrible, these people are madmen." His dismay seems genuine, but with some embarrassment I find myself wondering just where he is from, whether he is a Muslim, and what his sympathies really are. He explains that the decks descend from the bridge in alphabetical order, that the British officers and Filipino crew all have their own quarters, and that he and four other junior officers are my neighbors on C deck. Most of the crew bunks on D; the ship's laundry, hospital, and book and video library are on E; a spacious galley is on F, flanked by almost identical dining rooms, each with the same imposing, official color photograph of Queen Elizabeth looking properly solemn and regal in a floor-length white satin dress, blue sash, and bejeweled necklace and crown. "We call F the food deck and E the entertainment deck," Shakeel says, adding with a shy smile that while I am onboard C will stand for club class.

Down one more flight is the upper deck, the ship's first continuous watertight deck; it houses the engine control room, the ship's office, and the refrigeration lockers for stores. Shakeel decides that the machinery spaces below can wait, and we ascend in the elevator to A deck, where we run into the captain, Peter Davies, just returned from shore with my fellow supernumerary, his wife, Elizabeth, who has flown to Hong Kong from their home near Newcastle to join the ship. After cordial introductions (he pronounces his name "Davis"), he asks for my passport; I hand it over wondering when I will see it again and realize that for the first time since my army days in the late fifties I am under someone's command.

We sail just before 1900 hours, on September 13, gently pulled away from the berth by a tug that nudges us into the harbor, her laboring engine churning up a ferocious foam until, after about fifteen minutes, she slips away and leaves us to our own power. The evening is hot and sticky, the air thick with pollution; "fragrant harbor," the Cantonese meaning of Hong Kong, has not applied for some years now. We are under the temporary guidance of a harbor pilot, whose forerunners have been navigating the channels, shoals, tides, and currents in and near ports since at least 500 BC, when *The Periplous of Scylax of Caryanda,* a comprehensive pilot guide for the Mediterranean starting at the mouth of the Nile, was written. Unlike Captain Davies, formal in his summer whites, the young Chinese pilot looks, in his sandals, wrinkled shorts, and soiled shirt, as if he had just rushed to work after an afternoon of gardening. His competence is plain, though, as he surveys our path and gives periodic orders to the Filipino able seaman at the helm, which at about a foot in diameter looks like the steering wheels at game arcades rather than a mechanism for prompting the *Colombo Bay*'s rudder, a thirty-foot-high steel fin that weighs seventy tons. Captain Davies, also known as master, remains in the background while the pilot makes marginal course and speed adjustments as we inch through the harbor, threading among other container ships and tankers, ferries and barges, as smaller craft scoot around us like models on the Central Park boat pond operated by remote control from the shore.

The pilot departs after about an hour, riding down in the elevator to the upper deck and descending the sloping gangway, now suspended many feet above the water like an unfinished stairway. At the bottom he swings onto a rope ladder and lowers himself onto the deck of the pilot boat keeping pace beside us. Pilots leave and board ships this way thousands of times each day and night in ports throughout the world, moving up and down the swaying rungs like circus aerialists, the foul and treacherous waters their only net.

We are pushing out of the Pearl River Delta, the main sluice for China's flood of exports, a region roughly the size of Connecticut that stretches east to west across the estuary from Macau to Hong Kong and some eighty miles upriver into Guangdong Province. It was here in what is now Dongguan city that the imperial commissioner Lin Zexu ordered the destruction of more than 2 million pounds of opium in 1839, initiating the opium wars that forced

China to open its doors to foreign trade and investment. Now Dongguan is just one of the many manufacturing hives that dot the province, where scores of factories daily ship hundreds of containers by truck and barge to Stonecutters' and half a dozen other terminals only a few hours away.

In 2001 these docks handled some 25 million TEUs, about the same number processed by all U.S. ports combined. The Pearl River quays account for some 40 percent of China's exports, and more than a third of the goods flowing out of the delta—6,000 containers a day—are bound, like those on the *Colombo Bay,* for the U.S. market, contributing to a persistent trade deficit with China that in 2002 totaled more than $100 billion. China's exports to the United States grew by 20 percent during the year, and the country is soon expected to surpass Mexico for the number-two export spot, behind only Canada, as the roar of the sluice increases with each passing month. There is talk of constructing a fifteen-mile bridge-tunnel between Macau and Hong Kong's Lantau Island, with a new deepwater terminal near the Macau end to accommodate manufacturers on the southwest side of the delta, which over the years has lagged well behind the northeast bank in output. The delta's commercial engine is evident in the water traffic all around us, but as night falls the running lights of these vessels string the outer harbor with a glimmering serenity.

A crewman pulls a floor-to-ceiling curtain across the width of the bridge, blotting out the illumination around the communications area, weather chart table, and small galley at the rear, and creating a darkened stage on which Captain Davies now stars, delivering his lines in polite, uninflected tones.

"One-hundred and forty-nine degrees, Helmsman."

"One-hundred and forty-nine degrees, Captain."

"Thank you."

Insistent radio voices impinge on this colloquy, a vexed Greek chorus whose message sounds urgent but is made unintelligible (to me at least) by the crackle of static. With its two radar screens and other glowing panels, the bridge is the center of a galaxy that extends out to the lights of passing ships, the glitter of Hong Kong, and the canopy of moon and stars. For a better look, I go onto the starboard wing, one of the two outdoor porches that flank the wheelhouse, and am mugged by the clammy night, smacked with the realization that the land is falling away, that I am heading into the South China Sea at this awful moment in my city halfway around the world. I lean on the rail and try to take comfort in the surrounding shimmer, but the television pictures keep intruding, along with a certainty that the terrorists will strike New York again at any moment.

This is crazy. I never should have sailed. I belong with Diane and Amanda. We'll be in Singapore in less then a week. I'll fly home from there.

Get a grip, Pollak. This trip was your idea. See it through like a big boy. Diane and Amanda are strong; they'll be fine.

But . . .

No buts, just do it!

I whisper this exchange into the wind, like an actor rehearsing dialogue sotto voce on the Broadway bus, then look around, relieved to see that everyone is inside the bridge's air-conditioned cocoon. It is almost 2300, and I'm exhausted. I step back into the chill, say good night to Captain Davies, and en route to the stairs check out the closet-size galley behind the curtain. On the counter is a bubbling electric kettle and a selection of Yellow Label Lipton Tea, Nescafé, Cadbury's cocoa, Taster's Choice instant decaf, and a round tin, above which a sign reads: "Please Reseal the Cookies After You Open As They Go Soft. Ta, The Cookie Monster." I take a cookie, close the tin, and slip down to C deck like a guilty six-year-old.

After breakfast the next morning, the crew gathers in the lounge across from their dining room so Captain Davies can introduce me. I tell them I am writing a book about this voyage because I think the work they do is important and too little known. They nod and smile.

Any questions? They shake their heads and smile, looking eager to get on with their duties. "Call me Dick," I urge, clumsily. As they file out, two or three say, "Welcome aboard, Dick," stressing the name as if it were my rank. At 1730 the captain and other officers gather in their lounge with Elizabeth for predinner drinks. They seem a little more curious about my mission than the crew, but not much, perhaps distracted by P&O Nedlloyd's request that its ships join the rest of the world this day in mourning the terrorists' victims. At 1800 Captain Davies asks for three minutes of silence. Shakeel and two or three other officers seem to be praying, and their subsequent commiseration leaves me fighting back tears, not the persona I had hoped to present at my first meal among these seamen. I make a minimum of small talk, quick work of the roast beef, skip the "sweet," and am in bed shortly after 1900.

I awake to a travel alarm clock that reads 0220 and a wall clock frozen at 0200. I get up and climb the stairs to the bridge, where Shakeel is standing the midnight to 0400 watch. He makes me a cup of tea and explains that the ship's clock is being "retarded" an hour so we'll be in phase with the time at our next port, Laem Chabang, in Thailand. The sea is calm, as it has been since we left Hong Kong; the vibrations of the engine provide a far greater sensation than the feel of the ocean, which is virtually nil as the *Colombo Bay* cuts through the South China Sea at twenty-three knots. This is her maximum speed, and the huge ship seems to race through the dark water, though a fit cyclist could pedal at this rate of twenty-six miles per hour. Shakeel turns up the BBC World Service on the shortwave radio, the British voices reporting, with a welcome lack of histrionics, on the rising death toll in New York and Washington, and the speculation about retaliation against the Taliban and Al Qaeda in Afghanistan. He sees that I am worried and draws my attention to the crescent moon on our port side; it hangs just above the horizon and, like Jupiter, Cirrus, Venus, Vega, and the other celestial bodies Shakeel identifies, is luminous in a night sky now free from pollution's scrim. For a moment the tranquil scene banishes thoughts of terrorists; then Shakeel speaks of his mother.

Her name is Zhida, and in 1948, when she was sixteen and pregnant with her first child, she migrated to Pakistan, the Islamic state created the year before by the British partition of India. The trains carrying Muslim refugees were often attacked by various Indian factions, including Sikhs, who massacred many passengers on the train bringing Zhida and her family to Karachi. "There was blood all over the railroad carriage, my mother told me; she survived only because it was guarded by soldiers," Shakeel says. His father, Mohammed, who was about eighteen and like Zhida came from Kanpur in northern India, where they had been wed in an arranged marriage, was already in Karachi. Both families had left everything behind, knew no one in their new country, and at first lived in tents in a refugee camp. Mohammed eventually managed to obtain a plot of land, build a couple of rooms, and start selling soap door-to-door on a bike, a business that became more and more successful over the next few years and led to an association with Lever Bros. and a comfortable life for the family.

Shakeel, who now lives in England and is a British citizen, has not seen his parents in five years. An airline snafu subverted a previous effort to visit them in Karachi, and he has been planning a new trip for months, putting in extra time at sea so he will have a longer leave when he comes off the *Colombo Bay* on November 2. His siblings and other relatives in Pakistan will soon urge that he reconsider the visit in light of what U.S. military wrath might mean for the region in the coming months. Shakeel's own wrath seems reserved for the Islamic fundamentalists. "The Koran says pray, respect people, respect society; these people just use the religion to make trouble." He regards Pervez Musharraf, Pakistan's soldier-president, as an able leader, one who should give the country's pro-Taliban radicals "a good hiding." We are standing at the center of the windows that stretch across the width of the bridge, looking out at the placid sea, which I find comforting but which seems to offer Shakeel little solace. He says his mother suffers from a serious heart ailment; implicit in his voice is the fear that he may never see her alive again. "These attacks have affected everyone," he says softly, as more details issue from the radio.

As a boy Shakeel liked the white uniforms and white shoes worn by several members of his mother's family who served in Pakistan's merchant navy or with the British India Steam Navigation Co. Ltd., and like Jeremy, Conrad, and thousands of other teenagers over the centuries, he was drawn to life at sea. He attended a maritime college in Karachi in the 1970s but couldn't get a job because the shipping business was depressed. Sponsored by an uncle, he emigrated to England, served four years at sea, and then entered the well-regarded nautical college at South Shields, on the North Sea near Newcastle. By the time he passed his orals in 1985 and received his third-mate certificate, he was thirty-two, some ten years older than many of his classmates. He joined P&O Containers in 1989, stayed on after the British company merged with Holland's Royal Nedlloyd in 1997, serving nine years as a third mate before passing another set of orals and getting his second-mate "ticket" in 1999.

Shakeel is now in the middle of a three-month tour aboard the *Colombo Bay,* a typical stretch for P&O Nedlloyd officers; he talks lovingly of his wife, Susan, whom he met in 1982, when he was at South Shields, where they now live with their nine-year-old daughter, Sarah. When Sarah was younger, she and Susan came along on some voyages, but not since Sarah's schooling began in earnest. Shakeel is wistful as he tells me this, and melancholy, the reality of life at sea having long ago erased the romance of the white uniforms. He, too, is worried. Susan is Britain-born, a Christian; he is Pakistan-born, a Muslim. He says they have always been accepted in their community, but he knows there is a good deal of hostility toward "Pakis" in his adopted land and wonders how things will be when he gets home on leave. Already the BBC has reported random attacks on Muslims living in the West.

The next day we are off the coast of Vietnam, the shoreline invisible but the prospect of another quagmire, in Afghanistan, in bold relief. I mention to Matt Mullins, who met me when I came aboard two days ago and is now standing watch, that according to the chart we soon will be due east of Cam Rahn Bay. He smiles politely, the name of this harbor through which the matériel of our misadventure flowed seeming not to register. He is thirty, was not long out of diapers in Yorkshire when the helicopters strained away from the roof of the U.S. Embassy in what would soon become Ho Chi Minh City. This is Matt's first voyage as a chief mate, which gives him a good deal more to worry about than what lessons of the Vietnam War might be useful as Washington shapes its response to September 11. He is second in command, responsible for overseeing the crew and more than three thousand containers. He has a wife at home in England expecting their first child and also facing the possibility of wrist surgery for carpal tunnel syndrome. Matt speaks softly; he is a capable sailor more inclined to do his job than to talk about it. He has a quizzical countenance and repeatedly smooths the shock of sandy hair off his forehead; his whites are rumpled, but he looks fit and says that whenever he gets some free time—rare now that he is the first officer—he runs laps around the ship. He cautions that the steel decks are not knee friendly, an advisory that reinforces my decision to explore the one-third-mile loop at a sedate pace.

The sultry climate delivers another slap as I emerge from the accommodation's frost onto the upper deck, which rings the ship at the top of the hull. Eighteen ranks of containers rise from bow to stern, each one thirteen boxes across; the outermost stacks directly above my passage are supported by steel struts that the naval architects who designed the *Colombo Bay* doubtless vouch for but that look none too reassuring considering the four containers above could weigh some 120 tons. Though the upper deck is open to the ocean at the rail, it is otherwise boxed in, a three-sided tunnel that causes a paradoxical claustrophobia here in the middle of the sea. Despite the size of the ship, a sense of being squeezed in, of being a second-class citizen to stuff, prevails throughout; the living quarters and machinery spaces take up only about a twelfth of the vessel's length, hemmed in fore and aft by containers like a gleaming white palace set in a march of windowless, prefab housing blocks of red, blue, orange, and green.

I am close to the water for the first time since boarding in Hong Kong, the freeboard—the distance from the upper deck to the waterline—only about eighteen feet. A creamy wake rushes by, colliding with the modest swells angling in to create bursts of miniature rainbows in the spray, a phosphorescence that merges with a growing stench as I move toward the bow and a pool of brine and suet that has leaked from a container of wet hides. It is one of several such boxes that came aboard in Seattle, and their pungent drool accompanied the *Colombo Bay* across the Pacific, requiring the crew to spend hours hosing down the decks. All of the containers but this one came off in Hong Kong; it will be lifted in Laem Chabang and, like the others, travel by rail or truck to Asian factories, where the hides will be transformed into knockoffs of high-end designer bags, wallets, and other leather goods, then shipped back to the United States in less aromatic circumstances.

I circumvent the fetid lake and climb a short flight of steps to the forecastle deck, mouthing it "fo'c'sle" like a proper salt. It is about the size and shape of a softball infield, with home plate at the ship's prow, baselines flaring along the contours of the widening bow, and a white foremast standing tall on the pitcher's rubber, the revolving radar scanner on top receiving signals from an invisible catcher. Twin windlasses taller than I am flank second base, braking chains with links as thick and wide as a weight lifter's tight embrace. These cast-iron tethers thread through hawsepipes in the deck to the two

12.5-ton anchors at their end, one held against the port and one against the starboard side of the bow. There is no outfield; the first row of boxes stands where it would begin and cuts off the view aft.

In the days of sail, the crew lived beneath the deck of the fo'c'sle, but on container ships it is an oasis of quiet and escape. The engine's thrum is absent, the only sound is the gentle swish of the bow parting the water; clouds shepherd us along, their shadows creating dark ponds on the intense blue of the sunlit main. I am navigating the South China Sea by myself, basking in the solitude that has enthralled sailors since the first crude rafts pushed from shore in the mists of antiquity. From the steel pulpit wedged into the fo'c'sle's beak, the watery congregation stretches to the horizon in curling pews, the white-capped parishioners calm now but prone to evangelical eruptions at any time. As I stand on this windswept podium, there is no mistaking what Ishmael meant when he averred that one reason he went to sea was for the "pure air of the forecastle deck"—purer still for being upwind of the hides.

They are dripping on the port side, so a return aft via the starboard upper deck seems advisable. This path also affords a better view of two swooping and darting swallows, black with white bellies, the first birds I have spotted since Hong Kong. Are they hitchhiking, or do these tiny creatures, like albatrosses, have the staying power to remain aloft for days so far from land? This may prove an academic question, for a kestrel circles above them, hovering like a Darwinian helicopter gunship. At the stern the containers are stacked so close to the rail there is barely room to stand, but one flight down is the poop deck, a covered area that even with a big band would leave space for a roomy dance floor. Like the fo'c'sle, the poop (from the Latin *puppis,* for stern) is usually deserted, though rarely tranquil. The engine makes the deck shimmy like a grating above an endless subway train, vibrations compounded by the churn of the ship's single propeller, a five-bladed screw twenty-seven feet in diameter that weighs fifty-six tons and when we are at twenty-three knots turns at one hundred rpm. The freeboard is lower here, the propeller's wash seeming close enough to touch as it boils up into our wake's disappearing freeway.

There is no pulsation when I wake up on the morning of the sixteenth; we are drifting, one hundred nautical miles southwest of the Mekong Delta. On the bridge Captain Davies explains that we are making just the sort of schedule adjustment I had imagined for the barges parked in the Hudson; we have made such good time since Hong Kong that unless we stop for a few hours we'll arrive in Laem Chabang tomorrow before a berth is available and all the containers due aboard are ready for loading. While the engine is shut down, Steve Kingdon, the chief engineer, will oversee the replacement of a cylinder stud and invites me to watch and also take a tour of the machinery spaces. This requires that I don a boiler suit, the white cotton coveralls that all hands wear when rubbing against the ship's many dirty edges. I had hopes that this work suit would make me at least appear less of a supernumerary, but its unblemished whiteness amid the begrimed suits of the engineers only confirms my status as a nosy passenger as I descend like a freshly laundered baker's assistant into the noise, heat, and grease of the engine room.

Room, it is safe to say, is not quite the right word. The Sulzer 9RTA84C diesel engine takes up an area about the size of a basketball court and rises more than four stories, the silvery ducts at its top looking less like parts of a ship's bowels than like the arms and legs of a giant Tin Woodman in for repair and polishing. Gazing down on this power plant is akin to peering under the hood of an exceedingly large car: there are pistons and cylinders, a fuel pump, fuel injector, camshaft, crankshaft, turbocharger, flywheel, and several other familiar automotive components, all so big that Kingdon and his crew, when standing beside the row of nine cylinders, seem cast in *The Incredible Shrinking Boilermen.* Each piston weighs more than 7,000 pounds and has a stroke of almost 8 feet, in a cylinder with a bore of 2.73 feet; the crankshaft weighs 254 tons.

The two studs on each cylinder have shown a tendency to fracture at the cylinder block. All eighteen must eventually be replaced by longer, more solid studs, one of which now stands at the ready near where Frank McAlees and Chris Marlow, the first and second engineers, have burned one in half with acetylene torches. Frank is a tall, taciturn Irishman, Chris a burly, jovial Welshman; both are perspiring profusely in the heat as they struggle to remove the halves, which despite the employment of a chain pulley are proving recalcitrant. Steve Kingdon looks on with the air of an experienced chief engineer who knows that, however difficult, this job will get done.

Through the clatter, he beckons me with his head, and we leave his two subordinates wrestling with the stud and resume negotiating the multistory maze of ladders and catwalks that surround the engine. Steve has seemed private, even guarded, in our few conversations so far; but here in his element he manifests the enthusiasm of a man who clearly likes his work and enjoys showing off the mountain of machinery that drives the *Colombo Bay*. He comes from an agricultural background in Cornwall, where when he was a teenager the only escape was either the armed forces or the merchant service. Like Shakeel, he is a graduate of the nautical college at South Shields, where he, too, met his wife, Teresa, with whom he settled nearby and raised a son and a daughter. At forty-seven, Steve has been at sea for three decades, and though he could relax a bit now that he has reached the engineer's top rank, he is working hard to increase his knowledge by taking a correspondence course in quantum mechanics at England's open university. He also likes his job because of its principal perk, the day of shore leave that P&O Nedlloyd senior officers receive for every day at sea. How does Teresa tolerate his long absences? "Oh, she loves them. She hates my being home after a while; I get under her feet."

Steve explains that when the propeller is spinning at its maximum of one hundred rpm the engine is developing more than 46,000 brake horsepower. Since each unit stands for the strength of 1.5 animals, this means we have in harness the equivalent of almost 70,000 horses, all presumably good swimmers and watched over by Poseidon, whose purview as a Greek god included both the sea and horses. At this top speed of twenty-three knots, the engine consumes upward of 140 tons of heavy fuel oil each twenty-four hours, at a cost that averages about $150 a ton. Steve points to three globes about the size of pup tents, in which the oil is heated to 248 degrees Fahrenheit to reduce its viscosity before it is burned, aiding an efficient combustion process that sends little smoke up the funnel. About 4 percent of the fuel does wind up as sludge, a muddy sediment that in days past ships had to pay to have removed periodically; now it is something of a prized commodity, especially in Asia, where it is used in the cracking process to make fuel or turned into tarmac and other bitumen products. In some Chinese ports, sludge removal is free or occasionally even draws a token payment—in one case, Frank McAlees recalled, some pirated Hollywood films.

Our next stop is a steel box about six feet square in which the ship's sewage is treated. A culture of bacteria in a sachet is mixed with warm water to get an anaerobic process started, and then the mix is introduced into the raw sewage, where the process continues until the waste is converted to water that "they say," one engineer would later tell me, is clean enough to drink. I did not inquire who *they* were, being content with Steve's assurance that the water was chlorinated and then pumped into the ocean. The water we do drink is sucked in from the sea under a vacuum, which reduces the boiling point in the tank we are now standing before. When the seawater boils, it cannot hold salt in suspension, and the distillate that emerges is desalinated; all other minerals are purged in the process as well, which is why the ship's water tastes so plain.

Our compact incinerator would be the envy of municipalities all over the world that must make do with expensive, noisy garbage trucks and choked, rat-infested landfills. All the ship's refuse—including galley waste, oily rags, cardboard, and plastic—is incinerated at about 1,800 degrees Fahrenheit, at which temperature all toxicity is purged and the garbage reduced to a bucketful of ashes, which are thrown over the rail when the ship is in deep ocean, where such dumping is legal. Our final stop is the electrohydraulic rudder mechanism, which would fill the free throw key to the height of the hoop and, when signaled by the diminutive wheel on the bridge, turns the rudder as if it weighed no more than a playing card.

We are still drifting when the tour ends. I thank Steve for his instruction and take the lift up to A deck for a talk with Captain Davies. He and Elizabeth greet me in his suite, a spacious perk of rank that includes, besides his office, an anteroom, a bedroom, and a dayroom larger than my cabin, which is drenched in light on this sunny Sunday. There is a bar and kitchenette on one side, a cluster of plants opposite, a television set and VCR, and a coffee table set before a curved sofa, where Peter, as he asks that I call him, sits relaxed. He will be fifty-six in a few days but looks younger despite the gray in his hair. He is affable and informal, and in the shorts and kneesocks of his summer whites looks less like the master of a 900-foot-long vessel laden with cargo worth millions of dollars than a tall, friendly Sea Scout leader. He and Elizabeth met in the summer of 1975, married in September, and he shipped out two days later; when he returned in January, she gave up her job teaching at a catering college so she could sail with him, and she has done so often since. She has a ready smile under a cap of brown hair and is genial and good-humored like her husband, albeit quieter, and listens attentively as he recounts his history.

He grew up in Yorkshire, in a place pronounced "Steers" by the locals but known as Staithes by everyone else. Though the town is on the North Sea, there was no seafaring history in his family, and he went to public school with no thought of pursuing a mariner's life. But he developed little zeal for conjugating Latin verbs and other academic challenges and in 1960, at fifteen, was encouraged by his father to enter Conway, a century-old nautical school that for decades had been housed on moored ships but was now in a mansion and a collection of spartan wooden huts on the Menai Strait in north Wales. After two years he apprenticed to the British India Steam Navigation Co., serving on general cargo vessels of 10,000 deadweight tons or less that sailed from Europe to India, the Persian (now Arabian) Gulf, the Far East, Australia, and New Zealand. In the years that followed he was often at sea for long periods, once for eighteen months.

He feels one thing that made this life appealing was his strained childhood; his parents divorced when he was five, and he and his siblings were raised by his father. "I think that if the marriage had been happier, I might not have gone to sea so readily, or taken to it so readily. I didn't have a mother to wipe my nose; I had to get on with it." He was also attracted by what always has lured young men to the sea: the wages and the chance to see the world.

In October 1979 he sailed from England on the general cargo ship *Qarouh'-Kuwaiti* with Elizabeth and their twenty-month-old daughter, Claire. At Rotterdam the authorities kept the ship in port for more than a week because the charterers had failed to pay stevedoring costs on a previous call; this left plenty of time to introduce Claire to windmills and for other explorations. After a rough Atlantic crossing, the ship sailed up the St. Lawrence River to Montreal and Port Alfred, where she picked up newsprint and needed an icebreaker to escape the clutches of the Canadian winter. By late December the vessel was plowing through the Bay of Fundy for a call at Saint John, New Brunswick, where the Davies family and all but three of their shipmates went "up the road" on Christmas Eve to a midnight mass at a local church.

The *Qarouh'-Kuwaiti* then headed south, passed through the Panama Canal, called at San Salvador, and crossed the Pacific to China, where the days required to unload and load cargo left ample time to tour Shanghai, Beijing, and other cities. Western visitors were still a rarity, and Claire, a strawberry blonde of fair complexion, proved a magnet for fascinated Chinese wanting to touch her hair, so many at one point that an alarmed Elizabeth had to retreat with her daughter to their waiting transport. In Japan the ship called at Yokohama, Nagoya, and Tokyo; then she sailed back across the Pacific and through the Panama Canal again to Barranquilla and Cartagena in Colombia. The *Qarouh'-Kuwaiti* then put in at Freeport, Texas, and the family flew home from Houston.

"We were gone seven months. It was incredible, really, but that is what it was like then," Peter says, to enthusiastic nods from Elizabeth. After their second daughter, Katherine, was born, in 1981, they continued traveling as a family for several years. Claire and Katherine were allowed time off from school because the trips were so educational; they kept a journal, and Elizabeth helped them keep up with their English and math lessons. "You visited all these extraordinary places and had time to do things, meet people, make friends," says Peter, adding that he also had time to indulge his passion for golf, which he has played on dozens of courses around the world. "In Calcutta I had a caddie *and* a ball boy," he says, savoring the memory as if it were a hole in one. He does not have his clubs aboard the *Colombo Bay;* he knows that in the twenty-first-century world of container shipping the chance of getting in a round is about as likely as making that long shot.

CHAPTER TWO

By the middle of the twentieth century, merchant ships had advanced from oar power through sail and steam to the forerunners of monumental diesel engines like the *Colombo Bay*'s; well-maintained vessels staffed with skilled officers and crews were becoming increasingly stable and safe thanks to improvements in naval architecture, engine design, and modern technologies such as radar and satellite navigation systems. But the loading and unloading of cargo remained largely the same as it was in the thirteenth century BC, when Phoenician round ships traded at Mediterranean ports; the sinew required on the docks of Tyre still ruled by the time Marlon Brando's ur-longshoreman Terry Malloy worked the New York piers in *On the Waterfront*. Freight still came in drums, boxes, bags, barrels, bales, and crates; cranes lifted this "break-bulk" cargo, but human hands, arms, and shoulders pushed, shoved, and positioned it on the ships and docks. This stevedoring was both laborious and often dangerous: heavy lifting caused back strain and other sometimes disabling conditions; ropes and cables snapped, sending crates splintering onto docks and decks; workers stumbled into the holds or the water. These hazards bothered most shipowners less than the routine damage to goods and endemic theft—from petty pilfering by individual longshoremen to the "loss" of entire consignments arranged by mob-controlled union bosses—that led to costly claims by shippers and escalating insurance rates. But the chief drawback, as it had been for centuries, was time, since merchant vessels earn money only when they are under way. At every port the loading and unloading of break-bulk cargo took at least a few days and with large ships often a week or two, good for golf enthusiasts and seamen looking for other recreation when they went up the road but bad for the bottom line.

It is now an article of maritime lore that in 1937 a budding entrepreneur named Malcom McLean, not long off the farm in Maxton, North Carolina, imagined a different future. The ambitious twenty-four-year-old ran a fledgling trucking business and had driven a load of cotton bales north to the docks at Hoboken, New Jersey, where he sat around all day watching stevedores loading other cargo. "It struck me that I was looking at a lot of wasted time and money . . . that it would be easier to lift my trailer up, without any of the contents being touched, and put it on the ship," McLean recalled years later. This concept was not original. In 1928 a new company called Seatrain had equipped ships to carry railcars in their holds in a service between New Orleans and Havana that soon expanded to other ports along the Gulf and East Coasts. It proved cheaper to move the cars and their contents by sea than overland on tracks, not least because no longshoremen were needed to transfer the cargo at the ports. Not surprisingly, Cuban *estibadores* greeted this development with restrained enthusiasm; in a harbinger of worldwide dock-worker resistance to containerization, they demanded that they unload at least some of the products from the shipborne cars and reload them onto Cuban trains.

During World War II, the War Shipping Administration discovered that loading military vessels with crates of the same size was so efficient in saving time and costs that it decided to employ standard-size containers for all cargo, but the conflict ended before the plan could be implemented. The concept was there for the private sector to pick up in the late forties, but the conservative shipping industry, which had shown little interest in Seatrain's resourcefulness, ignored the WSA analysis as well, sticking with the break-bulk system it knew and continuing to grumble about its inefficiency.

By the mid-fifties McLean Trucking had become one of the leading long-distance haulers in the country, and the founder sold his share of the firm and went into the shipping business with enough capital to try what he had been envisaging for almost two decades. One insight McLean and others had had in these intervening years was that rolling entire truck trailers onto ships made no economic sense. The chassis took up too much space that could be used for income-producing cargo; moreover, because of these wheels and undercarriages, the trailers could not sit on top of one another, limiting the number any ship could carry. McLean spurred his staff to develop a new kind of trailer, one that could be detached from its chassis and was strong enough to permit stacking. To carry these prototypes he invested in several aging T2 tankers that during the war had carried, besides oil, airplanes on special skeleton platforms set above their main decks. He replaced these with solid platforms and fitted them with sockets that locked in the stubby legs at each corner of the redesigned and reinforced containers.

On April 26, 1956, one of the tankers, the *Ideal X,* made the maiden voyage carrying these boxes, which were hoisted by shipboard cranes at the Port of Newark and dropped onto the chassis of trucks waiting on the dock after the vessel arrived in Houston. McLean never made a profit on the T2 service because each tanker had a capacity of only fifty-eight trailers and his plan to augment income by carrying oil simultaneously was scotched by the U.S. Coast Guard for safety reasons. Nonetheless, he persevered, borrowing heavily to lease specially constructed ships, more containers to fit on them, and terminal space, betting on an idea that most shipowners considered "an utter folly."

McLean's newfangled vessels first served only East and Gulf

Coast ports, but in 1958 they began calling at Puerto Rico, then at West Coast terminals via the Panama Canal; in 1960 McLean christened the company Sea-Land Service, Inc., and by 1966 transatlantic runs had begun to Holland and England, along with military supply service to the Philippines and Okinawa. The following year Sea-Land established container operations at Cam Rahn Bay and three other ports in South Vietnam, dedicating 7 ships to sustaining the growing U.S. military involvement there; they carried some 10 percent of the supplies for the war effort, while it took 250 other vessels to haul the remaining 90 percent, a disparity that demonstrated the potency of McLean's folly, his strong endorsement of the U.S. military engagement, and his sharp eye for business. "Malcom's genius was really numbers," said Paul Richardson, a salesman who worked at both McLean Trucking and Sea-Land, noting that he could analyze bank loans, ship construction costs, and freight rates in his head and was a human calculator at cards. "Don't ever play gin rummy with Malcom for money," he said. "It just won't work."

By 1969 Sea-Land's gray containers with their bright red logos were ubiquitous in dozens of ports, and McLean sold the company to the R. J. Reynolds Tobacco Company for $160 million in stock (some $800 million in 2003 dollars). This gave him a seat on the Reynolds board, time to pursue real estate and other business ventures, and the wherewithal to operate First Colony Farms, a 400,000-acre spread in North Carolina where he required visitors to dress in sterile lab suits before viewing the animals. But McLean was a high-risk capitalist at heart and in 1978 bought United States Lines hoping to replicate Sea-Land's success, gambling on a new fleet of container vessels, each costing upward of $60 million and capable of carrying 4,400 TEUs. He optimistically dubbed these behemoths Econoships, but they proved anything but; their maximum speed was only eighteen knots, the cost of operating them ballooned beyond expectations, and the cargo necessary for profitability failed to materialize. By 1986 McLean's gift for numbers had deserted him, and United States Lines was headed for bankruptcy; he tried subsequent shipping ventures but never came close to creating another Sea-Land.

Nonetheless, the force he had set in motion in 1956 proved unstoppable, even by striking longshoremen in the United States and abroad, who saw, correctly, that each additional container arriving in port meant fewer jobs. In 1971 members of the West Coast's powerful International Longshore and Warehouse Union struck for 134 days in the face of burgeoning containerization and the technology that came with it. Three decades later the union's rank and file had shrunk from 100,000 jobs to just over 10,000. As more and more shipowners followed Sea-Land's example, containers multiplied so that by the end of the century the annual total passing through the world's ports exceeded 330 million TEUs.

McLean's simple idea had launched the greatest revolution in the international transport of goods since the coming of steam propulsion in the early nineteenth century; his innovation caused a seismic change in the world's economic life, one that drastically reduced the cost of shipping goods across both water and land. Between 1980 and 2000, the ubiquitous boxes and the "just in time" deliveries they helped make possible allowed U.S. companies to drastically reduce costly inventories, by one estimate from 25 percent to 15 percent of the nation's gross domestic product. The total value of U.S. business inventory was $1.5 trillion in 2000, 1 trillion less than it would have been had McLean's folly not taken hold. His innovation made inexpensive products available to millions who otherwise would not have been able to afford them. As one colleague put it, "He made the Wal-Marts possible." When McLean died in 2001, at age eighty-seven, he was widely hailed as a visionary by the international shipping fraternity, compared with Edison, Ford, and Bell by some; yet his name remains virtually unknown to the general public.

■ ■ ■

There are more than 3,000 containers on the *Colombo Bay*, most of them forty-footers, filled with hundreds of commodities—baby garments, puzzles, dolls, lamps, sporting goods, auto parts, Christmas tree lights, beauty shop furniture, belts, laminated bags, hand tools, machinery, meat, fruits, and nuts. Most of this cargo is bound for the United States, including twelve containers headed for KB Toys, a company with headquarters in Pittsfield, Massachusetts, that operates more than thirteen hundred stores throughout the country. Much of this shipment consists of jeeps, jungle fighters, soldiers on motorbikes, battle stations, and other military action figures made by a firm whose name would not have been likely to pass muster in the days of Mao—the Dabu Great Profit Toy Products Company, Ltd. Dabu is just one of the many manufacturers in Guangdong Province and other areas of southern China that now produce some 90 percent of the imported toys sold in the United States.

KB Toys doesn't deal directly with Dabu but works with vendors like the M&C Toy Centre, which have showrooms in Hong Kong, where they put the toys on display twice a year for buyers like KB's Bob Alarie. These vendors usually design the toys, and Alarie sometimes asks for refinements. "In military toys we try to get the details very correct; you want to be as realistic as you can be," he told me. Once the design is agreed on and the price and size of the order set, the toys are manufactured by Dabu or one of the other factories, then trucked to Hong Kong. The twelve KB-bound containers arrived at the port on September 12 and were loaded onto the *Colombo Bay* immediately after she arrived from Taiwan the next day. Such tight scheduling is typical, especially between July and October, when large retailers are stocking up for Green Friday, the day after Thanksgiving, when U.S. consumers invade stores to begin the

Christmas buying season. All twelve containers are due off the *Colombo Bay* on October 18 at Savannah, Georgia, a major receiving port for large retailers; once the boxes clear customs, they will be trucked to KB Toys's closest distribution center, in Montgomery, Alabama.

Shippers can now avail themselves of at least a dozen variations on the general-purpose steel boxes like those packed with the KB's military action figures. There are fantainers with hatches for electric extraction fans that suck out air, to prevent condensation from damaging perishable cargo like coffee beans; half-height containers with ramp doors and tarpaulin tops to accommodate building and other bulky, extraheavy materials; containers housing tanks for hazardous and nonhazardous liquids; hanger containers for the shipment of garments, and boxes that are forty feet long, seventeen feet wide, and thirteen feet high, especially built to carry fuselage parts from Japan to Seattle for Boeing. The *Colombo Bay* also has 174 plugs on deck and 66 in the holds for "reefers," refrigerated containers that can transport frozen prawns at minus 20 degrees Fahrenheit, cucumbers at plus 50 degrees Fahrenheit, and bacon hovering around the freezing point. The content of these jumbo horizontal iceboxes, especially if it is 60,000 pounds or more of meat or seafood, can have a market value of more than a million dollars; if the food spoils because a reefer's microprocessor-controlled refrigeration unit is missed or breaks down, or the 440-volt shipboard power fails, the financial hit can mean the difference between profit and loss for the voyage. The gauges on the reefers are checked—and, if need be, adjusted—twice a day, a task that falls to Alexander Gill, the *Colombo Bay*'s third engineer. On a previous call at Laem Chabang, some 200 reefers came aboard; plunging down vertical ladders into the holds and squeezing through the crevasses between the stacks of boxes on deck to check them all, Alex told me, was a twice-daily nightmare.

Alex is twenty-one, though a certain cockiness makes him seem younger, a likable wisecracking teenager on a summer job rather than a newly minted engineer in the British Merchant Service charged with keeping a lot of expensive food at the right temperature, or else. He looks jaunty in his whites but tends to disappear into his bulky boiler suit, like a child whose snowsuit is too big. He grew up in a small town outside Newcastle, in County Durham, and left high school just before his sixteenth birthday to work in a steel foundry, where his father worked and his father before him. The father of his girlfriend at the time was a second mate on tankers and general cargo vessels, and over drinks one night in a pub he asked Alex if he'd ever thought about going to sea. He had, as an engineer in the Royal Navy, but he lacked enough high school education to qualify. "I had never heard of the merchant navy. You never read about it in the papers, unless a ship crashes on the rocks, and then it's all about pollution," Alex says, a complaint several other shipmates would make—and Jeremy already had made—about the invisibility of their calling. At eighteen, Alex started his cadetship at South Shields, then went to the nautical college in Glasgow for a year, did ten and a half months of sea time, went back to Glasgow for another year, and emerged with his class four ticket.

Besides checking the reefers, he watches over the purifiers that extract water out of the diesel fuel and the evaporator that distills seawater for drinking, and every three days he's in charge of the engine room. "It's quite scary, really," he says. He receives the standard junior officer's .59 days of leave for each day he's at sea, and his annual salary, which is tax-free if he is out of England more than six months a year, is equivalent to about $30,000. Alex joined the eastbound *Colombo Bay* in Singapore on August 4, yet despite his heady responsibilities, the "fantastic holidays," and a salary he concedes most of his landlocked peers envy, he has handed in his notice and will leave the ship when we reach Malta on October 5. The immediate reason is Diane, the woman he lives with in Glasgow, who is battling cancer. "When you have problems at home, the last place you want to be is stuck on a ship thousands of miles away," he says. He plans to go to work in the Glasgow bar that Diane manages and hopes to enroll soon at the University of Leicester to take a master's degree in mathematics. Might he eventually come back to the sea? "Not on container ships; it's just work, work, work."

As computers and other advanced technology have come to merchant ships, P&O Nedlloyd and most other liner companies have cut costs by steadily reducing the number of officers and crew on vessels, hardly a new trend. In the seventeenth century, Venetian maritime statutes required that the buss, a 240-ton ship, be manned by fifty sailors; soon cargo was moving on vessels called cogs, square-sailed ships about the same size as the buss but needing only twenty hands—and, more important, mouths, since the cost of feeding hungry seamen on long voyages cut into profits. "We are now asked to do half another person's job, for no extra pay," says Captain Davies, a view shared by his subordinates as they recall the days when ships had radio and catering officers. Peter himself must now take the monthly inventory of the ship's bond locker, where items such as beer, wine, spirits, cigarettes, shaving cream, and toothpaste are locked away. He laughs and, mimicking a postaccident inquiry, says:

"What were you doing at the time of the collision, captain?"

"Counting toothbrushes, sir."

After four decades as a seafarer, the last twenty-two years as a master, Peter earns about $68,000 a year. "Considering what we are in charge of, what we are responsible for, the wages are a pittance," he says, with an uncharacteristic edge. "The company argues profit margins, as they always have," and as the owners of the *Pequod* did when Ishmael sought to join the ship. Captain Bildad offers him a very long lay, a mere 777th share of the voyage's profits, should there be any; in the would-be crewman's presence, Bildad tells his coprincipal, Peleg, that they must consider the duty they owe "to the other owners of this ship—widows and orphans, many of them—and that if we too abundantly reward the labors of this young man, we may be taking the bread from those widows and orphans."

Melville's irony would not have amused Bildad and Peleg's non-fictional counterparts, whose capital-intensive ships foundered by the scores and even if they survived their months at sea could never count on finding and harpooning enough whales to produce sufficient lamp oil and ambergris to make a voyage pay. Container ships rarely sink, but freight rates and the supply of cargo are always prey to economic cycles, like the Asian downturn of 1997–98, and capital expenses are higher than ever. The *Colombo Bay* cost $50 million by the time she came down the ways at the Ishikawajima-Harima Heavy Industries Co. shipyard and requires between $25,000 and $35,000 a day to operate at sea. The 14,000 reefers delivered to P&O Nedlloyd in 2002 cost the company more than $200 million. According to *Containerisation International,* the industry's monthly trade publication, in the last decade of the twentieth century, container shipping "clearly underperformed the S & P 500 index, failing to recover its cost of capital and creating limited shareholder value, if any."

Such lackluster financials have driven a continuing rush of mergers. In 1980 the twenty largest shipping lines moving containers controlled 26 percent of the world market; by 2002 the top twenty commanded an estimated 83 percent. P&O Nedlloyd ranked number two, the result of an equal partners merger in 1997 between Holland's Royal Nedlloyd and Britain's P&O Containers, both of whose roots go back to the coming of steamships in the early nineteenth century. The primary rationale for the deal, as in most such consolidations, was that economies of scale would save costs, and they have; not enough, however, to bring profits during the Asian economic crisis, when the supply of vessels and number of containers exceeded shippers' demands. As the Asian picture improved, so did P&O Nedlloyd's balance sheet; by the end of 2000 it was showing an operating profit of $201 million. But in 2001 it dropped to $87 million, and along with the rest of the industry, company executives began nervously speculating about the economic impact of September 11.

Despite the prevailing overcapacity at the turn of the century, most of the major liner companies continued to purchase larger ships, a trend that took its initial dramatic jump in 1987, when American President Lines (APL)—then a U.S. company but by 1997 a subsidiary of Singapore's Neptune Orient Lines (NOL)—ordered the first container ship that was too wide to pass through the Panama Canal. A decade later the Danish shipping combine A. P. Moller, which sits comfortably atop the Big Twenty, took delivery of the *Sovereign Maersk,* a vessel some 200 feet longer than the *Colombo Bay* and capable of carrying upward of 7,000 TEUs. By 2002 there were 250 such "post-Panamax" vessels in service around the world, among them at least a dozen sister ships of the *Sovereign Maersk.* P&O Nedlloyd counts twenty-two similar ships in its fleet, including four the company added in 2001, at a cost of $75 million each. The industry's reasoning—or hope—is that population growth and rising living standards, especially in Asia and Europe, will create the market demand to fill all these boxes, and many more.

Designs now exist for ships with a capacity of 9,300 TEUs, and a British study has argued the feasibility of an ultra large container ship that could carry 12,500. As envisioned, this ULCS would have a beam of 187 feet, 82 feet wider than the *Colombo Bay.* Already several major ports around the world, including New York, and Long Beach and Oakland in California, have or have ordered gantries that can reach out and pluck containers from the far sides of these leviathans. Nor does draft appear to be an obstacle at the ports where ULCSs would call; the British analysis concluded that the big ships would draw a maximum of 48 feet fully loaded, and that by the time they enter service in 2008 or later, at least twenty-eight ports would be dredged to accommodate them. Only propulsion remains problematic. The most powerful marine diesel engines in 2002 could not get the ULCS up to an economically viable twenty-five knots. Twin engines would bring the ships up to speed but would increase costs considerably. Still, the potential markets, the economy of scale mantra, and the industry's historic enthusiasm for bigger and bigger ships are likely to remain as seductive as Parthenope, Ligeia, and Leucosia, the mythic sirens who charmed Mediterranean sailors with their songs.

CHAPTER THREE

By early morning on September 17, we are in the horseshoe of the Gulf of Thailand and drifting again, waiting outside Laem Chabang harbor for another ship to clear our berth. Clouds hug the hills on our starboard as dragonflies circle the bridge wing, emissaries from the first land visible since we left Hong Kong four days ago. In the distance, the terminal's four-legged gantries look like dinosaurs constructed with an Erector set, their raised booms reaching up more than twenty stories, necks that crane warily as we approach. Peter orders slow ahead just after 1200; the harbor pilot comes up the ladder, arrives on the bridge after getting stuck in the elevator for a few minutes, and we make for the quay, passing a small general cargo vessel called the *Harmonic Halo,* which appears neither melodic nor angelic but dissonant with rust. Tradition dictates that whenever a ship enters a port she fly the colors of the host nation, so the red, white, and blue horizontal stripes of Thailand now flutter above the bridge along with the blue and orange flag of P&O Nedlloyd and the red ensign of the British Merchant Service, the "red duster" that in England's nineteenth-century mercantile heyday flew over more tonnage than the flags of all other maritime nations combined.

Peter appears on the port wing in his light blue company cap, the gold laurel leaf of his rank on the bill. A tug fore and another aft prod us laterally toward our berth between two other container ships, the APL *England* and the *Ming Union;* it seems an impossible fit, like trying to park an SUV in a VW space, though Peter says that there will be some 50 feet between us and the *Ming Union* and 164 feet separating us from the APL *England.* From the perspective of the wing, that doesn't seem like much leeway for a ship the size of the *Colombo Bay,* but no fenders get scraped as we dock, the stevedores stir on the wharf, and the dinosaurs go to work under the broiling sun.

Now seems a good point to satisfy the curiosity of readers who

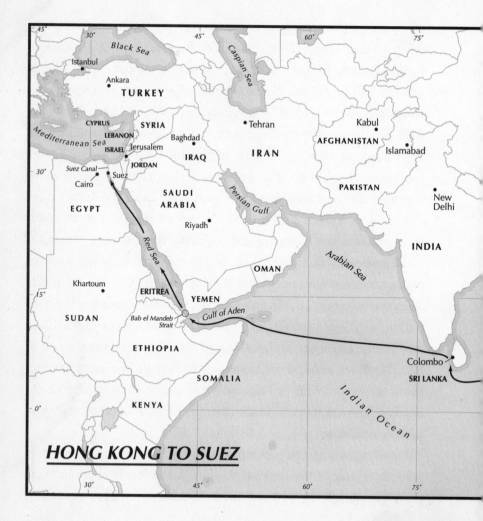

HONG KONG TO SUEZ

may be wondering if I have ever operated one of these mammoth box pluckers. The answer, of course, is yes—and not just any gantry, but a state-of-the-art Fantuzzi Reggiane super–post-Panamax number. This dizzying adventure took place at the Port Newark Container Terminal in New Jersey and began when I meet Mario Zucchi in the shadow of a "bogie," one of the seven-feet-high trucks that house the wheels that roll the crane back and forth on rails parallel to the berthed ship. Mario is the mechanical engineer in charge of crane maintenance at the terminal, and soon we were squeezed into

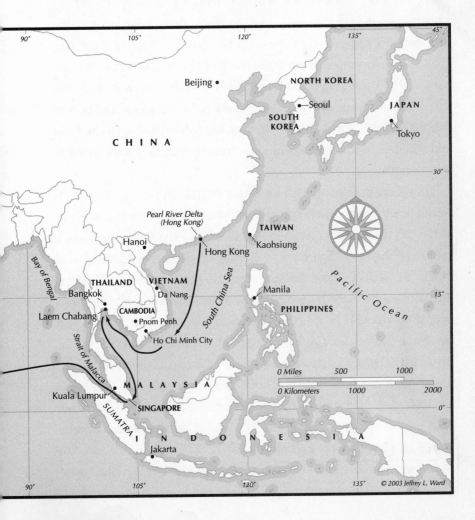

© 2003 Jeffrey L. Ward

a hoist slightly larger than a phone booth that took us up 150 feet. We stepped out into a labyrinth of ladders and catwalks, steel grating that with every step afforded a vertiginous view of the twelve-story drop; I concentrated on the Manhattan skyline across the harbor. In a large room full of panels and pulsing lights, Mario explained that 13,200 volts of AC current were being converted to the DC power for the electric engine driving the gantry. "Basically, a container crane is a sophisticated, three-dimensional elevator. It can move the boxes up and down, left and right and forward and backward," he said, as the boom, which reaches up another ten stories when raised, slowly lowered into its horizontal working position. We now entered the cab slung beneath the boom, where Stefano Negrini, who is overseeing the shakedown of this and the Italian company's three other new gantries at the terminal, was instructing three veteran crane operators—James Brown, Hayward Davis, and John "Catfish" Lewis—all of whom seemed delighted with the bells and whistles of this new six-million-dollar toy as they took turns at the controls.

They were practicing with an empty container, picking it up from the dock with the crane's spreader, a rectangular frame just in front of the cab that lowers on cables and locks into the four slots at each corner of the box. "You have to have good depth perception," said Mario, as Catfish placed the spreader into position and grabbed the box, a move he made by eye but that after thousands of repetitions over three decades he executed as reflexively and smoothly as I lock my front door. After Catfish brought the spreader and box up, he drove them before us on a trolley toward the end of the boom, which has enough reach to handle a 7,000-TEU ship with eighteen boxes across on deck. He stopped over a spot where, were there a container ship below, he would lower the box and slide it into the cellular guides in the hold or stack it on the deck, and then release the spreader and return it over the dock for the next grab. Skilled operators like Catfish, James, and Hayward can move more than forty boxes an hour with a modern crane, the main reason my shipmates get so little time up the road. The crane wobbled as we went along, sufficiently to make me lose my balance and accept the offer of a seat that hinged down from the wall. "The crane must be flexible or the steel would crack," Mario explained, as we continued the Fantuzzi shimmy. If winds blow up beyond 40 mph, an alarm goes off and the crane shuts down automatically. Below that force, wind doesn't have that much impact because the spreader alone weighs ten tons and the box it is moving can be up to forty tons.

"Have a seat," said Mario, pointing to the Captain Kirk chair in the center of the cab. I demur, not feeling much like William Shatner as we sway back and forth. "Come on, you can do it," echoed around me, so I stumbled the few feet from my drop seat into the fat embrace of the command throne. At each arm were two dozen lights and buttons and in front two joy sticks, the left-hand one to move us along the trolley, the other one to raise and lower the spreader. "You want to take it out to the end of the boom," Mario said of the practice box, now just in front of me. As my hand hovered over the knob, the grind of stripping gears filled my head, the sound I produced repeatedly when learning to drive our stick-shift Chevy in the Indiana Dunes. I first touched the knob so gingerly that nothing happened, then gave it a tentative nudge and the box lurched forward and started moving along the boom. When it reached the halfway point, I began to panic and pulled back on the stick. "Keep going," Mario said, assuring me that the trolley would automatically slow down as we approached the end of the 162-foot arm, which stretched almost halfway across the channel. I moved the container forward again, and when it was well over the channel grasped the other joy stick and lowered the cargo toward the imaginary ship berthed below. "Don't drop it in the water," someone behind me shouted, to a good deal of laughter. With visions of the box splashing into the drink, I jerked it up and brought it and us back along the boom to where the exercise had begun. "You have now driven the Ferrari of cranes,"

Stefano announced—without buckling my seat belt, I noticed as I dismounted.

■ ■ ■

Taxi drivers scramble up the gangway and jostle outside the ship's office, angling for passengers to take up the road. Bangkok, which is about a hundred miles to the northwest, is tempting; but the round-trip alone would eat up at least five hours, leaving time for little more than a quick meal since we are scheduled to sail again at 0200 and all hands must be back onboard an hour before. I opt instead to accompany Peter and Elizabeth to Pattaya, the beach resort twelve miles to the south. As Peter finishes dealing with the port agent, a Thai customs official departs with several cartons of Marlboros; there are, it turns out, scores more in the bond locker, without which procedures in Asian and Middle Eastern ports tend to be sluggish.

The ride to Pattaya is a NASCAR event set to music, we and the driver's deafening radio simultaneously rocking past a blur of cars, trucks, motorbikes, and cyclists, who seem oblivious to the internal combustion around them. We are driving on the left, old hat to Peter and Elizabeth but to me a prospective head-on with every swerve. We reach our destination in twenty minutes, surely a record. Peter recommends that we meet later at the Ruen Thai restaurant, and he and Elizabeth go off to relax on the palm-fringed beach. "My whole being was steeped deep in the indolence of the sailor away from the sea, the scene of never-ending labor and of unceasing duty," Conrad writes. "For utter surrender to indolence you cannot beat a sailor ashore when that mood is on him, the mood of absolute irresponsibility tasted to the full."

Pattaya was just a sleepy fishing village until U.S. troops began coming here for R & R during the Vietnam War. Now it's a major tourist mecca, a playland that offers sun, sea, sand, hotels, shops, and restaurants, a Burger King and two Starbucks, all cheek by jowl with a well-advertised abundance of sex. My shipmates had assured me, with the requisite winks, that I could find anything my aging loins might desire in the private rooms of the Dollhouse, Charlie's Angels, or the many other moist emporia, which promise forty women to choose from, three-girl specials, or whatever it takes to satisfy the discriminating visitor.

As I walk by Cats to Go Go, I find myself humming "Venezuela," whose recording by the folk singer Richard Dyer-Bennet I had spun many times as a kid and not thought about for years. In this lilting ballad, a sailor meets a woman and decides that, regardless of whether she had loved others, she would do to pass away the time in Venezuela, especially given "all the tricks" she knew. An eight-year-old schooled in the triple-X specificity of the Internet would have no trouble translating this euphemism; in my more innocent youth, the meaning proved elusive, the more so because for some mysterious reason the woman had a basket on her head. When the sailor bids farewell to his transitory companion, he tells her to cheer up because there'll always be sailors ashore with leave in Ven-e-zu-eh-eh-eh-eh-eh-eh-la. This was long before AIDS. When today's merchant seamen have time for dalliances in port, which they rarely do, most are inclined to heed Bildad's warning to Flask, the *Pequod*'s third mate, to "beware of fornication."

Not so the lathered Western businessmen lounging around the pool at the Royal Garden Hotel, where I go to pass away some time myself. Thai girls, wearing no baskets on their heads and little else, flit like pilot fish around these well-heeled *farangs*. One of them is a tall, beefy man of about fifty with a large, oval face and shaved head. He wears black trunks and a torso-hugging white T-shirt, and sits near the poolside bar consuming fistfuls of nuts and flirting in monosyllabic English with a slip half his size; she looks not more than fifteen, a common sight in Southeast Asia, where an estimated one-third of the "sex workers" are poverty-stricken teenagers, male and female. The man looks familiar and after a minute or two comes into focus as Jesse Ventura, though the notion of the married wrestler-governor of Minnesota publicly squiring a nymphet in this sybaritic retreat six days after September 11 is hard to credit. As I struggle with this cognitive dissonance, he rises and shepherds his diminutive consort toward a cluster of men with their own girl-toys. The back of his T-shirt declares: "Jesse Ventura for President."

I ponder how to introduce myself. "My daughter went to Carleton College, governor, and really loved the Minnesota winters. By the way, what brings you to Thailand?" Before I can refine this gambit, he and the child disappear into the lobby, leaving me to speculate about this odd couple until, weeks later, I Google the Minneapolis *Star Tribune*. The paper records that the governor was at home on September 17, honoring the victims of the terrorist attack, and a call to his office reveals that his Pattaya double, name unknown, has been traveling the world impersonating him for months. "We get calls like yours often," says a bemused aide.

At Ruen Thai, Peter and Elizabeth arrive with Steve, who has managed to escape his arduous engine-room duties for a few hours. We dine under tall palm trees while a half dozen dancers perform on a raised stage, their jet-black hair pulled tight and adorned with tiaras and bejeweled combs that sparkle in the spotlights, each bobbing head a miniature constellation. The floor-length costumes are a kaleidoscope of gold brocade and multicolored silks as the dancers glide demurely, their chastity as implied as Charlie's Angels' availability. The performance seems genuinely Siamese, especially the music, played by five men who strum, pluck, slap, and blow on authentic wooden instruments, one of which looks like a large butterfly, another like a small alligator. Their sound, like the dancing, is delicate and restrained, a spell broken when they take their break and recorded, amplified rock fills the air. We order six dishes to share: shrimp, carp, chicken, and beef in sauces both hot and sweet, accompanied by side dishes of rice and vegetables, and finish up with a plate of fruit.

At 2130 we meet our taximan and hurtle along the dark speedway back to the ship. The quay is bathed in yellow light from the gantries, which still have so many boxes to load that our departure has been pushed back to 0500. Peter groans and ascends with Elizabeth to their quarters to grab what sleep he can before rising to set course for Singapore.

At sunup an email rustles under my door, delivered by Peter as if he were a bellhop at a four-star hotel instead of the sleep-deprived master of a container ship that he had just maneuvered into the Gulf of Thailand. The message is from Diane, who reports that our travel agent has booked tentative reservations on two flights from Singapore back to New York. I had asked that she arrange this option, and now young Alex Gill's words about his Diane echo in the isolation of the cabin: "When you have problems at home, the last place you want to be is stuck on a ship thousands of miles away." We will be in Singapore in two days, and the prospect of seeing Diane and Amanda a day or two later pulls like a riptide. Diane says they are safe, coping with the aftershock as well as can be expected, and urges me to swim hard against the impulse to come home; she relays the same counsel from Amanda, on whom I have bestowed much unsolicited fatherly advice over three decades and who now, a documentary film producer, points out that it is my journalistic duty to sailor on. Peter adds his encouragement when I see him on the bridge after lunch. As master he is privy to all incoming and outgoing email, so my dithering is no secret. "Have you decided what you're going to do when we get to Singapore?" he says. When I hesitate, he urges me to stay onboard at least as far as Malta, where he and Elizabeth will debark. I am touched by his support but remain torn.

Later in the afternoon Peter hands me an advisory just arrived from P&O Nedlloyd fleet operations in Rotterdam; it is an email, forwarded to all company vessels bound for the United States, from Alex Ball, master of the P&O Nedlloyd *Genoa,* a container ship that called at East Coast ports in the first seventy-two hours after the attacks. He reports that U.S. officials were permitted shore leave at Charleston but not at Norfolk, likely because of the large Navy base there; for New York, the U.S. Coast Guard ordered that he email ahead a list of the ship's dangerous cargo and the names of all aboard, advising him that specific attention would be paid to nationals of Cuba, Iraq, Libya, North Korea, Sudan, Syria, Yugoslavia, Afghanistan, Algeria, Egypt, Kuwait, Maldives, Malaysia, Pakistan, Qatar, Saudi Arabia, Somalia, Tajikistan, Tunisia, Turkey, Turkmenistan, Yemen, Uzbekistan, and the United Arab Emirates, as well as the "Palestinian People."

Because of a shortage of Coast Guard personnel, the *Genoa* rode at anchor outside New York Harbor for eleven hours before a six-member inspection party, two of them armed, came aboard. They ordered officers and crew to assemble on the bridge, where they checked passports and briefly interviewed each seaman; all hands then stayed on the bridge except for one officer, who accompanied a team member on an inspection of the accommodation and machinery spaces while others examined the upper deck areas. After the inspection, which took about an hour and a half, the ship remained at anchor another two and a half hours, until two tugs were available to escort her into the harbor, a procedure newly instituted to guard against vessels ramming the Verrazano-Narrows Bridge or other strategic targets. When the *Genoa* finally reached her berth, no one was allowed ashore.

Until this moment it had not occurred to me that the *Colombo Bay* and thousands of her sisters were potential weapons, or that one of the millions of boxes aboard these utilitarian vessels could contain the shoe the terrorists drop next. For years smugglers have secreted drugs and other contraband in containers; now the ante is up, to conventional explosives sandwiched between a shipment of sandals from India, chemical or biological poison packed among dates from the Middle East, or a dirty radiation bomb hidden inside a container of wicker chairs en route from somewhere in Indonesia.

Once the container arrived at a U.S. port, it could be trucked almost anywhere to do its destructive work: on the Golden Gate Bridge, at the Capitol in Washington, in Times Square. Looking out at the hundreds of boxes stacked in front of the bridge, I ask Peter if they are ever inspected. Rarely, he says, confirming what I already know, that the whole point of containerization is to seal the goods at the factory and keep them moving as fast as possible along the supply chain until they reach the consignee's loading dock. In the week since September 11, official hand-wringing over lax airport security has surfaced repeatedly on the BBC; port security has rarely been mentioned, but in the months to come it will loom larger and larger as the container is recognized worldwide as a potentially lethal Trojan box, a subject revisited in the epilogue of this book.

I am contemplating these cheerful matters in my cabin when, at 1615, the ship's general alarm sounds. As earlier instructed, I report to my emergency station on the bridge, taking the three flights two steps at a time, believing that we are in bona fide trouble. If we are, Peter and Matt seem remarkably calm. They smile at my anxiety and explain that this is a drill, a scenario concocted by Peter in which Steve Kingdon is missing. He was last seen underneath the aft mooring deck entering the CO_2 Room, which houses some 300 seven-foot-high cylinders, whose carbon dioxide can be pumped into the engine room or the holds to smother a fire. In this drama, Steve is played by a boiler suit stuffed with rags that is now lying on the floor of the CO_2 Room looking like a scarecrow napping in his pajamas. Alex Gill, the reefer monitor, and Johnny Villarta, one of the able seamen, form the rescue team and head below with an oxygen rescue pack, carbon dioxide meter, and stretcher; via walkie-talkie, Peter instructs them to find out whether Steve has a broken limb or is unconscious because one or more cylinders has leaked, sucking oxygen out of the enclosed space. Taking no chances, both men pull breathing apparatuses over their faces, enter the room, place the pliable bundle on the stretcher, and remove it to the poop deck, where all hands present receive instruction on the use of the rescue pack. The presumably resuscitated Steve is then removed to the hospital on E deck, and at 1632 the exercise ends.

The seventeen-minute drill was carried out both smartly and in earnest but is followed by a somewhat less sober lifeboat rehearsal. The ship's two lifeboats are not the open, oversize rowboats of the *Titanic* variety but enclosed orange pods that look, with their tiny aviation windshields, like small space shuttles. The dozen hands now gathered about the starboard pod, all in white boiler suits, would not look out of place at Cape Kennedy. No one warned me about this drill, so I show up not in my boiler suit but in shorts and a polo shirt, an outfit that draws predictable mirth, which only escalates as first I and then Steve, now fully recovered from his ordeal, try and fail to buckle my life jacket. "Well," he says, giving up, "I guess we're going to lose you." Shakeel comes to my rescue, yanking at the straps and clasps like a mother wrestling her four-year-old into his overalls. We pile into the capsule, where more straps await, pairs of yellow and red tethers alternating down the rows of seats on each side. I immediately challenge the logic of this arrangement by grabbing one yellow and one red and, like an airline passenger with one hand on his neighbor's seat belt, again struggle without success to buckle up. We sit in the sweltering pod for about five minutes, enough time for Steve to test the engine and for me to envision the craft swinging out on its davits and dropping ten stories into the water as I bounce off the ceiling.

My initiation continues the following day when, at 1200, Peter knocks with an official sounding "Are you decent?" He enters with Steve and Matt; it's the *Colombo Bay*'s hierarchy, intimidating in their well-laundered summer whites, come for inspection. All eyes, not least my own, sweep the room. There are running shoes on the couch, socks on the floor, and wet towels hung about the bathroom like torn sails on a stormed-tossed clipper ship; the closet door is flung wide, the desk buried in debris, and papers scattered on the coffee table. I take some comfort in the made bed, then realize that my dainty travel pillow is on full display, along with the red bandanna I tie around my eyes to keep out the dawn's early light. Mister Rogers Goes to Sea. With mock severity, Peter notes the smears on the bathroom mirror, moving Steve to propose a white-glove check of the entire cabin. Peter runs his finger over the porthole sill, laughs, and they withdraw, leaving me with vivid memories of Sergeant Chiaromonte ripping up my bunk at Fort Dix for its deficient hospital corners. Whether or not the "inspection" was aimed at making me feel like one of the mates, it does—and ends my vacillating; I will not jump ship when we reach Singapore.

■ ■ ■

Since leaving Laem Chabang, we have been heading almost due south, through the Gulf of Thailand along the eastern coast of Malaysia. Each turn of the screw brings us closer to the equator, which passes about eighty-five miles south of Singapore; the sea continues calm under a torrid sun, the humidity more oppressive with every hour. On a circumnavigation of the upper deck, I encounter two of the crew on their knees chipping rust from spots they will soon repaint, in the daily battle against the predations of salt spray. In this oppressive heat, their boiler suits are aptly named. "Good morning, Dick," they say, in unison and with embarrassing deference. "Hi," I reply, trying to signal that they shouldn't regard me as an officer, a message that doesn't appear to register. This submissiveness is welcomed by most British officers, who for years had to deal with often surly and hostile British crews that, in a constant collision of class, resented being dogsbodies for their fellow countrymen. The Filipinos' commitment to duty, cooperative demeanor, and willingness to work hard for pay well below the wages demanded by unions in the West has made them the crewmen most in demand by shipping firms worldwide. These sailors, whose seafaring tradition dates back at least to their enforced service on the galleons of their sixteenth-century Spanish conquerors, now constitute about 20 percent of the crews on merchant vessels—more than 200,000 mariners, who bring to the Philippines an estimated $2 billion annually and have made Manila the manning capital of the world.

"It is very difficult to earn money in the Philippines," Nemesio Ibarrola tells me. Nemie has come to change my linen, Hoover the carpet, and otherwise clean the cabin, as he does for all the officers once a week. I tell him I can do these tasks myself, but he politely dismisses my liberal guilt and asks if I'd like him to do my laundry; when I tell him I've already done it, in the machines down the corridor, he appears disappointed. He is thirty-nine, with a round face, a mass of black hair, and a shy, gentle nature. He joined the ship on June 7 and will remain aboard for nine months, the standard tour for crew members on most P&O Nedlloyd ships, three times that served by the officers. The *Colombo Bay* is Nemie's third ship with the company; he was on the first for eleven months, the second for a year. "I needed the extra money," he says.

Like most of his Filipino mates, he earns about $1,000 a month, twelve times the average income back home, where unemployment is rife. Almost all of his paycheck goes directly to his wife, Maria Teresa, who lives with their four sons—two in primary grades, two in high school—about ninety miles south of Manila. If he manages to get time off the ship when we reach Singapore, he will try to phone his wife; such calls are rare and always brief, because of the expense. Mostly the crew depends on mail for word of home, letters their families send to the P&O Nedlloyd fleet operations in Rotterdam that are forwarded to the agent at a port in advance of the ship's arrival, a system that often works better in theory than in practice. One crew member recalled mailing a letter from Taiwan to the Philippines that took a month to arrive. Email, an alternative for the officers (and me), is not much of an option for the crew; most lack computer skills, not many of their families have easy access to the Internet, the opportunity to send personal messages from the ship is limited, and there is no privacy. I ask Nemie how long he will spend at home after he comes off the *Colombo Bay* in early March. A few weeks at most, he says. "I am working for my family; if I have no more money I will go to C. F. Sharp and ask for another ship."

C. F. Sharp is one of the many crew management agencies in Manila, a sixty-five-year-old company that in 2001 placed some 7,000 Filipinos on more than 350 merchant vessels and cruise ships. The firm verifies the sailors' credentials, checks their references, tests their seamanship and command of English, and establishes a pool to meet the needs of companies like P&O Nedlloyd. Nemie and the other crew on the *Colombo Bay* are now part of the firm's dedi-cated pool, a status they achieve at the end of their initial contract that gives them a good chance of being rehired when they apply to ship out again. This is no small advantage, since the supply of seafarers in the Philippines far exceeds the demand.

Most *Colombo Bay* crew members feel they are treated fairly if not lavishly by both Sharp and P&O Nedlloyd, and are particularly grateful that their pay comes in dollars and is promptly remitted to their families. Still, the chipping, painting, greasing of machinery, cleaning of holds, and other scut work they perform seven days a week for months at a time take their toll, as do the periods some must stand watch. Regulations require that we have a permanent lookout on the bridge between sunset and sunrise and during daylight hours when visibility is limited. The officer on the bridge always has tasks to keep him occupied—plotting our course, correcting charts, tracking the weather, monitoring the radio and radar, and many more—but the crew lookout stands before the windshield and gazes out across the boxes and over the sea with little else to do but count the days.

Federico Castrojas had just finished standing watch for four hours one afternoon when we went to his quarters for a talk. His cabin is like those of his mates, a narrow, rectangular space less than half the size of mine; it is crammed with a bed, bathroom, closet, and small desk, and seems only slightly larger than a Pullman bedroom in the days of the 20th Century Limited. A boom box the size of a roller bag makes the area smaller still. It is hooked up to the TV so Federico can watch and listen to videos of his favorite groups, among them the Eagles, whose voices fill the room as he demonstrates the stereo sound of what is plainly one of his proudest possessions. He turns the music down and shows me pictures of his large family, including his son, Gabriel Hermie, and wife, Swanie. "We are separated, but I still love her," he says, unburdening himself as if I were an old friend instead of someone he is talking to for the first time. As if on cue, the Eagles sing "The Girl from Yesterday." On the wall is a picture of Jesus and a small silver cross; beneath them a Bible lies open on the desk. "I read the Psalms, because they make you strong," Federico says. A map of the Pacific Northwest hangs over the bed; I ask if he has a special interest in the region. "No," he replies. "I pasted it over the painting of a cemetery in Egypt that was hanging there; it gave me nightmares, I couldn't sleep."

Federico is thirty and has been a seaman since 1991, when he graduated from nautical college in the Philippines; he is balding, with a slim mustache and a goatee, features that suggest insouciance until the sadness of his voice intrudes. His father suffered a heart attack while Federico was on his previous ship and died less than a week after he sailed on the *Colombo Bay* on April 21. He did not learn of the death for several days, and attending the funeral would not have been an option even had he been notified promptly. Three of Federico's five brothers have been seamen, and two of his four sisters are married to seamen. One brother, Ronnie, was on a ship in 1997 when, at age thirty-seven, he fell to his death during a boat drill off Colombia. After this accident the wives of Federico's two other mariner brothers asked them to quit the sea, which they did. Federico, too, would prefer work onshore. In high school he enjoyed drawing and wanted to be an artist, a goal his family dismissed as unremunerative. He looks at his callused hands and says, "They're too hard now; you need soft hands."

By now his maritime skills are all he has, and like his Filipino shipmates he acknowledges that the money at sea is much better than he could make at home. "My uncle is a judge, but he earns half what I do," he says. Federico's nine-month stint ends January 2, when the *Colombo Bay* reaches Singapore on its eastward voyage back to Seattle and Vancouver. "I will be home in time for Hermie's second birthday, on January 21," he says, his eyes tearing as he speaks of the event, and then of the collapse of his marriage. I ask if his long absences were the reason. "No, it was more her family." He does not explain, and I do not press him. He has met a new woman, Mayet, who works at the Polytechnic University of the Philippines; divorce, however, is not permitted in his predominantly Catholic homeland, only annulment, a process that takes seven years. "I have six to go, and it is very hard for Mayet, very hard." He is weeping openly now, as he tells of how children of annulled marriages are often treated as outcasts in the Philippines, of how he fears for his son's future. He wipes his eyes with his T-shirt and apologizes for his emotion. "This is a very sad job, a very lonely job," he says, looking away.

The buildup of loneliness over nine months at sea would be ameliorated if wives or girlfriends could sail with crew members for at least part of the period, as Elizabeth has joined Peter for the three-plus weeks it will take us to travel from Hong Kong to Malta. But by long seafaring tradition, as well as P&O Nedlloyd policy and that of most other liner companies, only officers earn the perk of companionship and the right to bring their children on voyages. Crews of whatever nationality, ethnicity, or color must tough it out alone. Even if, improbably, this double standard were to end, the plight of Federico and his fellow Filipinos would unlikely change much. Most of their wives could not afford to fly from Manila to meet the ship in

Hong Kong, Singapore, or Kao-hsiung, much less return home from a more distant port; nor could they leave their children, who are doubly dependent on them in their fathers' absence. Even if these obstacles could be overcome, the crews' cramped cabins would become intolerable for two people after only a few days.

Whatever hardships Filipinos face aboard the *Colombo Bay* and other merchant ships, they know that thousands of their countrymen and seamen from China, Indonesia, Turkey, and other developing nations have it much worse trapped aboard vessels flying flags of convenience. By the middle of 2003, the world fleet of ships of 1,000 gross tons or greater totaled more than 28,000; at least half these were FOC vessels, registered in Cyprus, Malta, Liberia, the Bahamas, Panama, and some twenty other small nations. None of these countries has a significant shipping industry, but all provide shipowners cost-cutting havens where they can register their vessels without having to meet the manning, maintenance, safety, pollution, and seaworthiness standards set by laws and regulations in the developed world. Taxes in FOC states are minimal to nonexistent, safety inspections rare and perfunctory, the wages, living conditions, and treatment of crews nobody's business but the master's. Officers and crew aboard FOC ships frequently lack proper training and credentials: in 2001 an anticorruption prosecutor in Panama revealed that scores of fake seafaring licenses and other documents had been stamped with the seal of the Panama Maritime Authority.

Shipowners in all countries take advantage of flags of convenience: 40 percent of the vessels registered in Panama are Japanese owned; 16 percent in the Bahamas, U.S. owned; 10 percent in Cyprus, German owned. Greek shipowners are particularly fond of the FOC dodge; 72 percent of Cyprus's and 55 percent of Malta's flags fly over Greek-owned vessels, numbers that dovetail with Aristotle Onassis's observation, perhaps made while he was relaxing on his yacht, that it is "poverty that drives men to sea. . . . Otherwise, no one would bear the hardships and deprivations, the separation from hearth and home and country of the sailor's life."

In 2001 the International Commission on Shipping, an independent body based in Australia, published an angry, 266-page report that cataloged what everyone in the industry has long known: for "thousands of today's international seafarers life at sea is modern slavery and their work place is a slave ship." The masters of these indentured servants are often literally that, captains who are usually racist and regard their deckhands as so many expendable bodies in the devotion to produce profits for the ship's owner. The report's inventory of maltreatment includes delayed payment or nonpayment of wages, failure to provide adequate food and accommodation, denial of medical treatment and time off, physical and psychological abuse, and sexual assault.

In 1999 an Australian named Gordon Green was fishing outside Sydney harbor near where the *Tomis Future,* a bulk carrier flying the Maltese flag, lay at anchor. When he noticed several of the crew waving to him, he moved closer and they threw a bottle toward him. The message inside read: "Please, if you can, call ITF because we have big problem on board. No money, no food, no water." Green relayed the message to the Sydney office of the International Transportation Workers' Federation, a London-based organization that monitors the treatment of men and women employed in all aspects of transportation worldwide, which found that the crew had been without freshwater for two weeks, had been surviving on little food, and that no allotments from their wages had been sent to their families for four months.

Owners also abandon broken-down vessels in ports far from the seaman's home country where, penniless and often unable to speak the language, he can only hope that the charity of church missions will rescue him. The ITF reported that between July 1995 and the end of 1998 it received notification of 199 cases where shipowners had walked away from their vessels, leaving some 3,500 seafarers unpaid and stranded. One hundred and thirty of these ships were flying flags of convenience, seventy of them the blue and red stars of Panama. These are just the cases that reached the ITF, which maintains they represent only a fraction of the total.

The FOC expedient has produced hundreds of pariah vessels worldwide—aging, badly maintained, polluting hulks that were well-represented in both Hong Kong and Laem Chabang harbors. With their peeling paint, rusting hulls, and neglected accommodation structures, they look like tramps—not as in the time-honored use of the term to mean merchant vessels that don't ply a regular route but as in derelicts. In storms or after collisions they often become coffin ships, because of cracked plates, defective firefighting and lifesaving equipment, and malfunctioning machinery. The 50 percent of the world fleet that flew flags of convenience in 2000 accounted for 75 percent of the gross tonnage lost; Panama topped the list from 1982 through 1998, a year when thirteen ships registered there went down.

One of them was the *New Baron,* a general cargo vessel that in stormy January weather near Ulsan, South Korea, ran onto the rocks, then slipped off and sank, with the loss of seventeen Filipino lives. The day before the *Flare,* a twenty-six-year-old bulk carrier registered in Cyprus, was sailing from Rotterdam to pick up a load of grain in Montreal when she broke in two in heavy weather and sank in the Gulf of St. Lawrence. A Canadian helicopter rescued four of the crew from their capsized lifeboat, one with a broken arm, all suffering from hypothermia; the remaining twenty-one perished in the frigid waters.

Seamen who complain about the hazardous and other inadequate conditions aboard FOC vessels are sometimes beaten and usually blacklisted as troublemakers by manning companies and government agencies in their home countries. This kind of maltreatment and the lack of standards aboard FOC ships in general are in clear violation of regulations established by the United Nations Convention on the Law of the Sea, the International Maritime Organization of the UN, the International Labor Organization, and dozens of national maritime bodies, including the U.S. Coast Guard. P&O Nedlloyd and most other major liner companies abide by these rules for the most part, but the exploitation of crews on FOC and many other vessels is likely to continue indefinitely, encouraged by widespread lack of enforcement of the regulations and fueled by the greed of shipowners and the abundant supply of men from developing nations desperate to feed their families.

Their degradation is only the latest on a continuum that stretches back centuries. Sailors of all nations have always faced not just the winds of indifferent nature that have sent thousands of them to the bottom with their ships but the lash of unscrupulous owners and captains. Psalm 107 may have comforted many a mariner with its assurance that God looks after those who go down to the sea in ships, but when they found themselves at their wits' end, a more profane being usually stood on the quarterdeck. A litany of this inhumanity is laid out in *Poor Jack: The Perilous History of the Merchant Seaman,* Ronald Hope's compendium of letters and other documents testifying to the routine cruelty of seafaring life, merchant and naval. Hope quotes one John Nicol, an Edinburgh cooper aboard the *Surprise,* a twenty-eight-gun frigate, during the Revolutionary War:

One of our men was whipped through the fleet for stealing some dollars. . . . It was a dreadful sight; the unfortunate sufferer tied down on the boat, and rowed from ship to ship, getting an equal number of lashes at the side of each vessel from a fresh man. The poor wretch, to deaden his sufferings, had drunk a whole bottle of rum a little before the time of punishment. When he had only two portions to get of his punishment, the captain of the ship perceived he was tipsy, and immediately ordered the rest of the punishment to be delayed until he was sober. He was rowed back to the *Surprise,* his back swelled like a pillow, black and blue; some sheets of thick blue paper were steeped in vinegar and laid upon his back. Before he seemed insensible; now his shrieks rent the air.

Men were press-ganged off the streets, crews never paid; ships sailed with rotting salt beef and weevily biscuits and often ran out of food altogether, leaving the crew to scavenge for rats and drink their own urine; smallpox and other killer diseases raced along the decks, especially aboard ships making the infamous Middle Passage across the Atlantic from Africa to America with slaves chained in the holds. "The death rate among sailors in slave ships—perhaps 20 percent a year—was higher than that among the slaves, for the latter were valuable merchandise," Hope writes with deadpan irony.

An economic historian who for forty years directed what is now the Marine Society, Britain's oldest seaman's charity, Hope points out that the mistreatment and deaths of sailors during the growth of merchant shipping in the seventeenth and eighteenth centuries came in the service not just of slavery but of other new trades that were hardly essential: "Drugs and spices from the East did not cure any illnesses nor preserve any foods; rum and sack turned some into alcoholics; sugar rotted their teeth; and tobacco was and remains a killer of powerful proportions." At Laem Chabang, more than a dozen containers of that baneful vegetable came aboard the *Colombo Bay,* bound for R. J. Reynolds, the cigarette company that made Malcom McLean a rich man in 1969 by purchasing his Sea-Land Service, Inc. The tobacco was shipped by JTI, the international arm of Japan Tobacco, Inc., which purchased RJR's global operation in 1999, making JTI the third largest tobacco company in the world. Under contract with the Japanese company, RJR turns the tobacco into Camels, Winstons, and Mild 7s, and ships the cartons back to JTI, which has made the brands three of the world's five best-sellers. With the market for smoking shrinking in the United States, billions of cigarettes made from imported tobacco are now shipped overseas by container to satisfy the cravings in China, Russia, and other addicted nations.

■ ■ ■

Despite all the advances in naval architecture, navigation technology, and safety procedures, seafaring remains one of the world's most dangerous professions. In the last decade of the twentieth century, accidents, storms, collisions, sinkings, and other hazards took the lives of some 7,000 persons serving on merchant vessels of all flags. One of them was Danny Boag, whose story I heard one evening after dinner from Chris Marlow, the second engineer, who had grappled along with Frank McAlees to replace the cylinder stud. He had come to my quarters to talk about his life at sea, and as he leaned forward and spoke of Danny Boag, the voice of Conrad's Marlow, narrator of *Youth* and *Heart of Darkness,* seemed to fill the cabin.

"Boag was what merchant seamen call a professional third," he began, meaning a third engineer who for whatever reason—laziness, failure to pass his orals, contentment with his lot—never rises above that bottom rank. "In the late nineties, he and I were shipmates on the *Cardigan Bay,* one of P&O Nedlloyd's older container ships, when she had an engine room breakdown near Sri Lanka. It was Danny's job to repair the machinery, in an engine room with extreme temperatures and humidity. He worked many hours over a couple of days, at one point for eight hours straight. I told him he simply had to come up and take a break, get some sleep, which he finally did."

Marlow paused and shook his head, describing a drama that was clearly as fresh to him as if it had unfolded last week. "When the time came for Danny to go back to work, I phoned him in his cabin but got no answer. I tried the bar, then the engine room, but couldn't find him. Panic stations! Search parties scoured the ship from prow to stern. He was nowhere." The *Cardigan Bay* turned about and steamed back six hours, all eyes searching the sea to no avail. The police in Colombo took statements, as did the police in Bermuda, where the ship was registered. Boag's wife and children in Ireland were notified, but no one onboard the *Cardigan Bay* knew what to say. Had he been drinking and fallen overboard? Had the ordeal in the engine room literally driven him over the edge, a suicide? "He just vanished," Marlow said. "Nobody knows to this day what happened to him."

Such ship-related deaths and the incidents that cause them are reported in a few maritime publications, notably *Lloyd's List,* the centuries-old shipping newspaper that publishes a daily casualty report in print and on-line. Coverage rarely appears in the mainstream press or on television news, which reserve their alarms for major oil spills like those caused when the tanker *Torrey Canyon* broke up off the south coast of England in 1967 and the *Exxon Valdez* ran aground in Alaska's Prince William Sound in 1989. On November 20, 2002, the *New York Times* ran a dramatic page-one color photo showing the two halves of the tanker *Prestige* sinking off the coast of Spain. The twenty-six-year-old, 791-foot-long vessel had cracked in gale-churned seas, dumping some of her 20 million gallons of oil into heavily fished waters and onto miles of beaches before breaking in two and sinking in water two miles deep. The *Times* devoted a lead editorial to the catastrophe and gave the spill running coverage for several days, as did the rest of the world's media.

Like other such accidents, the *Prestige* spill was undeniably an ecological disaster, and demands that such aging, single-hull tankers be taken out of service make sense, as do the repeated calls for Americans to stop driving SUVs and to cut back on their oil gluttony in general. Still, some perspective may be useful. In 2002 the National Research Council of the National Academy of Sciences released a study showing that tanker and pipeline spills accounted for only a small fraction of the man-made petroleum pollution in North

American ocean waters. Some 85 percent of such pollution comes from fuel dumping by airline pilots, emissions from boats and Jet Skis, and runoff from motor vehicles and other land-based sources. Natural seepage of crude oil from the ocean floor totals an estimated 47 million gallons annually in North American waters and 180 million gallons worldwide, while tanker and pipeline mishaps off the North American coasts account for less than 3 million gallons. The council's study found that, thanks to advances in vessel construction, tanker spills had been reduced significantly in the 1990s even though the number of tankers in service had increased by 900 to 7,270.

The *Prestige* sinking caused no human fatalities, nor do most other tanker spills. They do kill off thousands of fish, birds, and sea mammals, deaths that can always be counted on to produce heart-rending photos of crude-soaked cormorants. Concern for such victims and befouled coastlines continues to spawn large, sympathetic headlines after every spill, while the deaths of merchant mariners daily all over the globe seldom draw a sound bite.

CHAPTER FOUR

The lights of Singapore come into view at around 2000. We are entering the world's busiest port, a trading center since 1819, when Sir Thomas Stamford Raffles, prime mover in establishing the British empire in East Asia, made Singapore pivotal in the China trade; once steam replaced sails and the Suez Canal opened, in 1869, the port became the thriving entrepôt it remains. Tankers, container ships, and other large cargo vessels make 25,000 calls here annually, 10,000 more than at Hong Kong, the world's second busiest port. Three dozen ships are anchored or moving on our starboard, looking on the radar screen like a school of pale green guppies. We pass a tug pulling a barge that, in the shadows, looms like a dead whale being hauled to its final resting place. A few stars poke through the clouds, and I'm about to tell Elizabeth, who has joined us on the darkened bridge, that I've spotted a shooting one when I realize it's a plane, the first I've seen since we left Hong Kong a week ago. The approach to Changi International Airport is across our bow, and each passenger jet slipping toward the runways carries second thoughts. I have already told Diane by email to cancel the Singapore flights, that I have decided to stay the course. I wonder if I have made the right choice, then think of the crew's nine-month enlistment, Shakeel's fear for his family in Karachi, Matt's worry that he might not get home in time for the birth of his first child,

Alex's concern for his ailing girlfriend in Glasgow—and am cha-grined that I have the luxury of a choice at all.

As we berth, a single tug pushes our stern about so we will face outward for tomorrow's departure. The dinosaurs are already clank-ing into position in the wharf's blazing yellow light, the trucks be-neath looking like Tonkas. We tie up at just past 2300, a half hour early. The date is September 19, a Wednesday, though it could just as well be Monday or Saturday; days at sea are so undifferentiated, the work so incessant, that the only hint a week is beginning anew is the traditional serving of steak at Sunday dinner.

In the morning, Yap Han Lianga, a cheerful P&O Nedlloyd em-ployee, drives me to the company's Singapore headquarters. It is in the Suntec Center, a complex of four towers set around a giant bronze ring that stands on four thick, bronze legs, in the center of which water shoots a hundred feet into the air. This Fountain of Wealth, at 19,000 pounds the world's largest spout, is just across from Suntec's three-story mall, one of some eighty shopping centers in this island city-state of 4 million inhabitants where wealth may be conveniently dispensed and acquired in air-conditioned comfort. We walk to the elevators in Tower Four surrounded by handsome, well-pressed Singaporeans striding to work on the floors above, instant stand-ins for the New Yorkers making small talk and carrying coffee and bagels as the planes struck.

In the office on the tenth floor, Yap leads me to his cubicle, where I plug in my laptop and download twenty-nine emails, which demon-strate not that two dozen friends and relatives are concerned about me but that I am never out of reach of entrepreneurs eager to have me earn big bucks working at home so I can take advantage of fan-tastic low-interest mortgages while contemplating the advantages of an enlarged penis and viewing teen sluts engaged with sundry farm animals. After purging this spam, I send off several emails I had composed yesterday and call Diane. We talk for forty minutes, the conversation crimped by the lack of privacy, a nagging sense that I

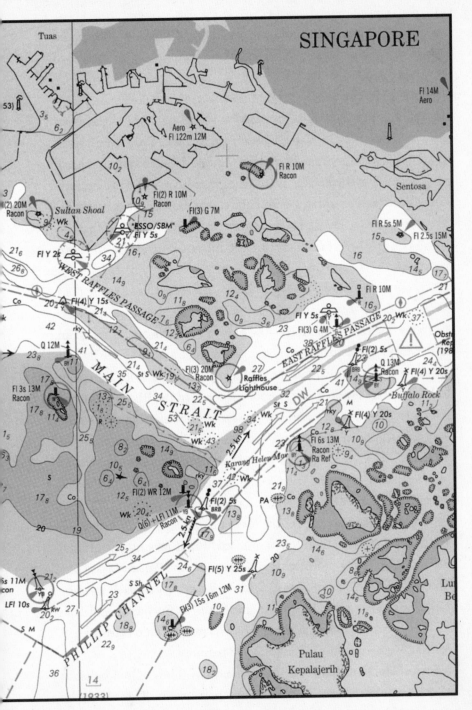

One of the World's Most Hazardous Passages: The Singapore Strait

am tying up Yap's phone, and the constant feeling that I should be by her side instead of playing jack-tar and trying to bounce my love off satellites.

By the time we hang up it is almost noon, and I take Kipling's advice to feed at Raffles. Britain ruled the waves when this sprawl of a hotel, named after Sir Thomas, went up in 1887; Prada, Tiffany & Co., Gucci, and other luxe stores now line its arcades and courtyard, but the whitewashed walls, palm trees, verandas, balustrades, burnished wood, enveloping wicker chairs, and vaulting lobby with its three handwoven Persian rugs remain quintessential Raj. In obeisance, I have lunch at the Empire Café, all ice cream chairs and marble tables.

My companions are the *Straits Times,* the *Financial Times, USA Today,* and the *International Herald Tribune,* fresh broadsheets that offer diverse distractions—the baseball standings, a story about a British mother who dashed 900 miles by taxis and planes to deliver her son's Game Boy, which she had forgotten to pack for him—but nothing much new on 9/11 to anyone steeped in the BBC's extensive coverage. The one exception is a piece, on the back page of the *IHT,* reporting that demand in the United States for American flags has been so great since the attack that domestic flag makers have been unable to meet it, prompting China to step into the breach. The Jin Teng Flag Co., in Zhejiang Province, reported U.S. orders of 600,000; Wu Guomin, office director of the Mei Li Hua Flags Co. in Shanghai, put his total at more than half a million. "Right now no one around the world can really compete with us flag makers. We have good machines and rock bottom labor costs," Wu said, claims I imagine achieving the singular feat of enraging both Pat Buchanan and Tom Hayden, though not the company whose container ship is transporting the "Made in China" star-spangled banners.

At the Suntec mall I get a haircut and buy a box of golf balls for Peter's birthday, after which all of Singapore awaits. There is the local history museum and the Asian Civilisations Museum, known for its Chinese ceramics and imperial porcelain; mosques and temples seem almost as ubiquitous as the shopping plazas. The Botanic Gardens are highly touted, 130 acres offering thousands of plant species, including 60,000 orchids; there's also the Bukit Timah Nature Reserve, a 200-acre primary rain forest replete with tropical birds. Both these outdoor destinations have their allure, though I tend to share Noël Coward's view, composed about Singapore and like tropical climes, that only mad dogs and Englishmen go out in the midday sun. Maybe a compromise is in order, a cable car ride to the beach on Sentosa Island for a cooling swim. Of course, all this speculation is wishful. It is now 1500, and the *Colombo Bay* is scheduled to depart in three hours, which means I must be back onboard in two, allowing at least a half hour for transit.

I am beginning to appreciate the revision muttered by my mates —"Join the merchant service and see nothing"—though the see-the-world days were not always a shoreside romp. On September 22, 1885, the sailing ship *Tilkhurst* arrived in Singapore after a three-and-a-half-month voyage from England with the twenty-seven-year-old Joseph Conrad aboard as second mate. The vessel stayed in port for a month while its cargo of coal was unloaded, giving all hands plenty of time to indulge in the outpost's exotic diversions; the crew grew so bored that they rioted, inflicting on one seaman a serious head injury. His behavior grew more and more erratic once the *Tilkhurst* sailed for Calcutta, and though his shipmates kept an eye on him, he eventually jumped overboard and drowned.

After retrieving my laptop from the office, I hail a taxi and head back to the ship. When the driver discovers that I'm from New York, he is briefly solicitous of the city's woes, then asks: "Would you like to see *our* World Trade Centre? It's not high, like yours, but it is very big." He assures me it is close to our destination, the Tanjong Pagar container terminal, and that a detour will take only a few minutes. I decline and change the subject by remarking on the couple darting in front of us against the light. Such jaywalking would not turn a head in midtown Manhattan, but aren't Singaporeans supposed to be among the most law-abiding people in the world? "They are probably tourists, and even they would be in trouble if the police were around," he says, adding, "The government knows what is best." What is best here are restrictions on freedom of the press and assembly; the filing of financially ruinous civil defamation suits against critics of the People's Action Party, which has ruled without serious challenge since before Singapore gained independence from Malaysia in 1965; mandatory caning—including of juveniles—for some thirty assorted crimes, among them illegal immigration and vandalism; and a mandatory death penalty for drug trafficking, murder, treason, and certain firearms offenses that, in all, yielded 340 hangings between 1991 and 2000.

Most citizens are properly cowed by this autocratic rule and bow to Orwellian pep talk such as "nation before community and society above self," though the message did not get through to at least thirteen Singaporeans arrested in January 2002. The government alleged that they were members of a clandestine organization called the Islamic Group, which had links to Al Qaeda and had been plotting for several years to bomb Western embassies, U.S. corporations, and naval vessels and other targets in the country. They were detained indefinitely without trial, another repressive wrinkle in this postage-stamp republic, one that would make the high moral ground quite muddy once the same tactic was employed after 9/11 in the great constitutional democracy of my birth. As I paid the driver at the terminal gate, he made one last pitch for the World Trade Centre, then urged me to visit Singapore soon again. "It is a very clean city, don't you think?"

It is, and the government also makes the cranes run on time. The operators work in three shifts twenty-four hours a day every day of the year at Tanjong Pagar and the port's three other container terminals, which together cover 830 acres and through which more than 17 million TEUs passed in 2000. The efficiency of this and other large Asian ports—much of it driven by increasingly sophisticated computer technology—draws high praise from the *Colombo Bay*'s officers and shipping executives like Jeremy Nixon, especially when compared with that of most U.S. ports. In Singapore, a single person working with a joystick at a video console in an air-conditioned control room can operate several straddle cranes, which move about the terminal on tires, straddle the trucks, lift boxes off, and ferry them underneath the gantries for loading onto the ships.

At Global Gateway South, the largest terminal at the Port of Los Angeles–Long Beach, the *Wall Street Journal* reported not long before I embarked, each straddle crane has "a crew of four: two drivers, who take turns at the controls, plus a clerk to coordinate their tasks and a signalman, who acts as the driver's eyes and ears." In some cases the crew knows which box to grab only because the clerk has written the container number on the bed of the truck in bright yellow chalk. One measure of port productivity is the number of TEUs handled per terminal acre per year. Hong Kong's Kwai Chung terminal leads the way with 18,500, followed by Kao-hsiung (18,000) and Singapore (11,000); the number for Los Angeles–Long Beach, which handles roughly a third of the United States' containerized cargo, was 4,540. By one estimate, this kind of lackluster productivity costs the U.S. economy $1 billion a year.

By the summer of 2002, West Coast longshoremen and the liner companies would face off on just this issue, the main sticking point being the introduction of new technology at the twenty-nine container terminals from San Diego to Seattle. In 2001 these ports handled some 40 percent of the nation's seaborne cargo, valued at more than $320 billion. The terminal operators and shipowners, represented by the Pacific Maritime Association, saw new automation as crucial to increasing productivity in processing this volume, which is expected to double by 2010 and double again in the following decade, to almost 30 million TEUs a year at Los Angeles–Long Beach alone. The International Longshore and Warehouse Union did not flat-out oppose this latest push for advanced technology but, having lost roughly 90,000 jobs since striking in 1971 over the coming of containerization, was determined to see that any newly created computerized tasks stayed within union jurisdiction. This the PMA opposed, especially for marine clerks, who were now taking electronic data about incoming consignments and rekeyboarding them, a redundancy for which some received a pay package worth up to $120,000 a year. The average annual pay package of ILWU members was lower, upward of $100,000, but still well above what most unionized blue-collar workers in the United States made, the result of both the ILWU's negotiating clout and the willingness of the liner companies over the last three decades to avoid strikes by settling, to keep the boxes moving.

The PMA took a harder line in 2002. On September 29, after weeks of negotiation had proved futile, the association locked out the workers, accusing the ILWU of an organized slowdown. Suddenly, the unseen world of containerization was on page one and the evening news, as scores of ships rode at anchor outside the idled ports and the supply chains for thousands of goods began backing up all over the world. By October 3, *The New York Times* reported, twenty containers of broccoli bound for Taiwan and Japan sat in danger of rotting at the Port of Oakland, a potential $320,000 loss to its California grower; a General Motors–Toyota auto assembly plant in the state had shut down because needed parts were still aboard ship; in Hawaii and Alaska, which are heavily dependent on imports, basics like toilet paper and canned goods were running out. With Green Friday less than two months away, the flow of toys and other goods destined for the Christmas shelves had ceased, panicking a business community already shaken by corporate scandals, an ailing economy, and the financial implications of President George W. Bush's threat to invade Iraq.

On October 8, with world commerce facing losses of billions of dollars, the president invoked the Taft-Hartley Act, ending the ten-day lockout because, he said, the nation's economic health and security demanded it. The act's requirement of an eighty-day cooling off period assured that holiday cash registers would jingle on schedule but infuriated the longshoremen and members of many other unions, who felt that labor's only effective weapon—the strike—had been wrenched from their hands by a Republican administration slavish to big business. "We now have a new dock boss," Richard Mead, president of an ILWU local in San Francisco, told the *Times.* "His name is George W. Bush. Will the workers listen to Boy George? I don't know."

The immediate answer was apparent to all aboard the *Colombo Bay* on October 22, when she arrived at Seattle after crossing the Pacific from Kao-hsiung, Captain Will Stoker now in command. The ship dropped anchor in Elliott Bay off the city's downtown and sat "swinging on the hook" for six days while the PMA complained to the U.S. Department of Justice that productivity at the port was 27 percent below normal because the ILWU had resumed its slowdown after returning to work. The union denied the charge, countering that the accumulated containers and "logistical disaster" on the docks were the result of the PMA's ten-day lockout. There was truth in both assertions, faint consolation to the men of the *Colombo Bay,* who spent the week bobbing in the harbor, doing routine engine room and deck maintenance, and mostly twiddling their thumbs as they gazed at the Space Needle and watched the skyline, in Stoker's words, "flare up in a blaze of orange as the reflection of the setting sun did its magic from all the windows."

Such postcard views were no substitute for going ashore, and a few hands looked into hiring a launch, only to be discouraged by price quotes of $450 to $600. When the ship finally did reach her berth, on the twenty-eighth, the congestion at the terminal was so severe and the pace of the stevedores so slow that she stayed alongside not for the several hours it usually takes to unload and load boxes but for three days. This allowed Captain Stoker enough shore time to get in a round of golf with the first mate, which doubtless would have made Peter Davies envious but may have displeased King Neptune; as the *Colombo Bay* steamed back across the Pacific, now running a week behind schedule, hurricane winds battered the ship for four straight days, delaying her further.

During the nine days the *Colombo Bay* was stalled in Seattle, the operations meter continued to tick, at a cost to P&O Nedlloyd of $25,000 to $35,000 a day. More important, the clogged pipeline meant that the containers aboard could not be circulated back into the system for unpacking and then repacking of new paying cargo. And once the ship had lost two or three days, she could not catch up to her original schedule without dropping ports, which ultimately leads to canceled voyages and more revenue loss. P&O Nedlloyd was fortunate in not operating any West Coast terminals, so the company lost no money because of the reduced container traffic during the slowdown-lockout; but Maersk Sealand, American President Lines, and several other liner firms that do own West Coast terminals were hit with a double financial whammy. By the end of November, the potential long-range economic pain had persuaded the ILWU and the PMA to settle on a six-year contract. Union members received modest pay raises but a pension increase of almost 60 percent, guaranteeing them an annual retirement income of $54,000 after thirty years on the docks. The liner companies and terminal operators got what they wanted most, a free hand to introduce optical scanners, remote cameras, and other advanced technologies to track containers both in port and on the oceans.

■ ■ ■

In Singapore, the *Colombo Bay* is berthed at Tango 3, a fifteen-minute walk from the Tanjong Pagar terminal gate by stack after stack of containers and their belching trucks in waiting. At the ship, three gantries move full tilt loading the last of several hundred boxes, an incongruous cornucopia of teas, glassware, bedding, fruits, nuts, furniture, seeds (fennel, coriander, caraway), jute, electrical cable, oils, optical lenses and prisms, natural sponges, engine parts, beverages, hats and caps, medical supplies, sports bags, leather goods, clothing, and greeting cards. I must pass beneath one of the dinosaurs to get to the gangway and feel every bit the landlubber standing amid the perspiring stevedores, ThinkPad in one hand, bagful of golf balls in the other. I wait until the gantry grabs a box from the sixteen-wheeler parked below; when the container moves over the hold, I make a dash and clamber up the quivery stairway, looking forward to my efficient shower and, for once, the ship's wintry climate.

In the lounge before dinner, Shakeel and others are batting about a rumor that we may not call at Malta as planned but instead go around the Cape of Good Hope. I think they are ragging me, then recall that at lunch yesterday Steve said we would be taking on 1,700 tons of fuel from a bunkering barge in Singapore even though we had enough to get to New York; he had explained that the oil was likely being added either because the price was favorable in Singapore or because we needed extra ballast to help balance the containers coming aboard. At dinner Peter offers a third reason: if hostilities break out, a Suez transit could be dangerous, and regardless, the war and terrorism surcharge levied by the *Colombo Bay*'s insurers might be so high for passage through the Red Sea and the canal that a Cape run would be not only safer but cheaper, despite the extra fuel burned and the missed transfer of boxes at Malta.

A look at the world map on the bridge confirms what any high school geographer knows: that the endless trip around the southern tip of Africa is just the voyage the creators of the canal sought to shortcut more than 130 years ago. A Cape run would begin in five days, after we leave Colombo, our next port; we would move southwest through the Indian Ocean, past the island of Diego Garcia and the east coast of Madagascar, round the Cape, and head northwest through the south and north Atlantic to Halifax. The passage would cover some 11,000 nautical miles and take at least three weeks in the best of weather, which is by no means guaranteed, as thousands of mariners have learned, among them Ishmael, who recalls the Cape winds howling around the eastbound *Pequod* as she "bowed to the blast, and gored the dark waves in her madness, till, like showers of silver chips, the foam flakes flew over her bulwarks. . . . Cape of Good Hope, do they call ye? Rather Cape Tormentoso, as called of yore." During the detour the *Colombo Bay* would put into no ports and see little or no land.

"Qué será, será," says Peter, which fairly describes his life view; he deplores the terrorist attack but also says of the victims, "If your number's up, it's up; you can catch it crossing the road, too." Still, he can't be too pleased at the possibility of a Cape run since he and Elizabeth are scheduled to fly home from Malta after he turns over the *Colombo Bay* to a new master. Matt and Alex are also due off at that Mediterranean island, which we are scheduled to reach on October 5. A Cape run could put us in Halifax as late as October 21, a week behind schedule, and could well cause Matt to miss the birth of his child. There does, however, seem to be an upside to the roundabout contingency, which turns out to be that I am a polliwog.

Polliwogs are sailors crossing the equator for the first time. There are no other polliwogs aboard the *Colombo Bay;* all hands are shellbacks, seamen who have crossed the line at least once and most of them many times. Elizabeth, too, is a well-tested shellback. The Crossing the Line rite has been traced back as far as the Vikings, who marked crossing the thirtieth parallel and may have passed their ritual on to the Anglo-Saxons and Normans in Britain. According to Ronald Hope's *Poor Jack,* the earliest known documentation of a crossing-the-line observance was recorded by two Frenchmen on their voyage from Dieppe to Sumatra in 1529: "On Tuesday, 11th May, in the morning, about fifty of our people were made knights and received the accolade on crossing the equator, and the mass *Salve sancta parens* was sung from music to mark the solemnity of the day." Solemnity does not best describe the modern ceremony, as suggested by my younger mates' knowing snickers and by Jeremy Nixon's account of his own initiation aboard the general cargo vessel *Nessbank* in 1979.

He was eighteen and heading from Oslo to South Africa with one Andrew Clements, both of them navigation cadets on their first trip at sea. In port, a fifty-six-gallon oil drum, into which galley slops were thrown, sat on the poop deck. Normally, these biodegradables would go overboard when the ship reached deep ocean; on the *Nessbank,* the drum was put inside the funnel, its contents left to marinate in the intense heat for the fourteen days it took to reach the equator. On the day of the crossing, the ceremony unfolded in what has become the classic routine. Both cadets were excused from duty and given a chance to hide while a group of officers drew up a list of charges against them, including citations for grievous naïveté, such as their discovery after standing around in the hot engine room for forty-five minutes that the "long wait" the chief engineer had promised to bring them was not a tool. Among Jeremy's more serious transgressions was asking, in the bar on his first day aboard, how long the "cruise" would last. Everyone not on duty turned out to search for the two green hands, who were soon found and tied by their wrists to the rail behind the poop deck; as an officer dressed as Neptune looked on in judgment, a Chief Executioner directed the induction.

"They first stripped off all our body hair with an electric shaver," Jeremy told me. "Because Andrew was so lippy, they cut off one eyebrow, one side of his mustache, and half of his body hair, so that he would have to cut the rest off himself." A necklace of chicken bones that had been stewing in the heated drum for two weeks was now draped over each initiate's head, after which they were slathered in antifouling paint and then gruel from the drum. King Neptune read out the charges, welcomed them into his world of seafaring, and then all shellbacks retired to the bar for a few drinks. "When they were of a mood, they came back and doused us with a high-pressure hose. That took off the necklaces and slops but not the antifouling lead paint. It stuck to our bodies for days and days. And of course you're totally bald. When we arrived in South Africa about ten days later, people thought I was either in the Army or a convict," Jeremy said.

Lest I hope that P&O Nedlloyd eschewed such jejune proceedings, Simon Westall, the third mate, assured me that when, at sixteen, he crossed the equator for the first time on the *Botany Bay,* another of the company's container ships, King Neptune and his assistants were very much on duty. "They covered my face in corn flour, red dye, and water, and made me drink a cocktail of cheap champagne, Tabasco, salt, vinegar, and other nasty things; I almost threw up," he told me. Like Jeremy, Andrew, and all other polliwogs, Simon received a certificate attesting to his ordeal and establishing that he was now a shellback in good standing and would never have to go through this baptism again—unless he lost the document. As a college freshman I had traversed a similar hazing to enter the hallowed brotherhood of Beta Theta Pi; it seemed unlikely, though, that the *Colombo Bay*'s shellbacks would find this fact at all mitigating, even were I able to produce a certificate.

■ ■ ■

There is hardly a ripple when we leave Singapore's sultry harbor after dinner, so the ship's sudden heeling as we turn to starboard takes me by surprise as I sit at my desk. Like a fumbling croupier, I scoop up pens, pencils, camera, tape recorder, and other chips, and stash them in a drawer as my shaving cream, razor, and toothpaste cannonball off the shelf below the bathroom medicine cabinet into the sink. Have we encountered a squall, or even a typhoon? A look out the porthole reveals only the ends of containers and a crack of darkness to port. A half hour or so later, the heeling ceases as mysteriously as it began, and in the morning Peter is still shaking his head.

"We had only half a meter leeway when we left the berth last night!" he says, meaning that despite the harbor's dredged depth of 41 feet, the *Colombo Bay*'s 900-foot-long bottom was about twenty inches from running aground. We rode so low because of the additional cargo that had come aboard in Singapore and the newly topped off bunkers; in order to keep the ship from scraping the floor, water ballast had to be sharply restricted. This reduced tonnage as desired but, with boxes now stacked five high on deck, gave us a high center of gravity, which was what made us heel so dramatically; once in deeper water we took on more ballast and regained stability. "Ships do want humoring . . . in handling," Conrad writes, "and if you mean to handle them well, they must have been humored in the distribution of the weight which you ask them to carry through the good and evil fortune of a passage."

He learned this lesson well when, in 1887, at age thirty, he shipped out on the *Highland Forest,* a 1,040-ton sailing vessel bound for Java from Amsterdam. He was sailing as a chief mate for the first time, was unfamiliar with the ship, and had ordered the general cargo stowed one-third above the beams, which in this case gave the ship too low a center of gravity and made her bottom-heavy, causing not heeling on turns but sharp rolling from side to side, especially in heavy weather. "Neither before nor since," he recalled,

have I felt a ship roll so abruptly, so violently, so heavily. . . . She rolled and rolled with an awful dislodging jerk and that dizzily fast sweep of her masts on every swing. It was a wonder that the men sent aloft were not flung off the yards, the yards not flung off the masts, the masts not flung overboard. The captain in his arm-chair, holding on grimly at the head of the table, with the soup-tureen rolling on one side of the cabin and the steward sprawling on the other, would observe, looking at me: "That's your one-third above the beams. The only thing that surprises me is that the sticks have stuck to her all this time."

A spar did fly loose and, with what Conrad would call "poetic justice," whacked him in the back and sent him sliding along the main deck and eventually into a Singapore hospital, where, while he recuperated from a spinal injury, the seeds likely took root for the episode at the start of *Lord Jim* in which that footloose sailor is disabled by a spar and enters a hospital "at an Eastern port" before sailing as first mate on the *Patna* toward the doom that came inexorably after he abandoned the steamer in a storm. A century after the *Highland Forest*'s voyage, Peter and Elizabeth rounded the Cape in high seas aboard a ship also bottom-heavy with cargo; neither was injured, but the vessel rolled with such a whiplike motion that Elizabeth and the second mate's wife, while trying to converse, were reduced to crawling about the cabin on their hands and knees.

These hydrostatic matters remind me that it was not only Melville I dodged in high school. All I remember of Archimedes is that he was supposed to have leapt from a bathtub and run naked through the streets of Syracuse shouting, "Eureka!" I recall thinking this was an implausible tale but also being vaguely comforted by my geometry teacher's assurance that what Archimedes had somehow discovered while soaping up guaranteed that any vessel I boarded, even the steel mass of ship and boxes on which I was now sailing so serenely, would not sink. Whether in his bathtub or not, what the Greek geometrician and inventor formulated in the third century BC were two sets of propositions collectively called "On Floating Bodies." Proposition 7 of the first set, which came to be known as Archimedes' Principle, states that ships float because their weight is precisely counterbalanced by the weight of the water they displace. All vessels—from wooden canoes to supertankers of half a million tons—bob on this fundamental law.

Why ships stay upright and how they behave when buffeted by waves and winds is somewhat more complex. The weight of a ship is concentrated at a single point somewhere inside the hull, a point known as the center of gravity. The forces that keep the ship afloat are concentrated at a different point, the center of flotation. A ship's center of flotation is determined by her design and construction; her center of gravity is determined by the way she is loaded and unloaded. The relationship between the two points determines the ship's "trim," i.e., whether she stays upright or leans one way or the other, and also her stability, how she responds when rocked in one direction or another. If there is no distance between the center of gravity and the center of flotation, the ship will float like a log half submerged in water. Such a log floats level, but if you step on one side of it, the log will spin and you will fall off—the center of flotation will not push against your weight and keep you upright on the log.

If the center of gravity is above the center of flotation, the ship will immediately capsize, which is what would happen to the *Colombo Bay* if her deck were loaded with containers without loading the holds first. If the center of gravity is to one side or the other of the center of flotation, the ship will lean to that side; if it is forward or aft of the center of flotation, the ship will float down by the bow or down by the stern. If the distance between the center of gravity and the center of flotation is relatively short, the forces keeping the ship upright will be weak, and the vessel will be "tender," which means she will right herself slowly when rolling. If the distance between the centers is relatively great, the ship will be "stiff" and experience the kind of whip that brought Elizabeth to her knees and the budding author Conrad to the hospital in Singapore. Two other hazards are "sagging," caused by too much cargo amidships, and "hogging," caused by too much cargo fore and aft; these conditions put extra stress on a ship's longitudinal steel and can break her in two in stormy weather.

The *Colombo Bay* is humored at every port. This process begins with vessel planners at P&O Nedlloyd operations centers in Singapore, London, or New York. Theirs is the task of making certain that the weight of more than 3,000 boxes is properly distributed, a job compounded by the often competing need to arrange them so that a container due off at Colombo is not buried in the hold eight deep beneath boxes going across the Atlantic to Halifax, New York, Norfolk, or Savannah. The planner's work is further complicated by yachts, military vehicles, and other oversize cargo shipped on flatbeds and whose sides could be damaged if regular containers were set down beside them; and by dangerous goods like explosives, chemicals, flammable gases and liquids, and radioactive material, which by strict code must be separated not only from one another but from certain areas of the ship, like the holds near the heat of the engine room. Then there is the garlic, four containers full just lifted aboard, thousands of heads neatly stored in bags of blue netting, enough for several chicken *marbellas*. These boxes, with their wire mesh at each end, must be stored on deck, open to the air; they are stashed

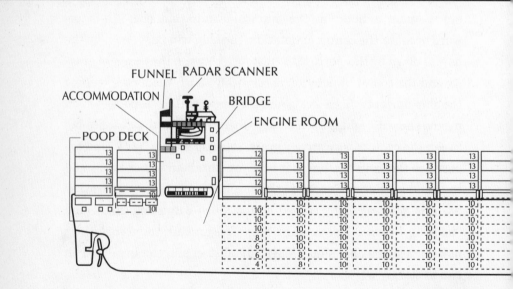

well forward, near the fo'c'sle, though their fragrance will frequently carry back to the bridge, where it is not to everyone's taste.

Before the *Colombo Bay* arrived in Singapore, the vessel planner there received a computerized bay plan file—sometimes called a BAPLIE—with the weights, sizes, types, and identifying codes of every box aboard. This was read into a software program called PowerStow, which provides a diagram of the ship's eight bays, with each container represented by a rectangle color-coded for its port of discharge. Taking into account the boxes coming on and off in Singapore, the planner created an updated BAPLIE, which the terminal managers and crane operators at Tanjong Pagar used as a blueprint to unload and load the ship. As soon as the *Colombo Bay* berthed in Singapore, Matt Mullins received a copy of the new BAPLIE on disk, allowing him to bring up on his computer screen in the ship's office the distribution of all the boxes that we would be carrying when we left port, cargo totaling 35,000 tons. With this information, he determined the ship's metacentric height.

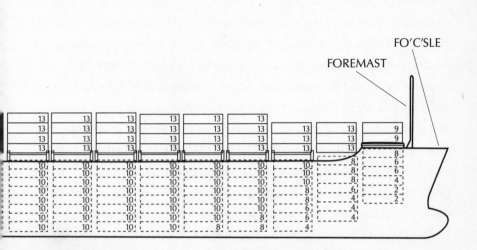

A GM of about a meter or a meter and a half is ideal and usually makes for a comfortable passage, though achieving it is frequently a challenge, PowerStow's color-coded rectangles notwithstanding. "You have to take into account the ballast capacity of the ship," Matt explains, as we head toward the Strait of Malacca with the container configuration he oversaw yesterday. "Plus there is always the desire to carry a minimum amount of ballast because it doesn't earn money; it's deadweight that slows down the ship. Technically, only seawater is ballast; but fuel acts as ballast and can be a major factor. To some extent the 140 tons of fuel we burn each twenty-four hours reduces stability because it makes the ship lighter as she proceeds. Either you compensate by adding seawater ballast to get the stability back; or if you're already full of ballast or riding so deep that you can't take on any more, then you should have sailed with enough excess stability to compensate for the loss. It's quite a complex calculation."

The strain of this balancing act is compounded by P&O Nedlloyd's membership in the Grand Alliance, a consortium of liner companies that also includes Germany's Hapag-Lloyd, Japan's Nippon Yusen Kaisha, China's Orient Overseas Container Line, and the Malaysia International Shipping Co. Such arrangements date back to the last quarter of the nineteenth century, when ruinous freight-rate wars plagued the shipping business as sail gave way to steam. At the Calcutta Conference, in 1875, a number of the hemorrhaging companies agreed to establish uniform pricing and to schedule set services and cargo shares in the trade between England and India. In the decades that followed, opponents of this kind of cooperation argued, especially in the United States, that it restrained competition at best and was monopolistic at worst; nonetheless, conferences became a fixture in the shipping industry and remain so in the twenty-first century, their adherents insisting that the cost of building and maintaining vessels the size of the *Colombo Bay* make them essential. The rationale is that a container ship will earn her keep only if she carries her maximum number of TEUs—or close to it—at all times; since ordinarily no single company can contract for enough boxes to make a given voyage profitable, combines like the Grand Alliance are necessary if all five members are to survive. Their boxes on the deck of the *Colombo Bay* offer a welcome variation of color against the monochrome of the sea; for Matt, though, this floating patchwork quilt means that he and his colleagues ashore must often humor the ship by coordinating containers from five different sources.

Matt looks tired, like a man who instead of getting ashore yesterday for a few hours of well-earned relaxation spent the day grappling with a Lego puzzle that he will face again in Colombo only a few days hence. He would not be much taken by Conrad's complaint that with the coming of steamships loading skills withered to the point where cargo was simply dumped into the holds "with clatter and hurry and racket and heat, in a cloud of steam and a mess of coal dust. As long as you keep her propeller under water and take care, say, not to fling down barrels of oil on top of bales of silk, or deposit an iron bridge-girder of five tons or so upon a bed of coffee-bags, you have done about all in the way of duty that the cry for prompt dispatch will allow you to do."

CHAPTER FIVE

In the corridor outside my cabin a wall poster depicts three menacing Asians boarding a large ship at the stern rail, one armed with a machete, another with a pistol, all under the warning: "Be Vigilant in Pirate Areas!" Though this vivid counsel confirms what Jeremy Nixon had told me about this threat, I initially find it hard to take seriously. Surely even the most determined band of pirates could not board so formidable an enterprise as the *Colombo Bay*, could not sneak up undetected by our radar and the alert watch keepers on the bridge and vault over a rail high above the waterline as we moved through the sea. The steel hull and embracing palace that are my temporary home seem a chrysalis of absolute safety, an illusion like that provided by the fuselage of the Boeing 777-200 that had enveloped me at 35,000 feet during the fifteen-hour flight from New York to Hong Kong.

My experience of pirates in the flesh was limited to the likes of Ralph Kiner, who hit fifty-four home runs in 1949, and Roberto Clemente, who won the National League batting title four times, though Pirates had always seemed an odd name for a baseball team in Pittsburgh, a coal and steel city some distance from any salt water. Mostly, piracy was the romance of sea chests overflowing with doubloons and parrots squawking, "Pieces of Eight! Pieces of Eight!"; of Errol Flynn shouting, "All right, my hearties, follow me!" in *Captain Blood;* of Burt Lancaster doing his own stunts in *The*

Crimson Pirate; of Gene Kelly as an actor pretending to be a Caribbean buccaneer to impress Judy Garland in *The Pirate.* In this Vincente Minnelli confection, they sing Cole Porter songs, including "Be a Clown," not a number calculated to persuade a fourteen-year-old in the Frolic Theater on Chicago's South Side that pirates were a particularly cutthroat lot, a view only reinforced when I gathered with my parents around our Steinway upright to render the tuneful jollity of *The Pirates of Penzance,* whose high-spirited protagonists turn out to be nothing more sinister than temporarily errant noble-men who dutifully love Queen Victoria. Nor did the literary takes I was exposed to in those days leave me with the impression that pi-rates were particularly fearsome; inept was more the case, like the wicked Blind Pew and Long John Silver in *Treasure Island,* who are outwitted by Jim Hawkins, a mere boy like me. As for *Peter Pan,* I was not inclined to quake at the prospect of Captain Hook, given that he was pursued and ultimately done in by a crocodile that ticked because it had swallowed an alarm clock.

My current reading, however, is more in line with the poster. No sooner do Ahab and his men chase several pods of whales into Sunda, the passage about 400 miles south of Singapore that sepa-rates the Indonesian islands of Sumatra and Java, than "rascally Asiatics" appear astern in hot, if vain, pursuit of the *Pequod.* "The shores of the straits of Sunda," Melville writes,

are unsupplied with those domineering fortresses which guard the entrances to the Mediterranean, the Baltic, the Propontis. Unlike the Danes, these Orientals do not demand the obsequious homage of lowered top-sails from the endless procession of ships before the wind, which for centuries past, by night and by day, have passed between the islands of Sumatra and Java, freighted with the costliest cargoes of the east. But while they freely waive a ceremonial like this, they do by no means renounce their claim to more solid tribute.

Time out of mind the piratical proas of the Malays, lurking among the low shaded coves and islets of Sumatra, have sallied out upon the vessels sailing through the straits, fiercely demanding tribute at the point of their spears. Though by the repeated bloody chastisements they have received at the hands of European cruisers, the audacity of these corsairs has of late been somewhat repressed; yet, even at the present day, we occasionally hear of English and American vessels, which, in those waters, have been remorselessly boarded and pillaged.

In the mid-nineteenth century, when the *Pequod* sailed, British and Dutch sea power had managed to punish and discourage piracy in the South China Sea and adjacent waters, where it had been rife at least since the Ming Dynasty tried to stamp it out with a force of more than 3,000 warships at the end of the fifteenth century. For most of the twentieth century piracy remained a negligible threat in the region, but spurred by political instability and widespread poverty in China, the Philippines, Malaysia, and particularly Indonesia, it began to grow again in the eighties and nineties, with pirates often fiercely demanding tribute at the point of their Kalashnikovs. By 1992 the problem had become serious enough for the International Maritime Bureau, a branch of the London-based International Chamber of Commerce, to establish a Piracy Reporting Centre in Kuala Lumpur. The ICC's annual piracy reports show a steady rise in worldwide assaults to a peak of more than 460 in 2000, a figure well below the total since scores of attacks go unreported, primarily because most masters and shipowners don't want to get bogged down in the time-consuming investigations that delay their vessels and the delivery of cargo.

When the *Colombo Bay* was drifting off the Mekong Delta so we would not arrive at Laem Chabang early, I asked Peter why we didn't proceed to the Thai port and anchor in the harbor until a berth became available. "Pirates," he said, and handed me a two-page message that had arrived on September 13, the day we sailed from Hong Kong. It was one of the PRC's daily bulletins, which are available free to all ships via satellite transmission; it summarized five recent incidents, four of them attacks on ships at anchor, one a general cargo vessel in the harbor at Jakarta that, on September 8, had been boarded by four men who assaulted a crew member, stole equipment, and escaped by boat. Such opportunistic hit-and-run attacks are the most frequent modus operandi, like the assault on the *Matsumi Maru No. 7*, a tanker flying the Singapore flag that was boarded at 0300 by fifteen armed pirates while under way in the Strait of Malacca in March. They took the second mate and a few crew members hostage, locked an officer who tried to resist in a cabin, then broke down the master's door, beat him, tied his hands and legs, and taped his mouth and eyes. Within minutes they had stolen cash, valuables, and equipment, and disappeared over the side in the dark.

The Strait of Malacca stretches more than 500 miles between Sumatra and the Malay Peninsula, from the pinched southern end near Singapore northwest to the 200-mile-wide mouth that opens into the Indian Ocean. It is one of the busiest seaways in the world; some 600 vessels, from pleasure craft, ferries, and fishing boats to bulk carriers, container ships, and tankers, use the passage daily, taking the shortest east-west route between the Indian Ocean and the South China Sea and Pacific Ocean. For centuries this funnel has been shipping's dark alley, where pirates have dashed out from their shaded coves and islets whenever a tempting target came close. Modern pirates, like those who attacked the *Matsumi Maru No. 7*, sprint from their shoreline hideouts at night in powerful speedboats and attack from behind, where they rarely register on the victim's radar, which has a blind spot behind the funnel and also can't always distinguish small craft from wake turbulence reflected on the screen. The speedboats come up under the poop, where they can't be seen from the bridge and where the freeboard is lowest, and throw ropes or hooked bamboo poles called *satang* up to the rail. Their chances of success are increased by the slow pace of large vessels like the *Colombo Bay,* which must proceed with extra caution through the tapered 200 miles at the strait's southern end because of the heavy traffic, irregular depths, and many wrecks and shoal patches, not all of them accurately charted or marked at all. Of the 469 attacks registered in 2000 by the PRC, 75 took place in the strait, a 66 percent increase over 1999 and ten times the number in 1991. In February 2002, after the ICC's annual report declared that the strait's waters remained the most dangerous in the world, the Indonesia navy put six warships on patrol in the passage.

When we entered the strait after leaving Singapore, Shakeel and his crew partner on the midnight to 0400 watch monitored the radar and scanned the sea with extra vigilance, and the steel doors on every deck were bolted tight. Such precautions, though routine in high-risk areas, are by no means foolproof. If pirates do manage to climb aboard, outside stairs on the port and starboard lead directly up to the bridge wings, where the invaders can smash or shoot out the windows to gain entry and terrorize the watch keepers by waving a gun or holding knives at their throats while the rest of the gang goes from cabin to cabin demanding money, watches, cameras, VCRs, and other valuables, and in some cases stealing stores and ripping the ship's safe from its bolts. There are no firearms aboard the *Colombo Bay* and most other merchant ships; it is P&O Nedlloyd policy, and that of most major liner companies, not to confront pirates once they get over the rail. "If pirates arrived when I was on the bridge I would lay out the red carpet," one master told me.

Sir Peter Blake, who headed the New Zealand crew that won the America's Cup in 1995 and 2000, did not do this when, in December 2001, six men in ski masks or motorbike helmets boarded the *Seamaster,* his 130-foot environmental research vessel, while it was anchored near the mouth of the Amazon River. As one of the pirates held a gun to the head of a crew member, the six-foot-four

Blake appeared from below with a rifle he kept onboard for fending off polar bears. He shot one of the bandits in the hand, but the gun then malfunctioned and one Ricardo Colares Tavares fired two shots into his back; the fifty-three-year-old yachtsman bled to death in minutes. The twenty-three-year-old Tavares and his accomplices were arrested within thirty-six hours by Brazilian police and eventually received sentences of from twenty-six to thirty-six years in prison, faint consolation to Blake's crew, friends, wife, and two teenage children mourning the cost of resisting a band that had made off with about $600 in cash, some photographic equipment, and an outboard motor.

Most hit-and-run pirates do not physically harm sailors if they don't resist, but their more ambitious brothers who hijack vessels are usually far more ruthless. In November 1998 pirates posing as antismuggling officers, a common ploy, intercepted the *Cheung Son* as she sailed in the Taiwan Strait with a cargo of furnace slag headed for Port Kelang near Kuala Lumpur. They bound, gagged, and blindfolded all twenty-three hands, hauled them on deck, shot or clubbed them to death, weighted their bodies, and threw them overboard; several turned up in the nets of fishing boats off Shantou, a port up the coast from Hong Kong often used by smugglers. The *Cheung Son* disappeared, but *The Economist* reported that, in August 1999, "Chinese police claimed to have found the mainland mastermind [of the hijacking], after supposedly chancing upon photographs of the pirates partying aboard the ship after the shooting spree." A Chinese court ultimately sentenced thirteen of the pirates to death and eighteen others to up to life in prison, moved by the photos and the fact that a dozen of the victims were Communist Party members. The proceedings marked the first time in more than a decade that pirates had been tried in China.

The country's reaction in the case of the bulk carrier *Tenyu* was much less harsh, and more typical. In September 1998 the Japanese-owned ship, flying the flag of Panama, disappeared in the

Strait of Malacca after leaving the Sumatra port of Kuala Tanjong with a load of aluminum ingots worth $3 million; she was manned by a Korean master and chief engineer and thirteen Chinese crew members and bound for Inchon, South Korea. In December a vessel called the *Sanei 1,* flying the Honduran flag and manned by sixteen Indonesians, arrived at the run-down port of Zhangjiagang near Shanghai. After harbor officials noticed that the name had been freshly painted on the bow and stern, a check of the engine's serial number revealed that she was the *Tenyu;* there was no trace of the aluminum ingots or of the fifteen original hands, who soon were presumed dead, either slaughtered by the Indonesian hijackers and dumped overboard or set fatally adrift. Chinese officials ruled that the *Tenyu* should be returned to its Japanese owner and that the sixteen Indonesia pirates be repatriated, despite the fact that two of them had been detained and released in an earlier hijacking.

The IMB and other organizations tracking piracy in the region lay such leniency to collusion between corrupt government officials in China and throughout Southeast Asia and the powerful organized crime syndicates that are behind most hijackings, which net a ship and her cargo worth millions of dollars. *The Washington Post* reported that "the *Tenyu* case involved South Korean planners, Indonesian thugs, Burmese dockhands and black marketeers, and at least some confederates in China." South Korea eventually succeeded in extraditing from Singapore one Lee Dong-Gul, who admitted in court that he had bought the *Tenyu* and her ingots from some Indonesians and, using forged documents, sold them to a Chinese company. Japan's Nippon Foundation, whose purview includes marine safety, estimates that from 1996 to 2001 Japanese-owned ships lost $45 million in cargo to pirates just in the Strait of Malacca.

One of them was the tanker *Global Mars.* On February 22, 2000, she left Port Kelang for Haldia, a harbor south of Calcutta, carrying 6,000 tons of palm oil. Two days later she was just north of the strait sailing at twelve knots in the Andaman Sea, off the west coast of

Thailand. As night fell most of the seven South Korean officers and ten Myanmarese crew were relaxing in their cabins when a fishing boat, running without lights, slowly approached from behind; within minutes, masked pirates had pulled themselves aboard. Armed with guns and three-foot-long swords, they threatened the seamen with death, bound and blindfolded them, and ordered them into the hold of the fishing boat. They remained there for more than a week while the pirates repainted the *Global Mars* as she rode at anchor, renaming her *Bulawan* and replacing her Panamanian flag with a Honduran one. When the job was finished, they forced their captives into an open boat and set them adrift with minimal rations; after five days they were rescued by fishermen and brought to a small coastal village near the tourist island of Phuket in southern Thailand, where their seventeen-day ordeal finally ended.

Three months later the *Bulawan* was sailing in waters off Hong Kong claiming in radio communications to be of Honduran registry; when Honduran authorities reported that they had no record of such a vessel, Chinese border police searched with patrol boats and aircraft until they tracked the ship down. They had found the *Global Mars,* but half the palm oil was gone. The crew of eleven Filipinos and nine Myanmarese was arrested but soon released, the police claiming, as in the *Tenyu* case, to lack evidence that any crime had been committed in Chinese territorial waters. This likely was just a cover for another case of collusion since law enforcement in southern China is notoriously lax and the market enormous for goods that have fallen off the back of a ship. But the freeing of the *Global Mars* and *Tenyu* crews also highlights the complex issue of legal jurisdiction over foreign nationals that has made it difficult for those honest justice officials to prosecute pirates even when they are caught red-handed.

The complicity of crooked officials along with the marginal budgets most cash-starved Asian governments devote to naval and coast guard forces have increasingly enabled pirates to act with impunity, as has the widespread view among impoverished villagers along the coasts that the bandits are not criminals who should be reported to the police but heroes, seagoing Robin Hoods who often share their spoils.

On September 25, 2000, the tanker *Petchem* left Port Dickson on the Strait of Malacca headed for the Sarawak city of Kuching with a cargo of diesel oil; in the South China Sea near the remote Natuna Islands, long a pirate haven, thieves boarded the vessel, overpowered the crew, locked them in their cabins, and soon rendezvoused with an unidentified tanker on which they sailed away after siphoning into it 2,200 tons of the oil, worth $700,000. The *Petchem*'s crew freed themselves the next day, but the getaway tanker was never found, its liquid plunder likely sold at bargain prices and used by hundreds of struggling fishermen and other boat owners, including pirates gassing up for their next sallies.

At the end of the nineties, piracy also began playing a role in the separatist struggle in Aceh, the Indonesian province at the northern end of Sumatra, where the Strait of Malacca meets the Indian Ocean. The people of the area are among the most devout Muslims in the world's most populous Muslim country, but their cause is based less on Islamic fundamentalism than on their anger at Indonesia's corrupt central government and western multinationals like Exxon Mobil, which they feel have robbed them of their share of Aceh's rich resources, especially its abundant fields of natural gas. The Free Aceh Movement (GAM) began a guerrilla war for independence in the mid-seventies and two weeks before the *Colombo Bay* entered the strait announced that all vessels passing through the waterway would have to get the movement's permission, a demand that put the government warships on alert even though the rebels hardly had the navy and firepower to establish an effective blockade.

In late August, however, armed men had succeeded in hijacking the *Ocean Silver*, a tugboat towing a barge with 7,000 tons of coal across the strait from the Aceh port of Padang to Lumut, in Malaysia. The pirates cast the barge adrift and took the tug to a small port on the east coast of Aceh, where they freed six of the crew and held the captain and five others, all Indonesians, for a ransom of about $34,000. Whether it was ever paid is unclear, though the tug was released on September 19 and made for Lumut. The Free Aceh Movement immediately renewed its threat to interdict shipping but at the same time denied responsibility for hijacking the *Ocean Silver,* accusing government forces of staging the action to discredit the movement.

True or not in this instance, the International Maritime Bureau and other maritime agencies do not doubt that the poorly paid drug agents, customs examiners, and seamen aboard the patrol boats of Asian governments sometimes moonlight as pirates. They either act on their own, grabbing what they can, or take their orders from politicians, businessmen, and law enforcement officials who know a ship's route and the value of her cargo. In this they are following in the illustrious wake of Sir Francis Drake, who in 1577 at the behest of Queen Elizabeth I set out from Plymouth to circumnavigate the globe aboard the hundred-ton flagship *Pelican,* ostensibly in search of Terra Australis Incognita and the elusive Northwest Passage between the Atlantic and Pacific. These lofty goals were largely window dressing for Drake's real commission, which was to plunder Spanish settlements and merchant ships, which he did with such competence that his ship, renamed *The Golden Hind,* returned to Plymouth in 1580 riding low with bars of gold and silver, coins, pearls, precious stones, and other swag worth forty-seven times the cost of the voyage. He bought Buckland Abbey, near Plymouth, with his share of the proceeds, and Queen Elizabeth knighted him for his predatory efficiency.

Such privateering flourished in the last half of the sixteenth century and beyond as armed private ships sailed out of English ports with letters of marque from the British Admiralty that granted them permission to attack the usually defenseless merchant vessels of the Spanish enemy, though these licensed-to-steal pirates were not always rigorous in limiting their assaults to ships flying the Spanish colors.* Generally, the Crown received 10 percent of the loot, and 90 percent went to the privateer's owners and captain, of which some trickled down to the crew, a distribution arrangement soon found congenial by most other maritime nations for their own privateers. The ratio is reversed for modern privateers in Asia, with most of the loot going to the corrupt parties onshore who facilitate the piracy and little to the patrol boat moonlighters who do the risky dirty work on the water.

By the morning of September 22, the *Colombo Bay* has transited the Strait of Malacca without incident when a reminder that piracy is no longer just a mercenary enterprise passes in the opposite direction on our port. Sitting in a row on the deck of this vessel are five half globes that, in their stark whiteness, look like igloos that have somehow been inoculated against the tropical heat. I am on the bridge with Simon Westall, who explains as he hands me the binoculars that the igloos are in fact complete spheres, the bottom halves hidden belowdecks; they are full of liquified natural gas, likely outbound from the Exxon Mobil operation in Aceh, the east coast of which we are now passing as we head into the Indian Ocean. She could be carrying a maximum load of 135,000 cubic meters of LNG, a cargo whose vapors are sometimes toxic and always flammable if exposed to air. About a mile of water separates us, but should she blow, Simon assures me, "she would easily take us with her." This notion that we are within the ship's explosive reach seems hyper-

---

*Piracy continues to have an elastic definition. On October 29, 2002, the *New York Times* reported that sailors of the U.S. and Australian navies boarded and searched scores of Iraqi vessels in the Northern Arabian Gulf, turning back those trying to smuggle out oil and other cargo in violation of the international sanctions against the country. Baghdad complained to the United Nations that these armed boarding parties were nothing more than pirates, a term the sailors happily embraced, referring to themselves as the Pirates of the NAG.

bolic, though I do imagine an instant tsunami rolling out from the disintegrated vessel and capsizing the *Colombo Bay* as if she were a Sunfish.

What is neither hyperbolic nor the fantasy of an overdramatic supernumerary is the chaos an LNG carrier could cause if hijacked by terrorists, a possibility that had begun to worry maritime officials even before September 11. The southern end of the Strait of Malacca is an international choke point, as is the even narrower Strait of Singapore just beyond, where the Phillip Channel is less than two miles wide. Day and night, scores of mammoth vessels squeeze through these passages, maneuvering among themselves as well as among rocks, reefs, shoals, and dozens of islands. If terrorists blew up an LNG ship in these waters with the kind of explosive force Timothy McVeigh concocted in Oklahoma City in 1995 or Muslim fundamentalists used at the World Trade Center in 1993 and at the U.S. embassies in Nairobi and Dar es Salaam 1998, the fiery carnage would be bad enough; if they did so after ramming a supertanker, the cost could be catastrophic in both lives and economic impact.

The wreckage and the pollution from the spill of millions of gallons of oil could block the passage for months, forcing thousands of vessels to make for the Lomboc Strait at the eastern end of Java, a detour that would add at least a day to and from Laem Chabang, Hong Kong, and other Asian ports. Singapore harbor might be so thick with crude that ships would be unable to berth there regardless of whether they came around by way of Lomboc. Freight rates would quickly rise to cover the added costs of the detour, with a potentially devastating impact on the fragile economies of Southeast Asia. Japan and South Korea, highly dependent on imported energy fuels, would be hard hit. Some two-thirds of the world's LNG trade passes through the Strait of Malacca, and the shipment of crude there is fifteen times greater than that through the Panama Canal and three times greater than that through Suez.

Since September 11, concern has grown that terrorists might now be eyeing that choke point also, one reason we filled our bunkers at Singapore and the talk of a Cape run continues on the bridge and at dinner. An Al Qaeda suicide team need not even strike the canal; they could achieve the same effect by hijacking a supertanker or LNG carrier and exploding it in Bab el Mandeb, the strait at the southern end of the Red Sea through which all east-west shipping must thread when bound to or from Suez. The approaches to Bab el Mandeb through the Gulf of Aden and the waters off the Horn of Africa are particularly lawless, an area where pirates from the coasts of Yemen and Somalia, both countries harboring Al Qaeda militants, often come armed with assault rifles, machine guns, and sometimes mortars. They would outgun most patrol boats that tried to intercept them, an encounter the pirates don't worry about much since neither Somalia, which has no effective central government, nor Yemen supports a forceful coast guard.

It was in the Yemeni harbor at Aden, which is less than 100 miles east of Bab el Mandeb, that a boat laden with explosives crashed into the U.S. Navy destroyer *Cole* in October 2000, killing seventeen sailors. Two years later to the month, another bomb boat rammed the French supertanker *Limburg* as she moved toward the Yemeni port of Mina al-Dabah; in the explosion and resulting fire, one crew member died and twelve were injured as thousands of gallons of crude poured into the Gulf of Aden, polluting some forty-five miles of the Yemeni coastline. An attack like these at Bab el Mandeb or Suez could force all shipborne east-west trade, as well as allied warships, to go around the Cape, as happened when Egypt closed the canal for eight years after its 1967 war with Israel. Al Qaeda or its sympathizers also could cause considerable loss of life and pollution, and sabotage the world economy, by exploding hijacked ships strategically in the Dardanelles and the straits of Gibraltar, Dover, and Hormuz, all heavily trafficked choke points.

Despite such high stakes, the thousands of container ships, tankers, LNG carriers, and other merchant vessels that pass through high-risk areas each year must, lacking weapons, develop what defenses they can. The first rule is bolted doors and sharp lookouts fore and aft, which on some ships, though not on the *Colombo Bay,* are augmented by high-tech motion sensors. Normally, the *Colombo Bay* runs at night with just navigation lights and those on the mooring deck and the palace; as an extra precaution in the strait the lights along the upper deck also were on. Some ships add floodlights that bathe the poop deck and, to give the impression of extra watch keepers, occasionally prop cardboard silhouettes of seamen at the rail. Tankers, which when fully loaded ride lower in the water than any other large merchant vessels, sometimes dangle fire hoses over the stern rail, ready to fend off would-be boarders with a high-pressure stream, an effective safeguard unless the pirates are firing Uzis or worse from below. Secure-Marine, a Dutch company, has developed Secure-Ship, a 9,000-volt electrified fence designed to surround a vessel at the upper deck and deliver an eight-joule jolt, the legal limit for shock wire, to anyone trying to breach the rail. In 2001 the Jumbo Shipping Co., of Geneva, which operates ships that specialize in lifting heavy cargo, announced that it would string these non-lethal but numbing wires around ten of its vessels, but there was no rush by other firms to do likewise.

In the late nineties, the International Maritime Bureau in conjunction with a French company, Collecte Localisation Satellites, developed SHIPLOC, an electronic device about the size of a shoe box that can be hidden anywhere on a vessel; its signal bounces off a satellite down to a data center that tracks a ship's location at all times. These fixes are available to both the Piracy Reporting Centre and the vessel's headquarters, which by accessing SHIPLOC's website can check the whereabouts of a ship several times a day. Should she deviate from her prescribed route and radio silence suggests a hijacking, SHIPLOC can track the vessel to any corner of the ocean that pirates might take her. Maritime authorities, notified by the owners or the PRC, could quickly give chase, assuming that they have the inclination and the naval wherewithal, are willing to risk jurisdictional disputes if their quarry enters another nation's territorial waters, or are not in cahoots with the hijackers. Even the most dedicated seagoing posse might not reach the ship for a day or more, though, giving the pirates plenty of time to escape in another vessel with their take, having left behind a crew at best traumatized, at worst dead. There is no shoe box aboard the *Colombo Bay,* or any other P&O Nedlloyd container ship, and few other liner companies showed much interest in the system in the months after it was introduced.

SHIPLOC may eventually catch on, but if it doesn't the reason rests primarily on the same arithmetic that explains the general lack of vigorous antipiracy efforts worldwide. By one estimate, some $1 billion was lost to piracy annually as the twenty-first century began. Since so many attacks go unreported and shippers, liner companies, and insurers are rarely enthusiastic about disclosing the cost of those incidents that do get recorded, the actual number is probably higher—but not high enough. In 2000 the value of world merchandise exports, including agriculture and fuels, was more than $6.2 trillion, according to the World Trade Organization. At least 80 percent of these products moved by sea at some point; thus, even if piracy losses had totaled $2 billion, they would have amounted to only .04 percent of the $5 trillion flow of seaborne products, or $4 for every $10,000 worth of cargo. These are not fractions that tend to concentrate the mind of the shipping community, whose risk management assessments tell it that spending money to install SHIPLOC or Secure-Marine's electronic fence makes no economic sense; better to accept the occasional piracy hit as a cost of doing business and get on with delivering the goods.

This view prevails in particular with major Western lines like P&O Nedlloyd, whose large container ships are targeted by pirates less often than are easier prey like bulk carriers and small tankers, especially those flying flags of convenience and manned by officers and crews from developing countries. These seafarers constitute the large majority of piracy victims, and since almost all of them are poor, are nonwhite, and lack union or any other effective represen- tation, they are generally viewed as expendable, their injuries and deaths also calculated as a cost of doing business. The IMB and other maritime organizations, national and international, have been try- ing to fight this cynicism, but they have no navy, only the ability to quantify incidents, send out alerts, and recommend defense strategies. This is useful, but piracy will be reduced only if liner com- panies, shippers, insurers—and especially the governments in high- risk areas like Southeast Asia—take tougher action. Few of these parties seem willing or able to do so.

■ ■ ■

Though the main alert in the Strait of Malacca was piracy, a good deal of attention was also paid to Peter's birthday, which we cele- brated on our first evening out of Singapore. At 1730, all officers ex- cept Matt, who is always on the bridge between 1600 and 2000, gathered in the lounge, which has at one end a well-stocked bar, be- side which a glass display case offers a sampling of insects captured onboard, among them dragonflies, grasshoppers, and cockroaches the size of half-dollars. Recently Shakeel had found a butterfly while checking the holds and, with the dedication of a true lepidopterist, climbed the vertical ladder with one hand, hoping to preserve his discovery; despite this valiant effort, the specimen flaked apart by the time its rescuer reached daylight. Shakeel had better luck on his last ship, P&O Nedlloyd's *Shenzhen Bay,* after discovering a multi- colored, inch-long bug, which he photographed as it crawled along the bridge's windshield. He submitted the shot to *The Marine Ob- server,* a quarterly published by the British Meteorological Office, which ran it with a short item identifying the insect as a shield bug from the family Pentatomidae and noting that Shakeel had responsibly returned it to the bridge wing from which he had removed it for the photo op.

For tonight's special occasion, the low tables in front of the couches feature bowls of peanuts and a mix of crisp, spicy noodles along with a platter of crackers on each of which salmon, cheese cubes, and sweet pickles compete. Drinks are duty-free cheap, their cost nightly deducted from each officer's contribution to the bar kitty, the ongoing subtraction recorded in a binder on the counter. Glasses filled, we toast Peter, who immediately thanks me for the golf balls, which I had delivered to his office earlier, hoping to avoid just such a public acknowledgment. Under the room's gaze, I shrink like a pupil who has brought in the only apple for the teacher.

As always, conversation must compete with the music emanating from the lounge stereo system. The principal enthusiasts for this steady rock beat are Alex Gill and his two age-mates, Simon Westall and Christopher Windsor-Price, both also barely into their twenties. Christopher, a trainee putting in his required sea time as a deck cadet, is tall, and lanky, and sports a buzz cut that gives him the aspect of a skinhead. This impression was italicized by his recent comment that he didn't much like Arabs and that, given September 11, maybe genocide was in order, a remark that would turn out to reflect a youthful impulsiveness rather than his true nature. Simon is the third mate, the lowest ranking deck officer; his compact build, square jaw, and glasses give him the look of a confident prep school senior who has lettered in swimming and track and just aced his SATs. He seldom takes part in the predinner banter, preferring instead to dreamily mouth the words as Steps, Queen, and the Backstreet Boys fill the room.

Peter seems to share my distaste for the intrusive "background" music and occasionally pulls rank and turns it down, conceding as

Alex, Simon, and the cadet groan that he is being a BOF, his daughters' shorthand for Boring Old Fart. "At least the Beatles had something to say," he says to the threesome, all of whom were born when
the Fab Four's catalog was being turned into elevator treacle. Their
eyes roll just as Amanda's did for years when I asserted my BOF status against music in restaurants. "Dad, *please*! Don't complain
again, it's embarrassing." I don't complain, even after Simon surreptitiously turns up the volume. Peter ignores these mutinies, feeling, I sense, that only a hard-hearted master would deny his young
subordinates a half hour or so of their cherished anthems. Against
the decibels, Frank McAlees, the first engineer, tells me a story. He
is from Belfast and speaks softly, with a brogue that in the best of
circumstances would fall on American ears with all the clarity of the
announcements on New York subway platforms. He looks down
from his barstool and unspools an anecdote that lasts two or three
minutes as I strain to decrypt it from an armchair about four feet
away. When he punctuates a point with a smile, I smile back; when
he laughs, I laugh; I understand not a word but during his pauses
nod vigorously and hope for the best.

At 1800 sharp we file across the corridor into the dining room.
This is the high social moment of each day, a formal dinner party at
which week after week the guests are the same and, with the exception of Elizabeth and me, the dress identical, white shirts and black
pants. The junior officers array themselves around the table nearest
the galley, and I join Peter, Elizabeth, Steve, and Frank at the other
table. The birthday menu includes batter-fried prawns, chicken à la
king, mashed potatoes, string beans and broccoli, with wine—Gallo
red and white—making a rare appearance. Frank, too, is making a
rare appearance, honoring his captain despite the chicken à la king.
He skips most dinners, finding them too bland and heavy, showing
up only for the occasional spicy fare, like the curry with condiments
and a medium-fiery Dutch sauce that would come next week. Elizabeth, with her catering background, is also sometimes a stern judge

of the galley's output, but tonight she is pleased. "Lovely," she declares, as she orders a second helping of the crisp prawns. All hands, including Frank, agree that the fluffy white birthday cake with its generous scoop of vanilla ice cream is a fitting conclusion to the meal and tribute to Peter.

Artemio Pangilinan is master of the galley. The chief steward, he has a cherubic countenance punctuated by a bushy, black mustache, will soon turn forty-three and has been working in kitchens on land and sea for two decades. This is his fourth P&O Nedlloyd ship, and his cheerfulness suggests that he has made his peace with the long separations from his wife, Consorcia, and their three sons, who live outside Manila. "I want all my boys to go to college," he told me. Artemio joined the *Colombo Bay* on April 30 and will remain aboard until January 30—nine months without a break of turning out, with the help of a second cook and two others, three meals a day, seven days a week for two dozen hungry sailors. In Singapore he oversaw a restocking of the ship's larder with sides of beef, chicken, pork loins and spare ribs, fruits, vegetables, long-life milk, and other stores, most of them frozen; we now have enough food, except for the occasional resupply of fresh fruit and vegetables, to last for eight weeks, when the *Colombo Bay* will call again at Singapore on its eastbound run and once more replenish the refrigerated food lockers. Artemio is, perforce, a master of culinary ambidexterity. Each evening he prepares dishes of fish, shrimp, vegetables boiled with beef or pork, rice, and fruit for his compatriots gathered at the four square tables with checkered tablecloths in their port side dining room, and British fare for the officers in their starboard mess.

These latter meals, like the birthday dinner, are perhaps best described as hearty, and their progression rarely varies: soup (cream of carrot, chicken vegetable), followed by what Americans call the appetizer but onboard was labeled the entrée (kippered herring, sliced melon), a main course (roast pork or lamb chops with cauliflower or green beans), and a sweet (rice pudding, peach cobbler), with salad and bread in abundance. Most of the meals are well prepared and all certain to put on weight unless you exercise restraint at the table or with laps on the upper deck, neither of which I did sufficiently to counteract Artemio's considerable gift for preparing potatoes. In an irresistible parade, these came baked in crisp skins, mashed with a generous dollop of butter, à la lyonnaise, au gratin, hashed brown, roasted, and French fried, a.k.a. chips. I did manage to forgo the M1 Special, which occasionally appeared at lunch and is named after England's major motor artery; it is along this route, as along U.S. interstates, that truckers are presumed to fall upon plates heaped with fried eggs, pancakes, sausages, bacon, baked beans, chips, and sundry other cardiac arrestables. Most of my British shipmates were not to be outdone by their lorry-driving brothers, though one did complain that "you can't get proper English sausages these days because of foot-and-mouth disease."

The captain's table, which would comfortably seat eight, looks out on the passing sea through two rectangular, floor-to-ceiling windows; the four windows that look forward are of similar size, but containers loom immediately outside and during even modest swells strain against their lashings, fingers on a blackboard as we talk. The courses are served by Primo Valmonte; he is thirty-two, wiry, and painfully shy, owing in part to his station, in part to the fact that he knew none of his Filipino mates when he joined the *Colombo Bay* in May. In 1990 his ambition was to be a U.S. Navy SEAL, but he did not pass muster and, like so many of his countrymen, drifted into the merchant service, a transition made easier by his uncle, who is operations manager at C. F. Sharp. Primo, too, is working for his family: his wife, Cherrie, and three daughters. He is a recreational diver and, applied for a job as a salvager because he wanted to be at home more, but the meager pay drove him back to crewing. Like his Filipino mates, he is unfailingly polite, demeanor Peter welcomes in a waiter. Both he and Elizabeth like the waiters in Italy, France, and the United States but regard English waiters as slack at best and surly at worst. "The English can't stand to feel inferior," he says, laughing.

This is about as contentious as conversation gets. It is clear, after a week aboard, that there is an unspoken mariners' agreement that in the closed society of a ship, where everyone must get along for months at a time, even moderately controversial topics are best avoided. Talk of September 11 was minimal beyond the repeated declarations of sympathy that all aboard expressed for the victims in the days after the attack. Peter did say during that first week that he thought Tony Blair should stop running around the world waving the Union Jack on behalf of us Americans and instead get on with the business of rescuing England's collapsing health and transportation systems, not a particularly incendiary position. I did manage to get into trouble early on, by praising the BBC World Service's comprehensive and thoughtful coverage of the terrorist assault and its aftermath. No one quarreled with this compliment, but it moved Peter to ask if I knew of Alistair Cooke's "Letter from America." Of course, I replied, he was famous for these radio reports, as he was for his years of hosting *Masterpiece Theatre,* which I explained was a weekly public television series that had brought us Yanks *Upstairs, Downstairs* and much other high-toned British teleculture. When Peter said he had heard some incisive Cooke commentaries just before shipping out, I assured him they must have been rebroadcasts because the man was, alas, dead. "I don't think so," said Steve, politely. "I heard them myself." Cooke was, in fact, still on the job at ninety-three, his "Letter" in its fifty-fifth year.

After the birthday dinner we return to the lounge, where to the continuing sound of rock Steve makes and serves coffee and the talk turns to sports and other safe topics. Peter, Steve, and Shakeel follow British football standings avidly, though all agree that hooliganism is hurting the game and that the salaries and egos of many star players could use some deflating. I assure them that professional sports in the United States suffers from the same wretched excess, and after citing the salary—$250 million for ten years—recently negotiated by Alex Rodriguez, the Texas Rangers shortstop, am certain my audience will gasp in disbelief. Hardly. Had I never heard of David Beckham, captain of England's national team and mainstay of Manchester United, the New York Yankees of soccer? He is married to Victoria Adams, formerly of the Spice Girls, and the royal couple lives on an estate in Hertfordshire dubbed by the tabloids Beckingham Palace, not such a stretch given that their combined annual income exceeds the queen's.*

Peter gives high marks to Tiger Woods, despite his seven-figure paychecks, but complains that U.S. fans are ruining the dignified game he loves with rude and noisy antics as they jostle against the ropes to get a better view of birdie putts. When the conversation shifts to American holidays, Peter expresses curiosity about Thanksgiving, which I try to satisfy with a brief discourse on Plymouth, Pilgrims, Indians, turkey, stuffing, cranberry sauce, pumpkin pie, and the gluttony in general with which we honor that distant harvest. I like to think it was the holiday itself rather than my explanation of it that prompted the perplexed looks. Occasionally, the postprandial talk gives way to a video, screened on the TV set mounted above the lounge refrigerator. One evening, the fare was *Snow White*—not Disney's but putatively the real Grimm thing, with Sigourney Weaver chewing up the scenery as the wicked stepmother, Sam Neill as her feckless husband and Snow White's father, and several full-size, if misshapen, men standing in for the dwarves. "This is crap," Peter decreed, not unreasonably. He and Elizabeth left around the time Weaver ate the heart of a pig that the huntsman had surreptitiously substituted for Snow White's. "Bon appétit," she said to Dad.

---

*Beckham defected to Real Madrid in mid-2003, but as of this writing he had not put the palace up for rent.

Peter, Steve, Matt, and Frank, the ship's senior officers, all have video players in their quarters. For the rest of us, viewing a video of our choice in private is something of a challenge. P&O Nedlloyd supplies the ship with 120 new titles every four months, all neatly arranged on shelves in the library on E deck. This would seem like more than enough to satisfy the cravings of the most devoted seagoing cineast; however, there are only three players in the library, one of which is broken. Thus there is a nightly scramble, and whoever wins it dictates what all of us will see if we choose to turn on our sets, since they are on a closed circuit. I was never fleet enough to commandeer one of the players after dinner, so I had to take potluck when in a video mood. As one result, I caught the end of *Rambo III,* in which Sylvester Stallone as the eponymous hunk throws in with the Mujahedeen so he can rescue his former Vietnam commander from the Soviet invaders of Afghanistan; the 1988 film is dedicated to that county's "gallant people." Most often the one-for-all system provides a steady stream of hard-core pornography, programmed by one, two, three, who knows how many of my shipmates; these videos offer grainy couplings, triplings, quartetings, and occasionally more ambitious entanglements, all apparently directed by someone with a keen interest in plumbing. For those seeking sexual stimulation of a more elevated nature, the library's bookshelves offer several possibilities, including Joyce's *Ulysses.*

■ ■ ■

On Sunday, September 23, I go up to the bridge just before 0700. The day is gray and the sea lively, causing rolls that would be a good deal more severe were we not weighed down with 35,000 tons of cargo. After exiting the Strait of Malacca around the northern tip of Sumatra, we fixed a course of 269 degrees—one point shy of due west—and are still on it, making a beeline across the Indian Ocean. Our next way point, or course alteration, will be near Dondra Head, at the southern tip of Sri Lanka, where we will begin moving north to

Colombo. The distance between the two way points is 872 nautical miles, and we are traveling at a steady twenty-three knots on what amounts to an aqueous interstate as eastbound ships pass regularly on our port.* The *Colombo Bay* has been—and will be—on autopilot for hours, like a car on cruise control from New York to Chicago; only service plazas are missing.

Peter hands me some literature about Sri Lanka, then downloads an email from his daughter Katherine back in England. She is worried that we are calling at Colombo, reporting that many tourists have been canceling vacations in Sri Lanka because of the latest eruption in the eighteen-year-old war between the separatist Tamil Tigers and the Sinhalese government. In late July the island went on increased alert after the Tigers, in a predawn raid at the international airport and adjoining air force base, virtually wiped out Sri-Lankan Airlines, destroying two Airbus jets, heavily damaging three others, and demolishing eight military aircraft. Some fifty British tourists fled the terminals as the separatists attacked with gunfire and mortar rounds. Katherine is also concerned about Suez, telling her father that warships bound for the Arabian Sea and closer proximity to Afghanistan passed through the canal yesterday with a cover of U.S. fighters. Does this mean we are now more likely to make the Cape run? Peter says he has not yet received instructions one way or the other but confirms what Shakeel, who keeps the charts, has already told me: There are none aboard for such a voy-

*The standard nautical mile is 6,076 feet, almost 800 feet longer than a statute mile, a difference owing in part to the curvature of the earth. A knot equals one nautical mile per hour, the term deriving from the knots on a chip log spaced 47 feet, 3 inches apart; the number of knots that played out in the sea while sand dropped through a glass over 28 seconds determined the number of nautical miles covered in an hour. These details are useful to know, but experience showed me that they may be less important than understanding that you risk a certain amount of cheerful derision if you say "knots per hour."

age. "I guess we'll just have to stay far from shore," Peter says, laughing as he wets his index finger and holds it up.

I have been drawn from the start to the charts we do have onboard, engrossed by them just as I was by the Esso road maps I spread across my bare knees as we drove in the family Chevy from the South Side to the Indiana Dunes in the summer. The miles that rolled off on the odometer between Whiting and Gary always matched the number printed above the blue line of Route 12 connecting those towns, which seemed a kind of magic, the creased, unwieldy map a security blanket of specificity and order in the bewildering forest of childhood. The charts neatly pinned to their hooded table in front of the bridge windshield offer similar reassurance, their certainty a soothing antidote to the chaos and uncertainty spreading daily since September 11. If God is in the details, nautical charts are Elysian Fields crisscrossed with lines of longitude and latitude, dotted with measures of ocean depths and island heights and with markers for rocks, reefs, buoys, and lighthouses. Scales indicate distance in miles and kilometers, Mercator projections flatten the curved planet, and sometimes what's beneath the waves makes an appearance. Soon after we set course for Sri Lanka, the chart showed us passing over the north end of the Ninety East Ridge, which pushes up from the ocean floor for some 3,000 miles along 90 degrees longitude east.

Every four hours whoever is on watch carefully marks our westward progress; you can *see* in the vast, undifferentiated sea exactly where the *Colombo Bay* has been and where she is headed, touch approximately where she is at any moment. It is doubly comforting that Shakeel and the other deck officers trace our course as I might have done in fifth grade, with a ruler and pencil, though such primitive instruments, like the charts themselves, are endangered tools on a bridge otherwise beeping and flashing with advanced technology. Already electronic charts are used on many newer ships, and the consoling paper on which navigators have plotted their course at least since Ptolemy laid the foundation of cartography nearly two millennia ago soon will be decorating cabin walls and sold for souvenirs.* I am being romantic, I know, a consequence no doubt of spending so much time afloat in the nineteenth-century world of my literary bunkmates. Yet even those two experienced seamen might have welcomed the convenience of easily updated and corrected electronic charts, and the protective eye of radar and pinpoint accuracy of the Global Positioning System (GPS).

I confess a certain attraction to these devices myself, and if pressed would concede that they are no less mundane than the magnetic compass and sextant were in their day. The GPS is by now a ubiquitous navigational aid based on twenty-four satellites orbiting some 11,000 nautical miles above the earth that send radio signals down to receivers that give positions within a matter of feet or, with the most advanced receivers, inches. The breakthrough system was developed by the U.S. Department of Defense in the sixties and was long a secret domain for intelligence gathering and other military purposes. The DoD still operates the system but has made it so widely available that backpackers use it like high-tech bread crumbs to find their way out of the Adirondacks and car renters to extricate themselves from LAX. The receiver on the *Colombo Bay*—an LMX 400 DGPS Navigator made by Litton Marine Systems—not only gives our precise longitude and latitude at all times but is programmed to indicate course, distance, time, and speed from way point to way point, adjusting the ETA whenever our speed changes. It also provides the time of sunset and sunrise at any position and, if

---

*In 2002 Peter Davies became master of the *Hudson,* a P&O Nedlloyd container ship put in service in May of that year; instead of standing on the bridge, as he did on the *Colombo Bay,* he guided the new ship enthroned on a chair, electronic charts embedded in the arms.

tide tables are fed into the system, predicts what the tides will be at our next port of call.

A few feet from the GPS receiver the radar crunches its own numbers, producing a broken red line on the flickering round screen that indicates our set course and a short green line showing our "course made good" due to currents and wind. The practical maximum range of the radar is twenty-four nautical miles, and any vessel that comes within that radius appears like a liver spot on the screen and can be fixed by the broken white electronic bearing line, which indicates the target ship's course and speed in relation to the *Colombo Bay*'s and determines to the minute how much time we would have to maneuver in the unlikely event that we were on a collision course. The screen also features a red safety circle that surrounds the *Colombo Bay* and can pick up a firm echo of a ship twenty nautical miles away; should the officer of the watch be bowed in paperwork or otherwise inattentive, an alarm rings on the bridge when an oncoming vessel crosses the circle. At the moment no ships appear on the screen, only a yellowish curtain indicating the dark rain falling from still darker clouds in the distance off to starboard. "Sometimes the crew asks the bridge to avoid the rain if they are painting on deck," Simon Westall tells me.

Simon stands watch from 0800 to 1200 and 2000 to 2400 and, because we are moving through a calm sea on autopilot, has had some extra time this morning to conduct this instruction on the bridge's electronics, which besides the radar and GPS include the shortwave radio, satellite telephones, a computer station, walkie-talkies, a copying machine, and the crucial electric teakettle, which keeps at a near boil twenty-four hours a day by toggling on and off automatically. Motion sensors are mounted near the doors to both wings; if a lone watch keeper goes out on the wing or is absent elsewhere so that no movement is detected in the wheelhouse over five minutes, an alarm goes off. With a grin, my guide concludes his tour by opening a closet at the rear of the bridge and revealing that everything we've said has been recorded. Inside is the ship's "black box," which is gray and about the size of a small safe. Every twenty-four hours this voyage event recorder captures on disk the readings from the GPS receiver and radar, all radio communications, and the voices in the engine control room and on the bridge, where three microphones are strategically placed to pick up all conversation. In case of a collision, fire, or other mishap, investigators have a record of almost all pertinent information from the previous twenty-four hours. "If we should be foundering, the captain's last duty is to retrieve the disk," says Simon.

His command of these details and the nuances of navigation is impressive for a twenty-one-year-old. He is soft-spoken and attractively direct and seems quite mature for his age as we talk about how he came to the sea. When he was fifteen he went on holiday with his parents, taking an overnight cruise ferry from Portsmouth to Bilbao. He wanted to get onto the bridge for a look, but the officers wouldn't let him up because of rough weather; he did manage a peek, though, and thought, I'd like to do that. He grew up in Lincoln, in the east Midlands, about an hour's drive from the North Sea, and had never given seafaring a thought until that voyage. When he returned home, he wrote to what was then P&O Containers, which hired him as a deck cadet just before his sixteenth birthday, in 1996. His first trips were to Australia—one eastbound via Suez from the Mediterranean, the other westbound from Europe around the Cape—during which he mostly worked week after week with the crew chipping, painting, and doing other dogsbody tasks. Like all cadets, he combined this sea service with nautical studies— at South Shields—over four years, during which P&O paid his wages and the fees for his courses and exams. He has been a third mate now for a year, always hoping to see a bit of the world. He managed four hours ashore in Singapore and like Alex Gill has wearied of life aboard container ships.

In the lounge before and after dinner, Simon has a tendency to hug a sofa pillow while lost in the stereo's embrace. "Is that your dolly?" he was teased on a couple of occasions, darts that seemed not to faze him any more than the occasional references to nancy boys and other homophobic remarks. These comments never seemed aimed at anyone in particular and were so infrequent and offhand that I gave little thought to the possibility that Simon—or anyone else aboard—might be gay, though shipboard homosexuality has a long history. Poseidon himself dallies with the adolescent Pelops on Mount Olympus, though the boy eventually returns to the world of mortals and seeks to wed Hippodamia. When her father insists that her hand go only to the man who can best him in a chariot race, Pelops asks his powerful erstwhile lover for help, and Poseidon proves a forgiving and understanding sea god; he provides the would-be groom with a golden chariot and, because he does double duty as the god of horses, the winged steeds needed to win the race.

Ishmael and Queequeg's relationship is among the most compelling love affairs in all literature, beginning when the young tar awakens in the marriage bed at the Spouter Inn to find Queequeg's arm thrown over him "in the most loving and affectionate manner." When Queequeg learns that they will be sharing the bed again the next night, he presses his head against Ishmael's, clasps him about the waist and announces that they are married. "Thus, then," says Ishmael, "in our hearts' honeymoon, lay I and Queequeg—a cosy, loving pair." Later, with a whale brought alongside the *Pequod,* Ishmael plunges his hands into the "musky meadow" of its sperm and, in a passage suggesting a call for mutual masturbation, exhorts his mates to "Squeeze! Squeeze! Squeeze! . . . Oh! My dear fellow beings, why should we longer cherish any social acerbities, or know the slightest ill-humor or envy! Come; let us squeeze hands all around; nay, let us all squeeze ourselves into each other; let us squeeze ourselves universally into the very milk and sperm of kindness."

Melville, who more than one scholar has suggested may have been gay, well knew from his own experiences how homoerotic life aboard ships could be when men are thrown together for months at a time. "Like pears closely packed," he wrote in *White-Jacket,* his fictional account of the weeks he spent as an ordinary seaman in 1843 aboard the frigate *United States,*

> the crowded crew mutually decay through close contact, and every plague spot is contagious. Still more, from this same close confinement . . . arise other evils, so direful that they will hardly bear even so much as an allusion. What too many seamen are when ashore is very well known; but what some of them become when completely cut off from shore indulgences can hardly be imagined by landsmen. The sins for which the cities of the plain were overthrown still linger in some of these wooden-walled Gomorrahs of the deep. More than once complaints were made at the mast of the *Neversink,* from which the deck officer would turn away with loathing, refuse to hear them, and command the complainant out of his sight.

In *Billy Budd* the menacing master-at-arms, Claggart, is so undone by his attraction to the "Handsome Sailor" that he slanders him, causing the innocent foretopman to lash out and unintentionally kill his superior, for which Billy, "as much of [a] masculine beauty as one can expect anywhere to see," is hanged. This ending was no fictional exaggeration of a mariners' world where for centuries homosexual acts sometimes drew the cruelest of punishments. In 1676 the trading ship *Asia* left Europe with a complement of 297 hands, including nine boys. One of the stewards, Christopher Schweitzer, reported that as she was sailing in bad weather near the equator, "the mate and his boy were catched together acting the abominable sin of sodomy. A council was held upon it, and sentence was given that they should be tied back to back (which was done by the boatswain) and tied in a sack and thrown alive into the sea." Almost three centuries later, in 1932, the poet Hart Crane was returning to New York City from Vera Cruz by ship when he was severely beaten by sailors after he had approached them seeking sex. He was not thrown overboard for his sins but jumped into the sea, ending his troubled life at age thirty-three.

By the end of the twentieth century, death was rarely a consequence of antigay attitudes, though machismo still prevailed aboard most merchant vessels and gay sailors continued to draw suspicion and often hostility. "Anyone who was gay found it hard going," Jeremy Nixon told me of his sailing days in the seventies. "The attitude toward homosexuals aboard ship paralleled what it was in the rest of society at the time." By the early nineties, however, P&O Nedlloyd and many other liner companies were allowing openly gay mariners to serve aboard their vessels, in part because the need for seamen was such that they could not afford to turn down qualified hands. This put their gender policies well ahead of the don't-ask-don't-tell regulations of their countries' militaries, which ended in Britain only in 2000 and by 2004 were still in force in the United States.

I did not learn that Simon was gay until I visited his website some weeks after leaving the *Colombo Bay*. Under a photo of him standing in bathing trunks on vacation in the south of Spain, he wrote that he was a twenty-two-year-old navigational officer in the merchant navy, liked to go out drinking, clubbing, and to the cinema, enjoyed pop and dance music, and had seen the Steps once or twice. He announced that he was a single gay man interested in meeting same for a relationship, friendship, or just email chat. "My best mates," he wrote, "say that I'm a bit insane/mad, but then you have to be to do my job!" By the time I read this Simon had left P&O Nedlloyd and was a navigational officer on the MS *Volendam,* a cruise ship of the Holland America Line that sails the Caribbean in the winter and from Vancouver to Alaska in the summer. In several email exchanges and a long phone conversation, he described what it had been like being gay in the broad-shouldered world of the merchant service. Even if you're not gay, he said, working at sea is 180 degrees from a normal job, reiterating a point he had made in one of our talks on the bridge about how constrained he felt to avoid friction at all times. "You learn to curb your frayed temper," he had said. "If a senior officer makes obvious or unreasonable demands, you sometimes simply have to bite your tongue and walk away."*

In the beginning he walked away from his sexual orientation as well. "I didn't know what to expect from working onboard a ship," he said. "I didn't want to rock the boat, so I watched what I did and said; I didn't want to pretend to be straight, but I didn't want to give the impression that I was gay, either. You have to live with your mates for many weeks in a male environment, and I didn't want to risk comments that would eventually make my life onboard unpleasant. I wanted to get things sorted out in my own head, too." He was often asked if he had a girlfriend, to which he replied, Not at the moment, explaining that he wanted to move ahead in his job before he got involved with anyone.

On one of his first ships he became friendly with a couple of straight sailors, with whom he sometimes went ashore drinking. In Sydney they suggested a visit to "the Cross," which Simon assumed was a pub but which turned out to be King's Cross, the red-light district, where he soon found himself sitting among lap dancers and watching strippers on the small stage. He was still a teenager, a sheltered boy who had grown up in a provincial town where his father ran a plumbing business and his mother worked at a school; when on leave in England he continued to live at home. Faced with so much exposed female flesh for the first time, he looked away in em-

*My conversations on the bridge with Simon and others, all of which were recorded on the eavesdropping voyage event recorder tape, gave me a new appreciation of the unwitting candor that led to Richard M. Nixon's downfall.

barrassment, nursed his drink, and kept quiet. "I look back on it now and find it very funny, but at the time it was, like, Oh my word!"

On his early voyages Simon mostly kept to himself when he wasn't on duty, retreating to his cabin to fine-tune his website, listen to his CDs, and read the Harry Potter books and the fantasy-world novels of the popular British author Terry Pratchett. "I didn't really come out on the ships until my first trip as third mate in the fall of 2000. It was on the *Newport Bay,* making the same eastbound run as the *Colombo Bay* does. The chief engineer's wife joined us in Hong Kong, and during the twelve-day crossing of the Pacific to the West Coast we would talk in the bar after I came off duty at midnight. She was very easy to get on with and made me feel comfortable. We were alongside in Oakland one evening when she returned from shore and came into the bar, and somehow I plucked up my courage; I'm not sure where it came from, but it was there, and I told her I was gay. She said she had picked up on it about three-quarters of the way across the Pacific, and looking back I can see that she often steered the conversation in ways that got me to hint at the fact. After that evening we spent most nights chatting about men and about my life at home and going out in London with friends. I now was so at ease that I felt, well, I can do my job and that's the important thing. She told her husband and this didn't bother me; if he or anyone had a problem with me being gay then that was their problem, not mine."

Simon said his stint on the *Colombo Bay* was a happy one, in particular because Alex Gill and Christopher Windsor-Price, the cadet, shared his enthusiasm for rock and much else in the twenty-something culture. He feels they understood and didn't judge him and that their occasional jibes were said in jest and never viciously. He sensed that his sexual orientation made the older officers a bit uneasy but said they kept their views to themselves and treated him fairly. Though he regards the training he received aboard container ships as invaluable, he has few regrets about moving to the

Volendam, which sails where the sea is mostly calm, the temperatures warm, and the skies sunny. His responsibilities have increased to include overseeing all bridge equipment and plotting courses between ports, and when we last spoke his capabilities had won him the promise of promotion to second mate. "And I am now completely out at work, and it's the best feeling ever," he added.

CHAPTER SIX

The *Colombo Bay* reached its namesake port in the early dawn of September 24, under clouds infused with a waning red glow from the lights of the Sri Lankan capital. The pilot boat meets us at 0630, delivering a darkly handsome pilot of about thirty-five whose Adidas and white Dunlop shorts suggest that any moment he might say, "Tennis, anyone?" He is accompanied by two eager teenagers, ball boys in identical whites with blue piping. As we heel toward the basin, they wander pop-eyed around the port wing, like high school sophomores on a field trip; when the pilot introduces them as "naval security," Peter manages to contain his laughter, though there is no shortage of bona fide security all around us. A buoyed barricade stretches across the northern entrance to the basin, designed to stop the suicide boats of the Tamil Tigers, one of which blew up against a government naval vessel only eight days ago, killing twenty-nine. A government boat patrols the other entrance, a narrow opening between two breakwaters that we are about to enter. The Sri Lankan flag's yellow lion, sword in paw, now flies above the bridge along with the red ensign and the P&O Nedlloyd colors as the sun pokes over the hills, backlighting the waiting dinosaurs and sending broad beams through the dark, low-lying rain clouds and the cirrocumulus cotton riding above them. The rays also glint off the windows of the white twin towers that dominate the downtown skyline; Peter's guidebook reveals that this tall welcome is the country's World Trade Centre.

Soon after we berth someone brings aboard the local *Daily News,* an English-language paper whose page-one banner reads: PROBE ON LTTE—BIN LADEN LINKS. The story offers scant evidence of any connection between the fugitive George W. Bush wants "dead or alive" and the Liberation Tigers of Tamil Eelam and seems little more than an attempt by a pro-government paper to make the separatists look worse by smearing them with guilt by association. Neither bin Laden nor Islamic fundamentalism is a significant factor in the Sri Lankan civil war, which is ferociously local, a bitter conflict between Tamils, the predominately Hindu minority that seeks an autonomous homeland in the northeast of the country, and the mainly Buddhist Sinhalese majority, whose leaders control the government, military, and most of the territory of this island nation off the southern tip of India.

It has long been a commonplace to liken the shape of the country to a teardrop, a description two decades of strife have made a good deal more than a cliché. In 1983 both sides began all-out hostilities after the Tamils killed thirteen government soldiers, deaths which prompted anti-Tamil massacres in Colombo on July 24 that left at least 400 dead; since then the conflict has claimed some 62,000 lives in a country with the same population—19-plus million—as New York State, a 9/11 annually for eighteen years. Between 1980 and 2001, suicide attacks worldwide totaled 188. In only half that period, from 1990 through 2001, the Tigers employed *thatkodai,* which means self-sacrifice or self-gift, seventy-five times, almost 40 percent of the total, killing 862 people. Except for the Al Qaeda planes of 9/11, the Tigers have proved more ruthless and persistent suicide bombers than any other group, including Hamas, Hezbollah, and Islamic jihad in their attacks on Israel.

The Tigers have decimated the Sri Lankan leadership by targeting ministers and other government officials. A third of the LTTE bombers have been women, spurred in part by a vivid, multicolored billboard on the highway that runs through Tamil territory; it shows a female in the midst of government soldiers exploding herself and them in a burst of flame. In December 1999 a woman took aim at Chandrika Kumaratunga, the Sri Lankan president, whose father, Solomon Bandaranaike, was assassinated in 1959, when she was fourteen, and whose husband, Vijaya Kumaratunga, was gunned down and died in her arms in 1988. The bomber, who wore two belts of explosives, blew herself up in Colombo about fifteen feet from the president, killing thirty-eight but not her target, who escaped with a blinded eye.

The government and its security forces have not been shy about employing terror strategies of their own, including—in the words of Amnesty International—"arbitrary arrest and detention, torture, 'disappearances,' and extrajudicial executions." In one two-week period in early 2000, the government detained 5,000 people for questioning after search operations in Colombo. At about the same time, Kumar Ponnambalam, a lawyer, politician, and outspoken supporter of the Tamil cause, was shot dead in a suburb of the city; a group calling itself the National Front Against Tigers took credit for the murder, declaring that it should be seen as a warning to all who support the LTTE. There is virtually no accountability for such acts or any of the other human rights violations rampant on both sides, from the frequent rape of women taken into custody by policemen, soldiers, and sailors to the kidnapping of children as young as ten years of age by the Tigers, who press them into their guerrilla ranks. Since the outbreak of the bloodshed, thousands of Tamils have fled the country, and upward of a million, most of them victims of the ruthless Tamil leadership, have left their homes in the northeast for dubious refuge elsewhere in the land.

At 0900 a car arrives to take Peter, Elizabeth, and me to the P&O Nedlloyd office near the port. En route we encounter three checkpoints manned by armed soldiers, some as young as the ball boys and all in disheveled brown uniforms. At each stop most of these sentries stand about in various states of boredom while one or two order us to roll down our windows, show our port passes, and open our bags. I have a tape recorder that a guard insists is a camera until he is unable to locate the lens. Peter does have a camera, which earns him a finger-wagging admonition not to take pictures in the port. He smiles patiently; he is a man who has dealt with such lectures before. At the office we are greeted by James Blewman, the company's man in Colombo, a New Zealander whose shaved head makes him seem both older and younger than his thirty-one years. A secretary brings in a tray of cups and an elegant white china pot of tea, and like a viceroy's wife, Elizabeth pours us back to the colonial decades, when the island was still Ceylon and the ruling British rode horseback through the tea estates. She, James, and I partake while Peter goes off to the British Admiralty agents in search of charts for a Cape run, "just in case." On the large world map that hangs near James's desk, the waters of the Indian and Atlantic Oceans seem vaster than ever, the Cape itself on some other planet. Peter soon returns, mission accomplished, and he and Elizabeth depart for a day of sightseeing. I make a date to meet James for lunch and set out to explore downtown Colombo.

Soldiers are everywhere, patrolling in pairs, behind barricades of rusted oil drums, in sandbag bunkers. The twin towers loom thirty-seven stories high at the end of York Street, where more soldiers stand guard at yet another checkpoint. One asks to see my passport, gives it and me a cursory once-over, and lets me pass unchallenged, as does the indifferent civilian security man just inside the large revolving doors of the east tower. The few people crossing the marble floors and riding the escalators under a squadron of tin mobiles suggest that the complex is not a resounding success, an impression reinforced by the absence of door nameplates on several upper floors and later confirmed by James, who says that the buildings have few tenants and are "a financial disaster." One reason is that these towers, too, have proved tempting targets: in October 1997, two weeks after the buildings opened, the Tigers exploded a truck bomb at the complex, which housed the Colombo Stock Exchange, the Central Bank, and several multinational corporations. The blast and street battles with government forces that followed left eighteen dead and more than one hundred injured, and shut down the center for six months of repairs. Despite such setbacks the impulse to build these temples to commerce is so overwhelming that a World Trade Center Association exists to keeps track of them; as of 2000, there were almost 300 in some 100 nations, more inviting symbols than may, in the post–9/11 world, be absolutely necessary.

Outside, there is "that swoon in the air that one associates with the tropics," as Mark Twain put it after visiting Ceylon in the mid-nineteenth century. To deal with it, I am wearing gray shorts, a blue polo shirt, and red baseball cap, and lack only a fanny pack to stamp me indelibly as an American tourist. As I walk along Lotus Road toward the ocean beach, one trishaw driver after another offers to take me on a guided tour of the city in his rickety three-wheel taxi. They lower their prices before I even respond, and look less disappointed than perplexed when I say I prefer to walk in the steamy morning heat. Several times men fall into step and introduce themselves. One is Silva, who approaches on Second Cross Street as I admire the redbrick and white Jama-ul-Zafar mosque, with its early twentieth-century clocks announcing prayer times. He says he is a government soldier on his day off, adding that he has a wife and three children. "Are you American?" I nod. "Bush should get the Taliban. I hate terrorism." I tell him I certainly understand, given Sri Lanka's travail, but this subject is now exhausted. "Would you like to see a ceremony with elephants? It's just up the road." I'm momentarily tempted but realize the pachyderms are in the opposite direction from the P&O Nedlloyd office, where I'm due to meet James in half an hour. I politely decline, but Silva persists, clearly frustrated that he hasn't set his hook. He abandons elephants and asks how long I plan to stay in Sri Lanka. When I say I'm leaving the next day, he asks on what airline, and when I say by ship he asks the name and where she is berthed.

I disentangle myself and walk back downtown through the honking snarl of traffic and human crush, passing along a two-block linear bazaar offering everything from dried sardines and fresh mangoes to T-shirts and batteries. Every few feet the crowd flows around a beggar, including an elderly woman who looks as if she will perish within hours. A sign announces, "Nobody Delivers Better." Domino's Pizza.

James's driver takes us to the Colombo Hilton for lunch. It is adjacent to the World Trade Centre but has its own set of sandbags and brown uniforms in the driveway, along with ersatz generals and faux Eastern potentates opening car doors at the entrance and bowing in the lobby. James guides me to the Gables, the hotel's premier restaurant; its theme of the moment is meals built around mushrooms and asparagus, but this gastronomic adventure is not to be. The maître d' takes one look at my tropical ensemble and stands frozen in embarrassment before a customer who not only dines regularly at the hotel but is now living there because the city has been turning off the electricity in his neighborhood late each afternoon for eight hours. James instantly divines the sartorial crisis, assures the flustered captain that it's okay, and we withdraw to the Lotus Terrace, one of six other restaurants on the premises.

We are seated with no fuss next to a glass-enclosed pond full of foot-long goldfish over which ducks and majestic swans glide as a fountain plays in the middle and James offers a thumbnail of his background. He took a business degree from New Zealand's Massey University, after which he landed an entry-level job with P&O Containers in Singapore, where his father worked for the company. After four years there and three in Dubai, he moved to the Colombo office twenty months ago. Like Jeremy, he is full of enthusiasm for the world of shipping. In Sri Lanka he would have to be; over the past eighteen months four suicide bombs have gone off within 600 yards of his house in central Colombo. One of them killed a cabinet minister and his wife, the in-laws of Romesh David, P&O Nedlloyd's agency general manager.

When I ask how this murderous atmosphere has affected the shipping business, James turns to the attack on the airport two months ago. The government-run SriLankan Airlines, he says, lost several hundred million dollars worth of equipment, which was covered by Lloyd's of London and other underwriters. Wanting to recoup that money, they increased the war-risk premiums in Sri Lanka, which for aircraft and ships had been "minuscule"—.0045 percent of a vessel's value. First they went up to .1675 percent; then insurance consultants came to town from London, checked out the port security, and went back with an unfavorable report. The premiums went up again, this time to .35 percent. This meant an extra $100,000 to $300,000 per vessel call for P&O Nedlloyd and the other big shipping lines, which passed the cost on to importers and exporters by tacking on their own war-risk surcharge, initially $350 per TEU.

This pass-along, which cut into the profits from the garments, tea, and other products Sri Lanka ships west, infuriated many local traders and government officials. James says he received several anonymous threats in the mail and over the telephone demanding that P&O Nedlloyd and the other liner companies rescind the surcharge, the implied or stated "or else" not easy to dismiss in Sri Lanka's climate of sudden death. "I've been told in certain rough language that myself along with other foreign shipping reps should leave the country," he says. Eventually a Sri Lankan delegation went to the underwriters in London and maintained in effect that, well, maybe the seaport was vulnerable to the Tigers; but if so it was no more so than before the airport attack, thus the risk had not changed. The argument carried and the surcharges began coming down—though where 9/11 would ultimately leave them, James says, was anyone's guess.

After lunch we go to the Queen Elizabeth Quay for a tour of the company's latest diadem, the port's new container terminal. James is now driving his own car, and when we reach the entrance soldiers order us onto a raised rack so they can inspect the underside for explosives. As we inch onto the narrow runners, a motorcyclist speeds into the checkpoint. Our handler shouts at him to stop, then yells to the guard on the other side of the rack to flag him down; the second guard ignores the order, either because he is preoccupied with guiding us over the rack or because he doesn't hear the command over the noise of the motorcycle, which quickly disappears into the port. The guards shrug as they watch it go, and we roll back to the tarmac and move on; no one looked under the car.

The quay is a confusion of bulldozers, backhoes, and piles of construction material that by the spring of 2003 would become the fully operational South Asia Gateway Terminals (SAGT), with berths for three ships the length of the *Colombo Bay,* each tended by three state-of-the art super post-Panamax gantries able to reach across the next generation of container ships. At the SAGT office, James introduces me to Tissa Wickramasinghe, the marketing manager, and together they tout the potential of the facility, which unlike the government-run terminal across the basin, where the *Colombo Bay* rests, is controlled by a consortium of private investors, including P&O Nedlloyd, and managed by its subsidiary P&O Ports.

For many months this move toward privatization was another source of anonymous threats, in part because of a certain we-can-do-it-better nationalistic pride but also because the port is a cash cow that helps underwrite the war. "Politics and fighting the war come first here, not commercial interest," says James, and statistics bear him out. Before the civil struggle heated up, military spending represented 1 percent of the economy; by 2000 it was nearing 7 percent, and more than five times as many people worked in the security forces than in the tourist industry. "The war has become an institution," a Western diplomat in Colombo told the *New York Times* a few weeks before we arrived. "Rich people are making money on commissions, kickbacks, selling supplies to the army. The soldiers are fairly well-paid too. Everyone seems to be making money."

The workers on the government docks might be excused for feeling left out of this bonanza. They receive two or three dollars a day for clambering over the *Colombo Bay*'s containers in the stifling heat to loosen and tighten lashing bars and do the other dangerous cargo tasks required while we are in port. James concedes that their base pay is low but is at pains to point out that it has long been augmented by "speed money," under-the-table cash that is a routine factor in the port's corruption, as are overtime pay and featherbedding. "In Singapore, they have about 5,000 workers moving some 18 million TEUs per year," he says. "Here there are more than 20,000 workers handling 1.5 million TEUs annually. Just before the last election, the government, to get votes, increased the number of workers on the docks by 4,000."

Whatever covert income and other benefits may come their way, the shirtless stevedores show few signs of being overpaid as they go about their work in flip-flops and often barefoot. "The conditions are appalling, and the same applies in the Philippines, Bangladesh, and some Indian ports," Shakeel told me, adding that he and some other officers did their best to collect used clothing and shoes to give the men. P&O Nedlloyd and other shipping firms maintain that these government "wharfies," as some call them, can't or won't do their job properly, a view shared by Matt Mullins and several other hands, who must spend hours inspecting the containers to make sure that the lashing bars are tightened, which often they are not, and dealing with other snafus. "They are a little behind in Colombo, to put it mildly," Matt says, noting that seventy boxes due for loading were still on another ship waiting in the harbor and that there were reefers due aboard whose location in the terminal he still hadn't been able to determine. Tissa Wickramasinghe speaks proudly of putting together an honest, efficient private workforce at SAGT, with no unions, "speed money," or overtime but instead a package of pay and benefits that is "solid" for Sri Lanka. When I ask for specifics, he demurs.

Privatization may well eventually come to the government termi- nal, as it has at ports in other developing countries, if slowly. One sign is that press coverage of SAGT, once hostile, has grown neutral in recent weeks, likely because the government, as is common with such projects, has a small equity holding in the new terminal. Colombo is strategically located on the principal east-west shipping lanes, making the port what a SAGT brochure calls, somewhat grandly, the "Hub of Tomorrow's World." The tea, garments, and handful of other products indigenous to Sri Lanka make up only a small fraction of the boxes loading here. Most have come to the har- bor on feeder ships of 2,500 TEUs or less from ports in Pakistan, Bangladesh, and Thailand, on the Persian Gulf, the east coast of Africa, and both coasts of India.

The containers of auto and truck parts now loading across the basin started out at a factory in New Delhi, traveled south overland to the Nhava Sheva terminal near Bombay, then moved by ship down the west coast of India to Colombo; they will come off the *Colombo Bay* at Norfolk, Virginia, and roll by truck or train to Day- ton, Ohio. Dried fruits and nuts brought by a feeder vessel from Mangalore will also come off at Norfolk, then travel by truck to a dis- tribution center in Jessup, Maryland. Six forty-foot containers of men's and boys' shirts from Madras are headed for Wal-Mart's warehouse at the Port of Savannah, Georgia. Marble from Hyder- abad is bound for New York, as are prepared and preserved mush- rooms and truffles loaded at Cochin and ten reefers of frozen shrimp harvested in the Laccadive Sea off Mangalore, where they were packed for the feeder lap to Colombo. The port charges for handling this "throughput" fill the udder of the cash cow, and if SAGT's pri- vate terminal proves creamy enough, Sri Lanka's business and government leaders may be unable to resist converting to a similar milking station.*

In the late afternoon we drive to James's home, where he introduces his house boy, Bala, and security guard, Lecheman, a short, rail-thin man who looks even less formidable than the ball boys. In the spacious living room, Veronique Liekens, who does charity work at a local school and with whom James lives, is scrutinizing two similar square coffee tables that have just been delivered so the couple can decide which size looks best. Their choices collide, so they solicit my view. It is fair to say that when I embarked from Hong Kong I anticipated a number of unique experiences, but posing as an interior decorator in Sri Lanka was not among them; still, I give it my best shot, circling the tables a couple of times, pausing for dramatic effect, and sagely announcing that the bigger table "works better" with their two large white sofas and matching armchair. This judgment seems to please Veronique; James is noncommittal. Happily, the symposium is truncated because it is now almost six o'clock and the electricity is about to die. We scoop up James's clean shirts and drive to the Hilton, en route passing the spot where the woman Tiger blew herself up in the failed attempt to assassinate President Kumaratunga in 1999.

At the hotel we run into Peter, Elizabeth, Steve, and Frank, and join them in the Echelon Pub as Veronique goes off to play tennis. A TV wall screen only a few feet from our table offers CNN: Christiane Amanpour looking competent and somber, Afghani fighters wrapped in bandoliers, President Bush and Secretary of State Colin Powell

---

*Private or public, the port's chances of flourishing, and of pay improving for the stevedores, would increase markedly if the war ended, and signs were already in the air that it might. A weariness with the slaughter had finally set in, and by February 2002 a cease-fire, brokered by Norwegian mediators, was in place; it was still holding by the fall of 2003, as the two sides continued wary negotiations aimed at giving the Tamil minority some form of autonomy in the northeast.

holding a joint news conference at the White House, a stock still of
Osama bin Laden. The sound is off, as if whoever controlled the volume had decided that whatever the words they would not matter
much. My mates are better able to ignore the screen than I am, and
as the drinks flow a happy-hour ambience soon prevails, made more
boisterous when several of James's expat friends join us. One of
them asks if I think Barry Bonds will break Mark McGwire's record
of seventy home runs. "He already has sixty-seven," he says, providing information I not only didn't know but hardly expected to hear
delivered with a British accent in a Colombo bar. I calculate that the
season, which was suspended for two or three days after 9/11, still
has about two weeks to go, time enough for four home runs, certainly. I predict that the Giants slugger will hit seventy-one homers,
confident that I am at least on surer ground than in judging coffee
tables.

There follows a lengthy discussion with Steve Kingdon comparing
the rules and relative merits of baseball and cricket, an inconclusive
deliberation in which the different meanings of *pitch* is just one of
the challenges. Peter is at the other end of the long table, and
through the cacophony I shout the question of the moment: "Any
word on the Cape?" He shakes his head. I pledge that if he can save
us from that lengthy deviation, I will put any extra Suez insurance
charges on my Visa card, an offer accepted with alacrity in front of
far too many witnesses. When Veronique gets back, she and James
take me to a nearby Thai restaurant, and just after 2200 we return
to the Hilton and say our good-byes; the *Colombo Bay* contingent
piles into a taxi and we again run the gauntlet of checkpoints. We enter the ship through the port door of the upper deck, almost stum-
bling over a half dozen ragged, barefoot stevedores grabbing what
sleep they can on the steel plating.

CHAPTER SEVEN

We nose out of the basin the next day just after 1200, to be greeted by a squall that reduces visibility to zero. This white-out lasts only five minutes or so but leaves us dangerously dependent on electronic navigation while several other large ships are close by. The sea is rougher than at any point so far, the cream-topped waves cresting at about nine feet. In the meteorological manual on the bridge there is a Beaufort scale, which measures winds and seas from zero (calm) to Force 12 (hurricane), when blows are at least sixty-five nautical miles per hour and seas thirty-seven feet high or more. The book provides photos of waves at every force level, and after comparing them with the swells breaking all around us, I guess Force 6. "Correct," says Shakeel, making me feel as if I'd just nailed my third-mate orals.

For the first time since Hong Kong, a small effort is required to maintain my balance, and I seek reassurance from an experiment I had conducted two weeks before embarking. After being advised by a website that anyone able to read in a moving car was unlikely to get seasick, I read most of the Sunday *Times* while Diane drove us to Manhattan from upstate New York, even managing to complete half the acrostic with no ill effects. This trial by interstate made me hopeful but not so cocky that I didn't ask Mike Bush, our family doctor, to prescribe an antidote for queasiness. He declined, explaining that for someone my age one nasty side effect of antiseasickness medication is the inability to urinate, a condition he suggested would be rather worse than a bout of mal de mer.

So I am on my own, and so far so good, though photos of the waves from Force 7 on up to the hurricane mountains make plain I had yet to be tested. "Only heavy weather makes you feel like a sailor, Dick, like a good old salty sea dog," the cadet, Christopher Windsor-Price, had said during a particularly placid day. "There's nothing like having to put your mattress on the floor, like fearing that when the ship rolls she won't right herself. It makes you realize just how insignificant you really are." I respected this philosophic insight, especially coming from one so young, but was less interested in having my cosmic standing confirmed than in not having to make obeisance before the toilet bowl.

As we forge through the moist Force 6, Shakeel hands me the binoculars and says to focus on a container up near the fo'c'sle, an open box that houses two tanks empty except for residues of nitrogen. Huddled near one of the tanks are two crows that made the mistake of sailing with us from Colombo. When they venture forth, they poke their bills into one container lug hole after another in a frantic search for food and water, or dart into the air, only to circle once or twice and return to the ship. Crows are notoriously tough birds, with a deserved reputation for survival, but they are land birds, unable to forage in the sea for sustenance and soar on the winds for days like albatrosses; the crows are trapped, and their twitching heads and desperate hopping show that they know it. If we go around the Cape they, as we, will not be able to get off the ship for three weeks, until we reach Halifax. Whatever route we take, they are now dependent on the kindness of strangers. Shakeel dispatches me to the pantry for some bread, and when I return the crows are on a container behind the funnel. We go out onto the starboard wing, where Shakeel tears up the slices and heaves the pieces, which fall on the box like a summer snow shower; I fear they'll blow away, but they are in the lee of the funnel and don't. The crows scramble away as the meal lands, then pounce.

On the second morning out of Colombo, an email arrives from Jeremy bringing good news for the birds and everyone else onboard. We are heading for the Suez. "You are now entering technically a war-risk zone," he writes. "Our normal insurance coverage has been revoked and all vessel operators have to take out additional premiums to cover themselves whilst passing through Suez and the Red Sea. On the Colombo Bay this is about an additional $25,000 per passage." He says that the outlook for trade in the wake of 9/11 is quite downbeat, with expectations for the North American Christmas market, toward which thousands of TEUs are now moving and will move in the coming weeks, are down 10 to 15 percent from the previous year. These bad financial tidings come on top of collapsing freight rates, which have been dropping for months mainly because of overcapacity in an industry whose fleet of container ships will have increased 12 percent by the end of 2001. Jeremy also reports that Wal-Mart has just announced record sales of American flags and ammunition. Mostly he urges me not to worry about coming under attack as we pass through the waters of the Middle East, since "the Taliban navy is not that well equipped!"

There is also an email from Diane, following on a call I'd made to her from James's office. It had been breakfast time in New York, and we'd talked for half an hour, the connection so good it seemed we were sitting across the kitchen table from one another. I'm fine, I said, looking into her eyes; I am fine, too, she replied, sipping her ritual morning tea. She said Isaac Stern had died; yes, so the BBC had reported. She had heard from conductors at the Buffalo and Lancaster symphony orchestras holding out the possibility of concerto gigs. Good news; surely at least one will come through.

She had just returned from Boston, where she had participated in a chamber music concert, her first performance since the attacks.

She had been unsure about it, because she and her colleagues had found it hard to concentrate on practicing and rehearsing. One of the works was the Brahms Quintet for Piano and Strings, a staple of the repertoire that Diane had played many times. There is a mournful passage just before the coda of the Finale, and the twenty measures now sounded to her like someone suffering unbearable emotional pain; as the performance had progressed she approached the section with increasing anxiety, fearing she would break down. A consummate pro, she did not.

That was more than I could say about my own reaction to the *Deutsches Requiem,* which was among the three dozen recordings I had brought along. I had played it a few nights before, lying in the dark, earphones clamped on my head and clutching the CD player like an oversize bedtime cookie, seeking solace not only in the choral beauty but in the melding of biblical verses assuring that out of death comes salvation and hope. "Blessed are they that mourn: for they shall be comforted," the opening chorus begins, quoting Matthew. But the solemn chords and voices soon became background music for images of the planes slicing into the towers, of children with coloring books on their tray tables consumed in fireballs, of people hurtling out of windows seventy, eighty, ninety stories above the street, and of the hundreds of others who had been suffocated or crushed in the impossible collapse. Ever since I was a child, music had been the one thing I could count on to drive away gloom, but the *Requiem* brought tears, not hope.

In her email Diane told of taking the West Side subway to the Franklin Street station, now the last stop in Lower Manhattan before the trains bypassed the decimated stations at what would come to be called Ground Zero. "The whole area is still cordoned off, but I went over to Broadway and walked south as far as Wall Street and could glimpse the wreckage down the side streets. Somehow the actual sight of the rubble and smell of burning weren't as shocking as seeing the big hole in the sky where the towers used to be." The sky-scrapers had always seemed to me prime examples of architectural preening, pegs driven into Manhattan's schist as if by nursery schoolers determined to impress their teacher with how high they could pile their blocks; but like Diane and everyone else, I had long ago taken the structures for granted as the twin anchors of the city's skyline. I could imagine the void, but not what the smoldering remains of two hundred-story towers looked like. Where do so much steel, concrete, and glass go? And what must it be like searching for bodies under so much debris?

I yearned for the hard lens of television, though my friend Michael Meltsner was probably right in saying, in an email message Diane had appended, that I was better off being out of it, that one more benumbed CNN watcher was hardly needed. Also appended was another email talking sense: "I think a lot of the feelings you described on the phone the other day—helplessness and distance—are no different than what we're all feeling right here in NYC. There's just nothing to do but go ahead with normal life, which is what we're all trying to do." This from the child I carried to school on my shoulders.

I am discomfited by the flash of self-pity these communications elicit, and later in the day get a needed if unintended jolt of perspective from Frank McAlees. We are sitting in his quarters on B deck, and even in this quiet setting the engineer's soft Irish cadences are hard to catch, though his message comes through. "We got used to bombs in Belfast," he says, as if talking about too much rain. "I had to leave school several times because of threats, and when I was thirteen my school bus was hijacked by men who made us get off and then set it on fire." When he was sixteen his parents moved out of Belfast to Whitehead, a small village about fifteen miles away. "We stayed away from pubs because you were likely to be blown up." He is not lecturing, merely recounting how it was growing up in Northern Ireland—as a survivor in Sri Lanka, Israel, Palestine, Rwanda, Liberia, Congo, East Timor, Nepal, Chechnya, Nicaragua, Guatemala, Colombia, Serbia, Tibet, Cambodia, Vietnam, or of the unimaginable slaughter in the two world wars might describe his childhood, a polite reminder of how self-indulgent we cosseted Americans are to feel suddenly singled out by man's lethal impulses, however dramatic the punch.

Frank is the son of a former chief engineer in the Royal Navy and, at forty-three, has been at sea himself for two decades. He is something of a loner, seldom hanging out in the lounge, usually skipping the evening meal, and spending much of his off-duty time studying the Old Testament through a course urged on him by a Methodist minister back home. Like Peter, Matt, and Steve, he has his own video player, and his library includes *American Psycho, Dune, Random Hearts, Philadelphia, Pearl Harbor, Tora! Tora! Tora!* and *How the Grinch Stole Christmas.* "I picked up *Grinch* recently in port only to discover that it was dubbed in Chinese," he says with a laugh. He is not long married, to Helen, who has introduced him to the Ulster Orchestra, and classical music. He shows me his collection, which includes the Carmen Suite and the William Tell Overture, and we agree to exchange CDs.

Our talk has been punctuated by my frequent snorts into Kleenex, evidence that the sniffles of the last few days have progressed to a full-fledged sinus infection. Microbes tend to travel fast aboard ships, circulating along with the gelid temperatures through the air-conditioning ducts. Have I started a plague or did I come onboard in the middle of one? Regardless, I accept Conrad's admonition that one "can't live everlastingly with one's finger on one's pulse." Still, my postnasal drip tends to focus the mind on a great unspoken of shipboard life: serious medical emergencies. "It is a curious fact," wrote the master British mariner and watercolorist J. W. Holmes of his sailing days in the late nineteenth century, "that a man untrained even in first-aid was presumed to acquire some miraculous life-saving power on taking command of a ship. As captain he was responsible for the lives of all on board in every circumstance, and he was equipped for the profession of physician and surgeon by the magic possession of the ship's medicine chest and a small paper-backed *Medical Guide*. With these alone, and without anaesthetics, in the complete isolation of a three to six months' voyage, he had to deal with all manner of accidents, diseases, epidemics and even insanity." The first edition of the *Ship Captain's Medical Guide* came out in 1867, and its use is instructively illustrated by the report of Commodore Sir James Bisset in *Sail Ho!*, the first of three volumes he wrote about his experiences at sea in the first half of the twentieth century. As a young sailor, he had come down with dysentery after leaving Melbourne. "The Captain," he wrote,

dosed me with chlorodyne twice a day for a week, with no good effect, until the chlorodyne bottle was empty. This bottle was Number 15 in the medicine chest, to correspond with the numbers in [the Guide]. I had eaten nothing since leaving Melbourne and had grown thin, weak and pale. I thought my last days had come.

The Captain said to me, "Well, m'son, I don't know what to do with you. According to the book, No. 15 should have cured you. . . . I think I'll give you some Number 10 and Number 5. That adds to fifteen."

I was too sick to care what he gave me. It happened that Number 10 was a brown powder with a nasty taste. It was a diarrhoea mixture. Number 5 was a syrupy cough mixture. The Old Man mixed these two in glass, diluted them with a little water, stirred vigorously, and I swallowed the dose. Almost immediately I felt better. After two more doses, I was cured.

On the *Colombo Bay*, the twenty-second edition of the *Medical Guide* is in the magic possession of Matt Mullins, who as first mate is medical officer and is giving me a tour of the sick bay on E deck. It consists of a closet-size medicine locker and an infirmary slightly smaller than my cabin, in the middle of which is a hospital bed with a wraparound stretcher stashed underneath. Surrounding these are a sterilizer tank, small sink, metallic urn for boiling water, blood pressure equipment, plastic gloves, first-aid kits, antiseptic solutions, catheters, inflatable splints, bedpans, oxygen bottles, a portable oxygen resuscitator, and oxygen and multigas meters to test atmosphere in enclosed places.

Matt explains that all officers must complete a recognized first-aid course and that the Medical Care Onboard Course he was required to take is the most extensive, possibly an overly generous word to describe training that covered "pretty much everything" in five days, during which he practiced giving injections to and sewing stitches on an orange. A book on the bridge lists centers worldwide where doctors stand by ready to give advice by radio, but if Matt is faced with a heart attack, third-degree burns, internal bleeding, or other life-threatening afflictions he has two choices: send for a helicopter or divert to port. The *Colombo Bay* is now midway between Colombo and the Yemeni port of Aden, farther from land—about 500 miles—than at any time since we left Hong Kong. Only a very few helicopters could make such a round-trip, and even fewer pilots would be inclined to attempt it; moreover, the likelihood of raising such a helicopter in Oman or Yemen is as remote as the *Colombo Bay* herself. By heading full-speed toward Aden, we would eventually come within helicopter range, but by then it might well be too late to get the stricken sailor to a hospital at the port.

"Very often people hide medical problems because they want to sail," Matt says. "This is especially true of crew members, whose pay stops if they are sent home for medical reasons." On the *Colombo Bay*'s eastbound crossing of the Pacific in August, Chris Windsor-Price was bedridden for five days. Matt made him comfortable and treated him for general malaise only to find when they got to Seattle that the cadet had not revealed he had a chronic kidney defect. A doctor in Seattle urged Chris to fly home for treatment in England; because he was a fledgling officer, his pay would have continued, but he refused to leave the ship, fearing in part that an illness that had already kept him out of the armed forces might now end his chance for a merchant marine career. I empathized. I have a long history of epilepsy that I had kept from Jeremy Nixon, worried that he or his superiors at P&O Nedlloyd might decide my presence aboard one of their ships was not worth the risk, even though anticonvulsant medication keeps my seizures almost completely controlled. Before Matt's tour ended I checked the *Medical Guide* to see what it told him to do in case someone had an epileptic attack. Its advice was reassuringly on the mark: Keep the victim comfortable, don't restrain him, let the convulsions run their course, insert diazepam (Valium) rectally if the seizures do not abate.

By the early morning of September 29, we have crossed the Arabian Sea and are about thirteen miles off the Horn of Africa, heading into the Middle Eastern heat of the Gulf of Aden, the ocean glassy under a cloudless sky. Before the year is out, these waters will be the prowling area of Task Force 150, a flotilla of eight warships, most of them flying the German or Spanish flag and manifesting a rare and little-reported involvement of European navies in post–9/11 defense. The task force monitors all maritime traffic in the region, searching for ships carrying contraband weaponry or Al Qaeda operatives fleeing Afghanistan for safe haven in the lawless outbacks of Somalia and Yemen.

After a year on patrol, the task force had not come up with much, but in December 2002 the Spanish ships *Navarro* and *Patino* intercepted a cargo vessel suspected of carrying Scud missiles. The captain radioed that his hold was full of only cement, then tried to outrun the Spaniards. The warships fired bursts of machine-gun bullets across the ship's bow and dispatched a helicopter, from which seven Spanish commandos slid down ropes onto the fleeing vessel's deck. They found missile warheads and fifteen Scuds from

North Korea, but when Washington discovered that the weapons were bound for Yemen, whose cooperation the Bush administration had come to count on in its war on terrorism, the ship was allowed to make its delivery. *El Mundo,* the Spanish daily, complained that the country's navy had been assigned to do the United States' dirty work and likened the sailors on the *Patino* and *Navarro* to police officers who arrest a criminal "only to see the judge release him through the back door."

After a day and evening of sailing, we reach Bab el Mandeb, the choke point at the southern entrance to the Red Sea. We pass through this "Gate of Tears"—so called because of its navigational hazards and because of those drowned, according to Arab legend, when an earthquake separated Asia and Africa—in the middle of the night. Yemen is on our starboard, Djibouti on our port, either coast less than ten miles away as the crow flies, and the several islets in the strait closer still. Our crows show no interest in flying, and at dawn, well after we have pushed into the Red Sea, they are still hopping about the boxes. Peter observes that this behavior demonstrates impeccable logic, since they are daily indulged with bread and other tidbits by Shakeel and me. We do appear to be the only softies aboard; after one of the avian freeloaders boldly entered and investigated the wheelhouse, Peter allowed that he didn't want any "flappy birds" on his bridge, a sentiment shared by Simon and the cadet, who for reasons they have trouble defining find the crows creepy. By 0700 the temperature is already almost ninety degrees Fahrenheit, and the birds are bothering no one, having sought refuge from the sun in their preferred quarters, the tank-holding container up near the fo'c'sle.

The Red Sea is an intense blue-green, its appellation applying only on those rare occasions when extensive blooms of algae die off, turning the water a temporary reddish brown. The sky remains clear, though sand blowing off the deserts of Yemen and Saudi Arabia creates a typical haze, mantling the many passing vessels in a

khaki shroud that summons up ghosts of the Egyptian and Phoenician merchant ships that sailed this 1,200-mile-long sea, the oldest
body of water in recorded history, as early as 2000 BC.

After breakfast I pull on my boiler suit and meet Matt for a visit
to the holds. "You would pick the hottest day to go down there," Peter says, telling his first mate to keep a close eye on me. We enter the
steamy boiler room, descend one flight, then walk forward along the
red floor of the enclosed underdeck, a tunnel strung with white pipes
of varying circumferences that carry electrical wiring, sewage, and
drinking water. After we enter the door that leads to Hold Number
4, one of the eight cargo compartments, Matt opens a three-by-
three-foot hatch to reveal a ladder leading straight down: twenty
rungs, at least a one-story drop to the steel decking below. My palms,
already moist from the heat, dampen further, less at the prospect of
the descent than at that of getting back up with upper-body strength
somewhat diminished from the brief moment at Fort Dix forty-five
years ago when I could do two sets of twenty-five pull-ups. I imagine
being stuck in this sweltering dungeon, Shakeel throwing the bread
crumbs to me. Matt senses my hesitation, tells me to stay put, and
descends this and two more vertical ladders to investigate a shallow
pool of liquid that has leaked from a container. His hand-over-hand
ascent brings him back to the hatch breathing as easily as if he'd just
climbed a step stool to change a lightbulb. "Probably organic stuff,"
he says of the leak, which will be cleaned up by the crew.

We next visit Hold Number 7, where the ladders, angled and with
handrails, are more senior friendly. We go down three levels, containers pressing in on all sides; they are stacked eight high and ten
across, and look, in the neatness of their arrangement, like boxes of
soap powder at a discount store up the beanstalk. At capacity, the
eight aisles of this ultramarket stock almost 2,000 TEUs. To my surprise, Matt says neither he nor anyone else aboard knows what's in
95 percent of the boxes that surround us, or those on deck. He has
content information only for the 200 or so reefers, because their per-

ishable goods require constant temperature monitoring, and for some three dozen boxes labeled Dangerous Goods.*

Simon oversees these DG containers, making sure that they are stowed as required by the International Maritime Dangerous Goods Code (IMDG), which the UN's International Maritime Organization developed in the early 1960s. The code lists nine general categories of hazardous cargo, ranging from various explosives through flammable liquids and solids to toxic and radioactive material, and its segregation table shows Simon how the boxes must be kept apart. Those with substances prone to spontaneous combustion must be separated by at least one compartment in the hold from containers loaded with any kind of explosive. For four decades complying with the code was voluntary, and corner cutting by both shippers and liner companies was common.

Two months after we passed through Bab el Mandeb, a ship unloaded ten containers filled with chromated copper arsenate at the port of Djibouti for transshipment overland to Ethiopia, where, much diluted, the wood preservative was to be used to coat telephone poles. The compound, which contains known carcinogens as well as arsenic, had been shipped from England by CSI Wood Protection, Ltd., a branch of Chemical Specialties, Inc., of Charlotte, North Carolina; it was packed not in metal drums as the code requires but in plastic jerricans, which began leaking before the ship reached Djibouti. Not long after the gantries deposited the containers on the dock, the contents began spilling out of at least 6,000 of the jerricans, the fumes rendering several stevedores unconscious. Three men admitted to Djibouti's Peltier Hospital died within days, and doctors could only guess at the number of others who may have succumbed after taking to their beds at home, or who will suffer the debilitating long-range effects of the chemical poison. The spill also

---

*I learned what was in most of the containers only when P&O Nedlloyd furnished me with lading details after I had left the ship.

contaminated an estimated 2,000 tons of soil around the quay and forced the closing for three weeks of a UN food program headquartered at the port. Partly because of such incidents, the IMDG Code was scheduled to become mandatory on January 1, 2004; but enforcement is likely to remain spotty in an industry where official inspectors are in short supply and more DG containers than ever travel around the world.

Most of the DG boxes aboard the *Colombo Bay* are category 9, "miscellaneous dangerous substances and articles." Several of them have been permeated with potentially volatile fumigants to ensure that the wooden pallets inside or the load of handcrafted wooden objects from the Philippines don't become havens for termites and other insects. There are twelve drums of flammable liquid extract flavoring in one box, and up near the fo'c'sle is the crows' open container, holding the two empty tanks with their residue of nitrogen. "We have a set of books on the bridge that lists all the different kinds of chemicals and what to do if they catch fire or someone touches or inhales them," says Matt, recalling a close call on a previous voyage. "Hydrogen sulfide is carried in reefers, and if it gets above a certain temperature it combusts. We lost the power for one such reefer and were about to turn the ship around and head back to port when the engineers finally managed to get it going again." Until Colombo we had onboard a container full of hand flares, parachute red rockets, and marine distress signals that, as Simon put it, would have made "a proper fireworks display" had the contents ignited.

More than fifty containers of fireworks did blow up on the *Hanjin Pennsylvania*, a vessel about the size of the *Colombo Bay*, as she was westbound south of Sri Lanka on November 11, 2002. What may have set them off, according to investigators, was an explosion that morning in containers laden with calcium hypochlorite, a widely used bleaching agent that, in the late nineties, also had detonated on at least two other container ships. The *Hanjin Pennsylvania*'s twenty-one-man crew fought the initial blaze, but when the fireworks blew, the rear third of the ship became an inferno that sent yellow flame shooting skyward wrapped in a plume of charcoal smoke from which white sparks arced into the sea. One crew member died of burns before the container ship *Wehr Altona* and then the salvage and firefighting vessel *Mahanuwara* arrived to rescue the remaining hands. The fire burned for more than a week, destroying the accommodation and engine room and reducing several holds and hundreds of boxes—those that didn't topple into the ocean—to sculpted steel. The charred vessel, leased to Korea's Hanjin Shipping by a German shipbuilder, had been launched only a few months before the explosion. She was eventually towed to Singapore and then scrapped, the total loss of ship and cargo put at more than $100 million.

Next to storms, fires constitute the most serious threat to a ship, as Conrad learned after sailing from Falmouth in September 1882 on the 450-ton barque *Palestine* with a cargo of coal bound for Bangkok. He was serving as second mate for the first time and making his initial run to the East, a heady adventure for a seaman not yet twenty-five when the ship embarked. In March, when the *Palestine* was off the coast of Sumatra, spontaneous combustion started the coal smoking, beginning a fire that despite round-the-clock efforts to tame it eventually exploded. "I seemed somehow to be in the air," Conrad wrote two decades later in *Youth,* his fictional account of the voyage, in which Marlow is his narrator for the first time. "I heard all around me like a pent-up breath released—as if a thousand giants simultaneously had said Phoo!—and felt a dull concussion that made my ribs ache suddenly. No doubt about it—I was in the air, and my body was describing a short parabola. . . . What is it?— Some accident—Submarine volcano?—Coals, gas!—By Jove! We are being blown up—Everybody's dead." No one was, but all hands were soon in the boats, watching with dismay as their ship, renamed *Judea* by the author, burned upon a disc of purple sea shot by the blood-red play of gleams; upon a disc of water glittering and sinister. A high, clear flame, an immense and lonely flame, ascended from the ocean, and from its summit the black smoke poured continuously at the sky. She burned furiously, mournful and imposing like a funeral pile kindled in the night, surrounded by the sea, watched over by the stars. A magnificent death had come like a grace, like a gift, like a reward to that old ship at the end of her laborious days. The masts fell just before daybreak, and for a moment there was a burst and turmoil of sparks that seemed to fill with flying fire the night patient and watchful. . . . At daylight she was only a charred shell, floating still under a cloud of smoke and bearing a glowing mass of coal within.

The sailors finally wrenched themselves from their sinking home of six months and after half a day at the oars of three boats made it safely to the island of Bankga and thence, on the British steamer *Sissie,* to Singapore.

When the coal first started smoking on the *Palestine/Judea,* the captain ordered the hatches and all other apertures battened down, hoping to stifle the incipient blaze by denying it oxygen. That tactic remains the first line of defense should fire break out belowdecks on a container ship, whose steel vents, doors, and hatches can be made airtight, unlike on the wooden barque, where the "smoke kept coming out through imperceptible crevices . . . [oozing] here, there and everywhere in slender threads." On the *Colombo Bay,* air is extracted continuously from the holds and a constant screening process measures carbon particles that set off alarms should a fire be smoldering. The compartment housing the "hot" container is sealed off, and carbon dioxide from several of the 300 cylinders under the aft mooring deck is released via pipes into the space to choke off any conflagration. Should fire break out in the engine room, a tinderbox of fuel oil and lubricants, it too would be sealed off, and carbon dioxide from some 200 of the cylinders would be pumped into the huge chamber.

The stifling strategy usually works, but if it fails, quelling a major fire belowdecks may be impossible in the middle of the Atlantic or Pacific, where a port's professional firefighters and equipment are not as close as were the Sri Lankan vessels that came to the aid of the *Hanjin Pennsylvania*. The officers and crew of the *Colombo Bay* go through regular firefighting exercises, but they are a brigade of only two dozen with no professional training for or experience in battling a serious fire. One that broke out in one or more buried containers, and could not be smothered, would require that Matt, Shakeel, Simon, Federico, and others climb down the ladders through asphyxiating smoke, a life-threatening descent even wearing oxygen tanks and breathing apparatuses—which several crew members resisted donning during the drills I witnessed because the masks made them feel claustrophobic. Even should the team manage to haul hoses down four or five vertical ladders, using water to douse the fire can compound the crisis. Cargo such as pulp, paper, and cotton absorbs the liquid, forcing containers to expand; more serious, as water pours into the holds it not only adds weight but the free surface effect of it sloshing around in the bottom of the ship can cause considerable instability. Fires that start in deck containers are easier to get at and using water to fight them less problematic; but these advantages are outweighed by the flame-feeding oxygen buffeting the ship and the uselessness of the carbon dioxide cylinders.

■ ■ ■

By midday the thermometer on the port wing reads 100 degrees Fahrenheit, but I go out in the noonday sun nonetheless, to find Federico and the bosun, Ernesto Robis, descending the steps from the galley on F deck. Each is holding one end of a spit on which is skewered a suckling pig, its shaved hide as white as their boiler suits; its eyes are closed, as if it were only napping while being helped to a deck chair so it can bask away its pallor while stewards bring drinks. "Follow us," says Federico, as the threesome heads toward the shade of the poop deck, in the middle of which is an oil drum that has been cut in half longitudinally, the halves overlapped to make a barbecue pit about five feet long that stands on four metal legs.

Federico and Ernesto prop the spit and its dozing passenger over the pit on vertical bars at either end, to one of which is attached a bicycle wheel; below the wheel, affixed to one of the legs, is an electric drill, its bit replaced by a pulley, around which is a rubber belt that is also looped about the bicycle wheel, like an automobile fan belt. Federico now pulls the drill's long cord across the poop and plugs it into a socket; with Rube Goldberg efficiency, the power (A) spins the drill (B), which activates the belt (C), which turns the wheel (D), which revolves the spit (E) and the pig (F) as its tongue (G) lolls. As we watch the wood fire heat up, Federico explains that roast suckling pig is the most popular meat dish in the Philippines and that it is a shipboard tradition for Filipino crews to barbecue a *lechón* once on every voyage.

At 1800 the pig, now crisp and brown, arrives by platter at the terrace of B deck, its open mouth seeming to express astonishment that those of us gathered, drinks in hand, would countenance its fate, much less the hacking about to come. The red sun setting on our port and full moon rising over the starboard bow provide distraction from the porker's reproach, as does the William Tell Overture, which pours over the Red Sea at top volume from Frank McAlees's stereo system, which he has brought out from his quarters. I tell Elizabeth about my radio introduction to Rossini in the forties thanks to *The Lone Ranger,* thinking this would be a scrap of American culture unknown to her. "Hi-yo, Silver," she shouts, adding, "We're showing our age." She is wearing a white T-shirt and dark slacks against the evening heat, her informality shared by the men, who have hung up their dress whites in favor of shorts and polo shirts or, in the case of Frank, Alex Gill, and Chris Marlow, no shirts at all. Beer and wine have begun to flow, and all hands are looking seriously relaxed as Rossini gives way to "Tea for Two" and then "Hatikvah," which seems loud enough to reach the Saudi Arabian coast, where the citizenry might be pardoned for thinking we are the Israeli navy.

Elizabeth winces at the sound level, agrees that it is impossible to converse, and asks that the decibels be reduced, a request not denied the captain's wife. Artemio has now appeared to oversee the dismantling of the *lechón,* which is undertaken by the second cook, Prudencio Modelo, whose imprudent foot-long blade soon creates a mound of pink shreds and chunks. For Shakeel, who doesn't eat pork out of religious conviction, or those who shrink from the prospect after witnessing the dissection, there are hamburgers, hot dogs, chicken drumsticks, beef kebabs, and it being Sunday, steaks, all ready to be thrown on the gas grill in the corner. There is also a tableful of coleslaw, salad, rice, and chicken chow mein. Artemio knows how to throw a barbecue, and there is much enthusiastic sampling, including of the *lechón,* which is tender and succulent and calls for two helpings.

The moon has risen bright against a dark blue sky when Steve joins me at the rail and recalls how his wife loved to go up to the quiet of the fo'c'sle and contemplate the night, how she could gaze at the bow wake for an hour watching the patterns swirl by. Like all veteran merchant seamen, he is used to being away from home and family for months at a time, but his wistfulness is obvious as he looks out over the water. Moments later Shakeel buttonholes me wanting to know if I'm taking the echinacea he gave me yesterday to counter my sinus woes. When I tell him that I'm suspicious of such holistic remedies, he gently lectures me against such shortsightedness and begins an explanation of the nostrum's miraculous curative properties, but his words are lost in a cascade of sound. Someone (Simon, Alex, the cadet?) has slipped a rock CD into Frank's player and maxed the volume. I yell a promise to take more echinacea before going to bed, and do after retreating to my cabin at about 2000 and choosing Mary Cleere Haran to lull me to sleep with "This Funny World" and fifteen other songs by Rodgers and Hart.

Diane responds to this and most other popular music with what W. S. Gilbert so deftly called modified rapture. She finds the tunes and lyrics kitschy and sentimental, and a lot of them are; but, as Lorenz Hart put it, "I'm a sentimental sap, that's all," and the words and music, which Haran honors with crystalline phrasing and a moving simplicity, only make me wish that I were watching Diane's eyes roll as I try yet again to convince her that Rodgers, Gershwin, Berlin, Porter, Kern, Arlen, and Sondheim have written art songs worthy of Schumann and Brahms. And isn't "Matelot," Noël Coward's song about a mother's longing for her absent sailor son, with its wistful melody and Schubertian shifts from major to minor and back, among the most moving ballads ever composed? I am still arguing my case when the clock again freezes at 0200, to put us in sync with the time at Suez.

By early Tuesday morning we have reached the Sinai Peninsula, where the minnow-shaped Red Sea forks into its smaller siblings, the Gulfs of Aqaba and Suez. A fiery ball rises on our starboard stern, and the crows stretch their wings with a few anxious circles above the boxes as we enter the Strait of Gubal and start the 200-mile run to the canal. Matt is finishing his 0400 to 0800 watch, guiding us at reduced speed and with extra caution along a two-way shipping lane less than a mile wide, with islands and hidden reefs close on either side that have brought vessels to grief for centuries, among them one of the *Colombo Bay*'s prouder antecedents, the Peninsular & Oriental passenger ship *Carnatic*.

The canal was three months from opening in 1869 when the seven-year-old, 1,776-ton vessel, powered by both steam and spanking square-rigged sails, left Suez on September 12 with thirty-four passengers—sahibs and memsahibs pampered by a crew of 176 on a floating extension of the British Raj bound for Bombay with a cargo of cotton bales, copper sheeting, Royal Mail, and 40,000 pounds in specie for the Indian mint. In the middle of the first night, the ship maneuvered to avoid Shadwan Island, only to grind onto Sha'ab Abu Nuhas, a reef less than a half mile off the *Colombo Bay*'s port as we pass through the strait. At sunup some passengers pleaded with the captain, one Philip Buton Jones, to let them make for the island by lifeboat; he refused, convinced that the reef would not further damage the iron-hulled vessel, that the pumps could handle what water was coming in, and that the *Sumatra,* a P&O sister ship inbound for Suez, would come to the rescue later in the day. She did not, and by evening more passengers were asking to enter the lifeboats, while others, lulled by the captain's confidence in a happy outcome, donned their formal clothes and enjoyed a sumptuous dinner.

In the middle of the night, water flooded over the boiler, leaving the *Carnatic* without light or motive power. By morning there was still no sign of the *Sumatra,* and Captain Jones agreed to put women and children in the boats. The operation had just begun when the ship suddenly broke in two, the aft section sinking in a matter of minutes, drowning five passengers and twenty-six crew members. As the fore section tipped over on its port side and began to slide off the reef, the rest of the panic-stricken people tumbled into the water. Almost all of them struggled into the seven lifeboats and made it safely to Shadwan Island, where within hours the *Sumatra* did come to their aid.

The *Carnatic* catastrophe is now recreation, just one of many sunken wrecks in the strait and elsewhere at the northern end of the Red Sea that, along with the profusion of opulent reefs, daily attract scores of snorkelers and scuba divers, many of them from Ras Mohamed and Sharm al-Sheikh, the popular Egyptian resorts at the tip of the Sinai Peninsula. Matt hands me the binoculars, which reveal that already at 0730 a half dozen boats are hovering over the sunken playgrounds on both our port and our starboard. The benign setting is a welcome antidote to the Middle East of hatred and war that daily pours from the BBC World Service, and I imagine delegations of Arabs and Jews in diving gear making permanent peace for their peoples, inspired by a few days' swimming around the multicolored, filigreed coral with blue-spotted grouper, bristly puffers, Spanish dancers, and the hundreds of other exotic fish in the amniotic warmth of these historic waters. The needles of reality daily prick such wishful fantasies, including in these waters, where in just a few weeks Israeli commandos will raid a rusty, blue freighter, the *Karine A;* onboard they will find a cargo of mattresses, sunglasses, and sandals, and fifty tons of rockets, mines, antitank missiles, and other munitions being smuggled to the Palestinians.

Oil rigs poke out of the depths as we push north. One looks like something Industrial Light & Magic might have conjured up for George Lucas, a menacing creature rising on four spindly legs from an evil subterranean world about to pounce on the innocent sailboat in its shadow. It is a jack-up rig, Matt explains, a platform whose legs can be hoisted, allowing it to float to another position, where the stilts are again pushed into the gulf's bottom and test drilling begins anew. We are passing through the Ashrafi, Hilal, and East Zeit oil fields, the burn-off turning several of the rigs into fiery inverted exclamation points. On the port shore stand some twenty white storage tanks, behind which rise the barren, serrated mountains of the Egyptian mainland, the bright sun searing their ocher flanks. I go out on the port wing for a better look with the glasses and am almost knocked off my feet by the head wind funneling down the gulf from the canal. Such conditions are typical for this stretch; still, I am surprised to spot a wind farm on the sandy port shore, some three dozen windmills spinning in smart unison. Energy upstarts warning the world's greatest oil region that its polluting days may be numbered?

CHAPTER EIGHT

"Come in, *Colombo Bay*," a radio voice squawks. "Ignore it," says Shakeel, who has just arrived on the bridge at noon to relieve Simon. "Come in, *Colombo Bay*, do you read me?" The two mates smile and continue to disregard the insistent pleas, which offer no official identification and likely come from an Egyptian vendor trying to drum up business, probably by selling us some stores. At 1230, Suez harbor control makes contact, and Peter, who has come to the bridge finishing his sandwich lunch, responds that our ETA is 1400 and our draft is forty feet. We are heading for the collection anchorage on the east side of the Bay of Suez, where ships gather to form the convoys that the Suez Canal Authority requires for passage in either direction. The chart shows twenty-nine spots in this marine parking lot, and Peter is hoping for one on the outside so we can make a quick getaway when entering the canal. We reach the bay right on schedule, with eleven hours to spare before the 0100 deadline that ships must meet to be included in the next morning's convoy, the only northbound transit of the day. Just a half dozen large vessels have arrived at the anchorage so far; nonetheless, harbor control directs us to a slot in the middle. Qué será, será.

I go up to the fo'c'sle to watch the anchor *drop*, the proper word, a somewhat testy Conrad advises. "Your journalist," he writes, ". . . almost invariably 'casts' his anchor. Now, an anchor is never cast, and to take a liberty with technical language is a crime against the clearness, precision, and beauty of perfected speech." He says *cast* is an "odious word" used by "benighted landsmen" who think an anchor is something thrown overboard, when in fact it is already overboard hanging against the hull and is simply allowed to fall. Thus, "the order is not 'Heave over!' as the paragraphists seem to imagine, but 'Let go!'" When will we be *letting go,* I ask Simon and the cadet, who have come to the fo'c'sle to oversee the drop but for the moment are preoccupied by the *Mahmood,* a small boat that has just chugged across the harbor and is now idling below our rail. A canopy covers the stern deck, where four men are eating lunch at a makeshift table. Do we have any rope or wire for sale? one of them shouts. Simon shakes his head and waves them away, and to his surprise, they shrug, return to their meal, and motor off. "Usually they're more persistent," he says of these approaches, a regular feature of the anchorage. At twenty-one, he already has passed through the canal more than a dozen times.

We are dropping just the starboard anchor, all that is needed to keep us from floating free in the calm waters of the bay. Ernesto, the bosun and top-ranking member of the crew, has loosed the gear of the starboard windlass and now awaits the order to release the brake, which comes at 1420 by walkie-talkie from Peter on the bridge. An explosion of clanks follows as, pulled by the anchor's twelve and a half tons, the chain's endomorphic links rattle over the windlass and down through the hawsepipe in the deck, throwing off a sirocco of rust that blankets the fo'c'sle as mud stirred up by the plunging iron swirls about the bow like an animated finger painting. The cadet now raises the symbol of a ship riding at anchor, a round wicker basket that when it reaches the top of the foremast looks like a homemade version of the ball whose descent in Times Square marks the new year.

The fo'c'sle is once again the most tranquil place on the ship, and we are about to take our reluctant leave when Peter reminds Simon via walkie-talkie to screw the covers on the hawsepipes. Last year at this anchorage, Peter didn't bother with the covers, and the next morning there were footprints in the dew on deck, signaling that thieves had shinnied up the anchor chain in the night and squeezed through the hawsepipes; they broke into a container and made off with a boatful of woolen garments.

In the morning the crows are gone, apparently having decided after nine days and almost 4,000 miles aboard the *Colombo Bay,* that the town of Suez and environs would provide them a more varied diet than bread crumbs. We weigh anchor and begin moving toward the canal as another hot, cloudless day dawns, a full moon casting a wan eye on the sunrise. We are number nine in the convoy; number ten, now maneuvering in behind us, is the *Al Salamah,* a sleek white yacht with four decks raking up to the bridge. The speculation at breakfast is that she belongs to a Saudi prince bound for sybaritic indulgences in the Mediterranean. Subsequent investigation, however, reveals that her owner is the aged King Fahd himself, and that the 482-foot vessel, built by a German shipyard in the late nineties at a cost of $250 million, is the world's largest "megayacht." Though she is less than half as long as the *Colombo Bay* and weighs a fifth as much, she is manned by sixty more seamen, none of whom seem to be stirring as I sweep her decks with the binoculars.

The harbor pilot, who arrived on the *Colombo Bay*'s bridge just after we left the anchorage, explains that *Al Salamah* means "peace" and assures me that the vast majority of Muslims want peace and hate terrorism. He offers his condolences for the 9/11 attacks, observing that everyone suffers from fanatics, including the Egyptians, whose peace-making president Anwar el-Sadat fell to the bullets of extremist Muslim soldiers in 1981. His point made, he returns to his navigational duties and is soon gone, replaced by the first of three canal pilots as, at 0725, we enter the 132-year-old waterway, which stretches some 100 miles to Port Said on the Mediterranean and under normal conditions like today's takes about fourteen hours to transit. "When the girls were small," Peter says, "we had contests to see who could spot the most camels. Chocolate was the prize."

The canal has been Egypt's prize since 1956, when the country's president, Gamal Abdel Nasser, nationalized it. Up to then it had been run by a private company with an international board of directors and was open to all shipping, under the 1888 Convention of Constantinople, though after the 1949 armistice between Israel and its Arab opponents, Egypt had denied use of the canal to Israel and any country trading with the new nation. Infuriated by Nasser's canal policies and by continuing raids by Arab terrorists, Israel invaded the Gaza Strip and the Sinai Peninsula, then Britain and France attacked Egypt after demanding without success that the country evacuate the canal zone. Nasser retaliated by sinking some forty vessels in the canal, closing it for several months until, in 1957, under international pressure, the three invaders withdrew and a UN peacekeeping force stood guard over the reopened waterway.

Egypt again shut down the canal after the 1967 Arab-Israeli war, and this time it stayed closed for eight years, becoming a fortified ditch in a war of attrition between the belligerents. Sadat, who had succeeded Nasser after he died of a heart attack in 1970, saw reopening of the canal as central to any détente with Israel, and—after Egyptian forces aided by the United States, British, French, and Soviet navies cleared the zone of mines, bombshells, and the other military detritus that had accumulated during the standoff—traffic resumed, on June 5, 1975; still, the canal was not opened to all nations, including Israel, until 1979, when Sadat signed a peace treaty with the Jewish state.

By then Egyptian leaders had recognized that shutting down the canal was like pulling a sustaining intravenous drip from their own arms. The government doubled the transit tolls when the canal reopened, in part to make up for revenue lost because the large tankers that had been constructed during the shutdown to carry greater volume around the Cape were too big to pass through the canal. Egypt began harnessing the waterway's economic potential with an ambitious modernization program, installing radar stations and other electronic navigation systems, and ultimately widening the canal to a maximum of 1,200 feet and dredging it to 68 feet, permitting passage of ships with drafts of up to 58 feet. When the canal opened it was 26 feet deep, 72 feet wide at the bottom, and 300 feet wide at the surface; in 1870, its first full year of operation, 468 ships passed through carrying 437,000 tons of cargo. By 1967, more than 20,000 ships were moving through, loaded with a total of 267 million tons. By 2000 the number of ships transiting had decreased to 14,000, but their much larger average size enabled them to carry cargo totaling 374 million tons, bringing Egypt some $2 billion annually.

The government-run Suez Canal Authority levies tolls based on a ship's net tonnage, the gross tonnage minus deductions for the space occupied by the accommodations, machinery, navigation equipment, and bunkers but not by cargo and passengers. The charge is highest for the first 5,000 tons, then decreases as the tonnage rises. Add-ons are plentiful, including pilot and port fees, pay for an electrician to operate a searchlight on the bow at night, surcharges for deck cargo such as boats, and penalties for showing up late for convoy formation. I was disinclined ever again to complain about the $6 toll on the George Washington Bridge after Jeremy reported that the cost of getting the *Colombo Bay*'s 45,429 net tons through the canal was roughly $250,000 per transit, not including today's $25,000 war and terrorism insurance surcharge.

We are proceeding down the center of the canal, the banks on either side an easy swim through the barely ruffled water. It is tantalizing to see land this close after more than a week at sea since Colombo, and I'd welcome an hour's stroll among the houses, gardens, and palm trees on the west bank, perhaps with a quick stop for some fresh mango juice and *foul medames,* the stewed fava beans in olive oil, lemon, and garlic that the Egyptians make so well, or even a short, nutritionless walk along the arid east bank, from which the baking desert of the Sinai Peninsula stretches to the horizon. But as always, moving the boxes comes first, and there will be no chance for anyone aboard to stretch his or her land legs until we get to Malta in two days.

At regular intervals we pass signal stations on the west bank, posts where the canal authority monitors our speed and the distance behind the vessel in front, which happens to be another, larger P&O Nedlloyd container ship, the *Rotterdam*. Regulations require that we stay one to two miles apart and travel at between seven and eight knots; pilots can be fined for speeding. A two-lane road hugs each side of the canal, the civilian traffic interspersed with armored personnel carriers and other military vehicles. We are less than an hour into our transit when we pass three lookouts atop a dune on the west bank where armed soldiers stand sentry around mounted machine guns. I wonder aloud if the entire length of the canal is fortified, and the pilot, looking up from the breakfast tray just brought to him from the galley, says no, what we have just passed is an army training camp.

His name is Ashraf Emam, and like the harbor pilot he looks a bit like a hospital orderly in his neat uniform of long pants, untucked open-necked shirt, and shoes—all white. He is in his mid-forties and has done this work for fifteen years, now commuting two hours by car from Cairo, where he lives with his family. He is voluble and friendly, revealing between drags on his cigarette and apropos of nothing that Moses parted the Gulf of Suez and not the Red Sea. "It is not known exactly where, but they were going to Sinai," he says. I do not challenge this revisionism, mostly because I am no biblical scholar but also because parting the waters, wherever it may have taken place, has seemed to me something of a doubtful achievement ever since I saw Charlton Heston do it.

I ask if any naval vessels have come through the canal recently. Yes, says Ashraf, seventeen British and U.S. warships transited south about two weeks ago; they are likely the flotilla that had set Katherine Davies to worrying, in the email she sent her father a week ago, about our safety during this passage. My question opens the gate for a polite but firm lecture about the United States' behavior as the most powerful nation in the world. "I love the American people," Ashraf says, "but your leaders are very bad. They only recognize terror when it is on your shores. Besides, you are responsible for bin Laden because your CIA supported him when he fought with the Afghans against the Soviet Union." Ashraf abruptly abandons this criticism and, echoing the harbor pilot, offers his sympathy for the 9/11 attacks and stresses that the Muslim religion does not condone terrorism. He punctuates this change of tack with a good-natured smile and returns to his breakfast, which he finishes while reading a newspaper, occasionally looking up through the haze from his cigarette and ordering the helmsman to give the *Colombo Bay* a tweak to keep her within the flanking channel buoys.

By 1000 we have reached Little Bitter and Great Bitter Lakes, so named because of their extra salinity; on the chart, their contiguous bulges make the canal look like a python that has swallowed but not yet digested a rabbit. Floating moorings on the west side of the lakes accommodate thirty-six vessels, and some two dozen are now tied up, part of a southbound convoy, the first of two that leave Port Said each day, one at 0100, the other at 0700. Despite considerable widening over the decades, the canal is too narrow to handle two-way traffic in ships the size of the *Colombo Bay,* which is by no means the beamiest of the vessels that regularly make the transit. Northbound convoys leave Suez only once a day; once the last of our twenty or so ships passes beyond the lakes, the southbound convoy will leave its lay-by and continue toward the Gulf of Suez and the Red Sea. On our port as we pass between the two lakes is El Kabrit, site of an airfield used by the RAF in the World War II battles of El Alamein and by MiGs when Egypt was a Soviet client in the 1960s; now, on a spit of land jutting toward us, a collection of grand whitewashed houses stand amid an oasis of lush greenery, a compound of second homes to which Cairo's elite repairs on weekends. At midday we arrive at the halfway point, Ismailia, on Lake Timsah, where a beach, like a taunting tongue, sticks its carefree bathers almost in our path. They suggest—as does the local museum devoted to the papers of Ferdinand de Lesseps, the French diplomat who oversaw the decade-long construction of the canal—that a pleasant and instructive twenty-four hours could be spent here by somehow going over the rail and catching another New York–bound container ship tomorrow.

Across the lake from Ismailia is a memorial to the Egyptian soldiers who died battling Israel in the 1973 war, a 216-foot-high bayonet whose silvery white blade glistens in the noon sun. Soon another memorial appears on the east bank, a statue of an Egyptian soldier holding the country's flag, in front of which stand two tanks, their guns pointing toward the canal. Ashraf left us at Ismailia, replaced by two pilots who will take us to Port Said. I ask one about the memorial, and he says, tersely, that it signifies Egypt's victory in the 1973 war, adding that the soldier was created from bomb scraps and that the armored sentinels are captured Israeli tanks. "You mean American tanks," his partner says, looking me square in the eye.

An awkward silence follows, one that lasts about an hour, until the pilots point with pride at the Mubarak-Peace Bridge, a four-lane suspension span that arches the canal at 230 feet, providing sufficient air draft for all vessels now using the waterway. Constructed over the past three years with the help of Japanese engineers and funding, it will be inaugurated within the week by Hosni Mubarak, the Egyptian president, opening a crossing that the government hopes over the next fifteen years will encourage more than three million people to move from the narrow Nile valley, where most of the nation's 67 million citizens live, to settle in and develop the Sinai Peninsula, now home to only 340,000 inhabitants. Whether or not this migration happens, the bridge will be a great improvement over the small ferries that periodically dart between the convoy's ships, like shoppers dashing across Fifth Avenue during breaks in the St. Patrick's Day Parade. They carry passengers and at most a half dozen vehicles, the lucky few who had made it to the front of a line that at some crossings totaled more than a hundred cars, vans, oil trucks, semis, and pickups which must wait their turn for two or three hours in the desert heat.

There is another bypass at El-Ballah, a six-mile-long channel that curves off and back into the canal like a highway rest area. More than a dozen vessels in the day's second southbound convoy are tied up here, most of them container ships—no surprise, since half the vessels transiting the canal each year are box boats. There must be at least 30,000 TEUs on the pausing ships, which together with the 4,000 we are carrying and the 6,500 just ahead on the *Rotterdam* offer a vivid snapshot of globalization in motion. On the east bank a packed, ramshackle bus chuffs north, its roof piled high with dusty baggage and freight, its passengers gazing through the open windows. A few may see the profusion of containers, and the thousands more that pass through their homeland daily, the way the World Bank, International Monetary Fund, and G8 powers would like them to, as a free-trade boon that improves their lives because of the increasing stream of hard currency the transits bring to Egypt; more doubtless sympathize with the antiglobalization protesters, who less than three months ago took to the streets at the G8 summit in Genoa and view the ceaseless procession of goods the way the world's poor do when watching the West's cushy consumer life flicker by out of reach on television.

My liberal reflexes, honed over fifty years, grab at the latter view, make me want to shout to the antis on the bus that, yes, I know that many of them will never benefit from the good life streaming daily through the canal, that thousands of the items packed in the containers emerged from Dickensian conditions in the factories of developing nations, that the free-trade fundamentalism promulgated by the United States and most other industrialized nations is sometimes nothing more than a cover for international corporate greed. But the many conversations I've had with the Filipinos aboard the *Colombo Bay* give me pause. They are, to a man, more than grateful to be earning relatively good pay, from jobs they landed largely because of globalization. The same applies to those "wharfies" in Sri Lanka lucky enough to win work at P&O Nedlloyd's new container terminal, where the pay and conditions will be, if not at ILWU levels, several notches above those across the basin at the government port.

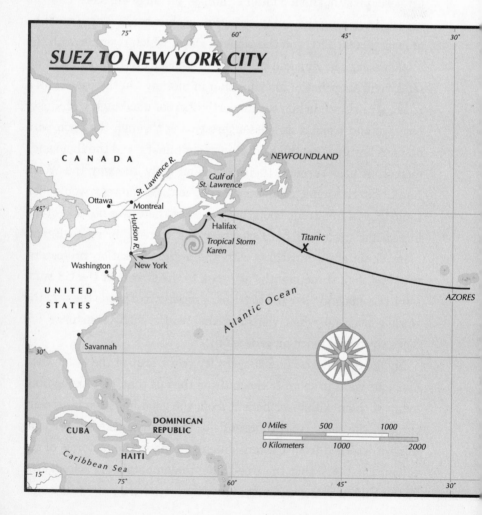

Just such incremental gains have helped lift more than 300 million people in East Asia out of poverty since the mid-seventies and turned China into the economic powerhouse it has become. Not incidentally, the country is now a more open society—as is India, which has developed a similar market thrust; together the two nations represent one-third of the world's population, people who slowly have become more democratic in part because of the pluralism that free trade encourages. None of this excuses the stinginess of the U.S. government, whose foreign aid as a percentage of GNP at

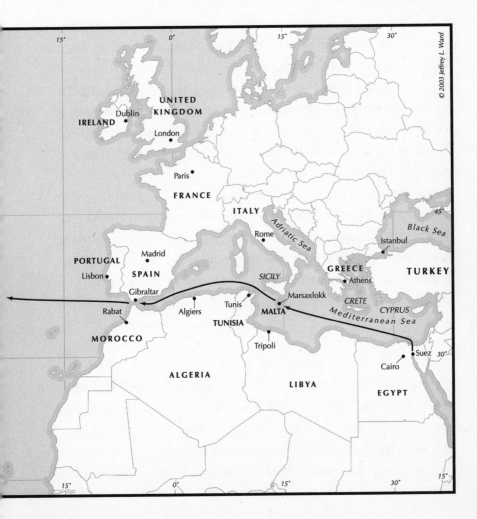

the end of the twentieth century trailed that of the Netherlands, Japan, France, Germany, and Britain; or its hypocritical grants of tariffs for big steel and subsidies for farmers at home instead of letting their prices rise or fall in the free market; or its willingness to look away from the sweatshops in the developing world while endorsing the "fiscal discipline" that has forced these countries to dismantle social programs so investors can be guaranteed high interest rates. Globalization, whatever its benefits for some, remains a cruel deception for most of the world's poor but its advance seems as uninterruptible as the flow of boxes through the canal.

We arrive at Port Said just before dinner, the *Colombo Bay* now lighter by several cartons of Marlboros. Their distribution began with the "quarantine" official who came aboard while we were still anchored in the Bay of Suez to inquire if everyone was vaccinated for yellow fever and if anyone was sick; he seemed quite prepared to let us proceed even were bubonic plague racing through the ship. The Suez harbor pilot was the next recipient, then Ashraf. Peter predicted that he would ask for two cartons, and he did, on the grounds that he had done the work of two canal pilots, the normal complement required by the canal authority's featherbedding regulations. Ashraf's two successors left us at Port Said with a carton apiece, as did a canal inspector and the electrician who operates the bow searchlight, after explaining that he was with us for the entire thirteen-hour daylight run in case of emergency—perhaps a surprise solar eclipse.

■ ■ ■

After dinner I go up to the bridge and out on the starboard wing. Port Said twinkles aft as diaphanous clouds slide past the rising full moon, a Halloween sky that is less spooky than a warm welcome to the West. We are in the Mediterranean, where through three and a half millennia beginning in 2500 BC the Egyptians, Greeks, Romans, and Phoenicians developed the art of navigation. This Latin Lake, Conrad writes, makes a tender appeal to the seaman: "It has sheltered the infancy of his craft. He looks upon it as a man may look at a vast nursery in an old, old mansion where innumerable generations of his own people have learned to walk." These waters, stretching west more than 2,000 miles from the canal to the Strait of Gibraltar, were well suited for maritime toddlers; they are tideless, the pinhole at the strait allowing only enough ebb and flow to raise and lower the inland sea's 1.1 million square miles of water an inch or so.

By the Renaissance, Spain and Portugal had come to dominate this sea, but like other European maritime powers they eventually pointed their ships across the Atlantic to the riches in the Americas. The commerce that had thrived for centuries in the Mediterranean diminished, as did the number of naval vessels that had protected it. Pirates sailed into the vacuum, for generations turning the sea into their private hunting preserve, plundering merchant vessels and coastal communities at will, as Odysseus had done after sailing from Troy through the Mediterranean's wine-dark eddy, the Aegean, to Ismarus, where he "sacked the city, killed the men," and dragged away wives and booty. The most notorious Mediterranean marauders were the Barbary pirates, ferocious and skilled Berbers who put out from the north coast of Africa in oared galleys until the seventeenth century, then under sail. The Catholic forces of Spain had driven many of these Moors into exile, and they found their revenge by capturing one Spanish ship after another, among them the *Sol* in 1575. Miguel de Cervantes was on this galley, returning to Spain from the eastern Mediterranean, where his left hand had been permanently maimed in the naval battle against the Turks at Lepanto. He was enslaved in Algiers for five years, sometimes in manacles and chains, and because he tried to escape four times, often under threat of torture and death. When he was twenty-eight, Cervantes's family finally was able to ransom him for about 300 ducats, a significant sum to them, a small price to ensure that *Don Quijote* would come to us.

Slaves like Cervantes were the Barbary corsairs' most prized commodity; by one report, in the first half of the seventeenth century they sold more than 40,000 Christian captives in the markets of Tunis and Algiers alone. Algiers remained a pirate stronghold into the nineteenth century, until by 1830 British and French colonial power had brought the corsairs to heel. But it was only after the opening of the Suez Canal in 1869 that the nursery again began teeming with merchant ships, which now steam through the Mediterranean in an unbroken procession of east-west trade.

All the blood spilled into the Mediterranean by pirates and warring states over the millennia, Conrad writes, "has not stained with a single trail of purple the deep azure of its classic waters." Gazing out from the sun-drenched fo'c'sle in the morning, I find momentary comfort in that image; but back on the bridge the BBC relentlessly confirms his lament on the same page of *The Mirror of the Sea* that "the nations of the earth are mostly swayed by fear—fear of the sort that a little cheap oratory turns easily to rage, hate, and violence." Car bombs have exploded in Jerusalem and Kashmir; the Israeli military may be out to kill Yasir Arafat; Pakistan's President Musharraf has given up trying to persuade the Taliban to surrender bin Laden and now regards a confrontation as inevitable; the bombing of Afghanistan by the United States and a subsequent invasion seem more likely than ever; the Red Cross there and in Pakistan faces the impossible task of feeding thousands of refugees; a hundred people have been killed in the run-up to the Bangladesh election this week; a reported plane hijacking in India turns out to be a false alarm, but Swissair may go bankrupt and a Russian plane has exploded en route from Tel Aviv.

One or two items of benign news do manage to elbow in—Barry Bonds has tied Mark McGwire's record of seventy home runs—and even some comic relief. The Swedish government has decreed that male circumcisions must be performed with an anesthetic and with a nurse present, a ruling that apparently has outraged many in the Stockholm Jewish community. There is much talk of appealing the new law to the European Court of Human Rights, meanwhile taking circumcisions underground so that mohelim may continue to wield their blades freely on eight-day-old boys properly narcotized with a little wine.

The next day—October 5—we are homing in on Malta, where Peter will turn over the *Colombo Bay* to a new master and fly home with Elizabeth to Yorkshire. A new first mate also will come aboard, relieving Matt Mullins, who absent the Cape run will now get home to Hampshire in time for his wife's delivery. Their imminent departure—and that of Alex Gill, who is leaving both the ship and the merchant service—feels like a violation, a sudden breakup of what for three weeks has seemed to be an indivisible family. But as the faces often show during the sometimes strained conversation and comradery in the lounge and at dinner, the togetherness is deceptive; shipboard relationships are usually tentative, and even when they are not are inevitably transient.

Chris Windsor-Price is particularly glum about no longer being able to listen to CDs and watch movies in the evenings with his pal Alex. As a cadet he generally works eight to five at his training tasks and would be happy to hang out after dinner with Simon, the only other person aboard his age; but as third mate Simon stands watch from eight to midnight. The older officers, most of them at least twice Chris's age, fade to duty assignments or to their cabins soon after dinner. "What I do is not physically challenging for someone my age, and I don't get very tired; if I go to bed early I just roll around," he told me, speaking wistfully of the *Texas,* on which he had sailed several months before. "She was like a home away from home, with leather sofas and armchairs, bathtubs, double beds, teak decking, canopies, a big swimming pool"—and more hands than on the *Colombo Bay,* so that the bar was full every night with a conviviality that made the weeks at sea pass more quickly. "By comparison, this ship is like a floating prison," he said, echoing Samuel Johnson, who remarked within his friend Boswell's earshot that being on a ship "is being in a jail, with the chance of being drowned." The good doctor notwithstanding, the cadet's judgment struck me as a bit harsh, though perhaps I would think otherwise if I, too, were doing an eighteen-week stretch. After only ten days at sea since Sri Lanka, I am more than ready for a few hours in port this evening.

■ ■ ■

The Maltese Islands cover only 122 square miles, but their location just east of the Strait of Sicily, where less than 100 miles separates the southernmost reach of Europe from the north coast of Africa, has made them a strategic prize ever since the Phoenicians brought their trading ships to the archipelago's three small islands—Malta, Comino, and Gozo. Over the centuries the islands fell to the Carthaginians, the Romans, Constantinople, the Normans, Aragon, Arabs, and various feudal lords. In 1530 the Knights of St. John, a religious and military order of the Roman Catholic Church, took over, establishing a navy and ancillary maritime enterprises that pushed trading vessels into all corners of the Mediterranean; this power flowed in part from the order's defeat, in 1565, of 30,000 soldiers of Süleyman the Magnificent's Ottoman Empire, a victory led by the knights' grand master, Jean de La Valette, after whom Malta's capital is named. Napoleon grabbed the islands in 1798 but soon lost them to the British, who like all their predecessors coveted Valletta's deepwater harbor for its commanding position as a naval and merchant shipping base. In 1814 the Treaty of Paris gave Malta to the Crown, allowing Britain's powerful navy to control the inland sea through the decades of empire. Malta became independent in 1964 and a republic within the British Commonwealth in 1974, and it is a key transshipment hub for containers bound to and from Europe. This commerce no longer passes through the much-fought-over harbor at Valletta, which now hosts mostly the cruise ships that help feed the island's flourishing tourist industry, but through Marsaxlokk, the port ten miles to the south, which the *Colombo Bay* enters at 1600 as the cadet runs up Malta's red and white colors.

A small tanker, the *Meriom Hope,* rides in the middle of the harbor, hooked up to a pipeline rising from the water that is siphoning off her liquid cargo. Only a few yards away, buoys and netting create four adjacent square ponds, a fish farm full of pampered darts and wriggles. Beyond these strange bedfellows bob the harbor's trademark fishing boats, wooden vessels called *luzzu,* whose sides of yellow, blue, and red stripes shimmer as they catch the setting sun's reflections off the water. On the docks the reds, browns, silvers, oranges, greens, and blues of several thousand containers, and the blue-and-white frames and black-and-yellow neck scarves of the dinosaurs become a Hopper in the late afternoon Mediterranean light. In the distance the four-century-old Fort St. Lucian, built by the Knights of St. John to fend off the forever-hectoring Turks, broods over this soothing scene, a gray stone warning not to be lulled by all the cheerful colors. Our pilot is smoking furiously and looks anxious as two tugs move us hard to port and we berth bow to bow with our mirror image, the *Singapore Bay.* As we descend in the elevator, I ask if he's finished for the day. Yes, he says, wiping his brow like Pavarotti with a handkerchief the size of a small pillowcase and damning a ship he had brought in earlier. "No elevators," he says. "I had to walk up 132 steps to the bridge. By the time you get there you have no horsepower left, only donkey power."

At about 1800, Shakeel and I catch a ride into Valletta, where he provides a forty-five-minute walking tour through the town's imposing Baroque architecture, ending at the Barracca Gardens overlooking the Grand Harbor, where the evening shadows slowly envelop two cruise ships. We go for good pepper steaks at the restaurant of a hotel where he and Susan have stayed and then return to

Marsaxlokk by taxi in time to join Peter and Elizabeth at Reno's, a family-run fish restaurant near the container terminal where they, along with Steve Kingdon, are digging into plates of fresh swordfish and prawns. A door near the table leads into a dark and narrow hallway where a pay phone hangs on the wall, the graffiti around it attesting to the boatloads of sailors who have stood in this gloomy space so they could, after weeks incommunicado, at last actually speak to someone who loves them, or did when they shipped out.

Diane's voice is a tonic, and we talk for half an hour, repeating stories we've already imparted in our email exchanges, reminding each other that it's only eleven days now, insisting we are just "fine," wringing words over the post–9/11 world, declaring our love and how much we miss one another, then, after a few more bytes of small talk, making the declarations again, and again. Young men periodically descend the steep stairs that lead from the hallway and stand next to me. What's up there? Ladies? Each time I think they want to use the phone; each time they just want me to move closer to the wall so they can squeeze by. My words get ever more stilted as the pressure mounts to hang up so Shakeel can call Susan and I can say good-bye to Peter and Elizabeth. Our exchanges are beginning to sound like a telegram. How's Amanda? STOP. Fine. STOP. I'll send you another email soon. STOP. I love you. STOP. Good-bye. END.

Back at the table, Peter is settling the bill and about to go to the hotel where he and Elizabeth will spend the night before flying home tomorrow. I will miss this skipper, who despite his long hours, his bitterness over the financial corner cutting that prevails in the merchant service, and his nostalgia for the good old days always seemed to be in a good mood. I thank him for treating me so well and for putting up with all my questions; he waves it away, we promise to keep in touch, and then, as abruptly as the phone call's end, they are gone, and Steve, Shakeel, and I are strolling underneath the dinosaurs back to the *Colombo Bay*.

CHAPTER NINE

We slip out of Marsaxlokk Harbor at 0600 on a course that will take us along the coasts of Tunis, Algeria, and Morocco to the Strait of Gibraltar. Our new master is Christian Urwin, who is surprised to find that he is blessed with a supernumerary from New York. "Had I known I would have picked up some Yank newspapers at the airport," he says, displaying a cordiality and thoughtfulness that, like Peter's, will turn out to be typical. He, too, is a passionate sports fan, and brings word that Bonds broke McGwire's record yesterday with home runs seventy-one and seventy-two. He is in his late forties, his crew cut whitening at the temples and beginning to recede at the forehead; he is trim and looks fit, an impression subverted each time he lights up a cigarette, which is often.

Christian grew up mainly in Kent, in a family he says is "best described as economic migrants from the north." The sea seemed the best option after he graduated from high school in the early seventies, because, "it gave me full support instead of the pocket money that other apprentice jobs offered." He has now served on container ships for three decades, and though he voices the same grievances that Peter did about how seafaring has changed from a noble calling with tradition and plenty of time in port to a cost-conscious profession pushing undermanned ships around the globe, he seems more resigned, perhaps because he is a decade younger than his predecessor. Like most officers, he enjoys the long breaks between voyages and has recently returned from a vacation with his wife, Jean, and their two teenage daughters to the West Coast, with a side trip to Las Vegas. "I couldn't believe the traffic in Southern California," he says, shaking his head as if he were still trapped on the Santa Monica Freeway.

In the afternoon Shakeel says as we listen to the BBC that Susan told him when they spoke last night the Home Office was recommending no British nationals travel to Pakistan, so he has canceled the trip he had planned to see his ailing mother when he came off the ship on November 2. The reason for the warning becomes clear the next day as U.S. and British warplanes begin bombing Afghanistan. But the *Colombo Bay*—like Conrad's *Narcissus,* "a fragment detached from the earth, [sailing] lonely and swift like a small planet"—has her own concerns, one of which is the weather. It is getting peppier, the wind now coming right at us at eighteen to twenty knots as we cut through the swells, which are shorter than they will be in the Atlantic because of the shores of Europe, Africa, and the Middle East that hug the nursery. The wind is at twenty-five to thirty-five knots out in the Atlantic, where a deep low has formed just north of our course to Halifax and a high just south of it. The hope is that by the time we reach the Azores in three days the low and high will have moved sufficiently north so that the high will be over our route, producing clear skies and compliant winds. We shall see. We also shall see about Hurricane Iris, now off the southern tip of Jamaica, and Tropical Storm Jerry, east of Barbados. Both are headed west at the moment, but as we East Coast residents are reminded every fall, such swirling dervishes often veer north and ravage Florida, the mid-Atlantic seaboard, and occasionally New England, off which we will make the run from Halifax to New York.

A routing chart of the Atlantic in October is now spread beneath the glass on the bridge table. It shows the weather patterns for the month as they have been reported over more than a hundred years: the average direction of the wind at given points in the ocean, the force of that wind on the Beaufort scale, and the duration of the blows in days. Besides this history a downpour of meteorological information falls on the *Colombo Bay* throughout the day and night, reports from weather ships, naval vessels, other merchant ships, and at the moment from weather stations in Athens (for the Mediterranean), Toulouse (for the eastern Atlantic), and Boston (for the western Atlantic). Every six hours the weather fax machine produces a synoptic chart, a sophisticated descendant of the forecasting technique developed by Admiral Robert Fitzroy, best known as captain of the *Beagle,* the brig on which Charles Darwin sailed in the 1830s, but also the first superintendent of the meteorological department Britain established in 1854. These weather charts, with their undulating isobars signifying lines of equal barometric pressure and their indications of cloud cover, rainfall, temperature, and wind speed over a wide area, normally give ships ample time to adjust course to avoid the worst of a storm. Bad weather may batter a vessel but rarely as a surprise.

After dinner I go to my cabin hoping that our proximity to the coast of Algeria will furnish a TV signal or two. The remote seems unable to find anything but the usual video close-ups of panting partners in flagrante; then, suddenly, there is Osama bin Laden. The picture is grainy and the sound minimal, but he is clearly in his lecture mode, speaking softly and wagging his finger slowly at the camera; even with a fatigue jacket over his white robes he looks less like a terrorist than like a spaced-out guru of some harmless cult. The MSNBC logo appears in a corner of the screen, but no voice-over supplies an English translation of the sermon. Periodically the program cuts away to bombs landing somewhere in Afghanistan, the explosions bursting on the screen like flashbulbs in a darkened theater. I try escaping to the *Pequod,* but Ahab's mad pursuit only underlines the hazards of retribution—by them or by us. "Ah, God!" Melville writes, "what trances of torments does that man endure who is consumed with one unachieved revengeful desire. He sleeps with clenched hands; and awakes with his own bloody nails in his palms." I am drifting toward sleep thinking that Islam is quite a large, if not white, whale when the *Colombo Bay* begins to roll, enough to get me up to cushion the ThinkPad in my shirt drawer. I assume we have hit some heavy weather, but after half an hour the rocking stops, and I fall asleep perplexed.

At breakfast Simon reveals, with some agitation, that during the second half of his 2000-to-2400 watch more and more ships began appearing on the radar. "By 2320 there were twenty-three ahead of us, ranging from three points to starboard to one point to port," he says. "They were all steaming west like we were, but we were overtaking them, and under the rules of the sea we must give them a wide berth." At about 2330 he was planning to pass south of the ships when one of them, and then another, made a U-turn. In something of a panic, Simon called the captain, who arrived on the bridge in about five minutes, by which time a half dozen ships had turned around and were steaming right toward the *Colombo Bay*. "They were generally playing silly buggers" is how Simon described this development. Christian now opted to pass north of the oncoming ships and swung hard to starboard, from 260 to 300 degrees, producing the rocking. "At this stage," Simon continues, "we didn't know what kinds of vessels they were but assumed they were merchant ships. I said to Captain Urwin, 'Do they know something we don't?' It was as if a message had come in to all ships but us, saying, 'Stay out of the area.' So I madly checked all the NAVTEX and other messages to make sure I hadn't missed something. What we also found weird was that there was no radio communication at all."

One of the oncoming ships passed about a half mile off the *Colombo Bay*'s port side, and as she drew closer the binoculars revealed that she was a U.S. warship, a destroyer or cruiser that Christian surmised was on maneuvers with the rest of the Mediterranean fleet. Several vessels cut across the *Colombo Bay*'s bow more than once, as helicopters flew about as if checking out an enemy ship. "There were four or five other merchant vessels getting messed around with as much as we were, so we had to be careful to keep out from under their feet as well," Simon went on, still high on this bump in the night. "Usually we run with only the external accommodation lights on, plus the mooring deck lights and the navigation lights; last night Captain Urwin switched on the lights that run up the side of the ship to indicate we were a large box boat, to tell them, 'We are big.' Around midnight, the warships all appeared to be migrating south, then a few turned north and cut across our bow one more time. There must have been at least thirty ships involved, but by 0100 it was all over." At dinner Christian confirmed Simon's account, adding only that British merchant seamen tend not to be overly fond of "your navy."

■ ■ ■

The encounter with my navy may be as close as we have come to U.S.-flagged vessels since we left Hong Kong almost a month ago, a measure of the virtual disappearance of American merchant shipping in the world. This absence came as something of a surprise, probably because I still harbored images of Rosie the Riveter helping to turn out a Liberty Ship every fourteen days during World War II and of the American merchant seamen caught in the crosshairs of Japanese and German periscopes in the Pacific and Atlantic. The heroic convoys that carried crucial supplies on the Murmansk run to the northern Soviet Union were indelibly imprinted on my young mind by *Action in the North Atlantic*, the 1943 semidocumentary salute to the merchant marine in which Captain Raymond Massey and First Mate Humphrey Bogart successfully get their Liberty

Ship and her cargo through to our desperate Russian allies, en route dodging torpedoes and shooting down a German plane or two.*

By the end of the war, U.S. merchant shipping was as muscular as it had ever been in the twentieth century; in 1948 the country's 5,200 merchant vessels, many of them converted Liberty Ships, represented 36 percent of the world fleet by tonnage and domestic liner companies had an opportunity to dominate world shipping as they had not since the square-rigged clipper ships made the mid-nineteenth century the United States' golden age of seaborne commerce. But in the 1950s, the industry began to sink like a bulker with a slow leak, despite efforts to cut costs by forming liner partnerships and the registering of hundreds of American-owned ships under flags of convenience; by 2000 the number of merchant ships in the world fleet had risen from 30,000 after World War II to almost 90,000, while the number flying the U.S. flag remained below 6,000.

Perhaps nothing symbolizes this decline better than the history of Sea-Land Service, Inc., the company started in 1960 by the container pioneer Malcom McLean, who led the containerization revolution for a decade until he sold the firm to R. J. Reynolds. In 1995 Sea-Land, by then owned by the U.S. company CSX Lines, formed an alliance with the Danish shipping giant Maersk, which four years later swallowed McLean's brainchild whole for $800 million. The deal made the new company—Maersk Sealand, a division of Den-

---

*The exhausted crew is greeted in port by Russians wildly shouting *"Tovarich,"* but once the Cold War set in this scene was often absent when the film appeared on television, as was the fadeout at the end when a voice-over, putatively FDR's, urged an alliance of united nations against the Axis. John Howard Lawson, who wrote the screenplay, and the one for *Sahara,* another popular anti-Nazi war film starring Bogart that came out the same year, had been a member of the American Communist Party since 1934. In 1948, after refusing along with other members of the "Hollywood Ten" to cooperate with the House Un-American Activities Committee investigation of putative left-wing influence in the entertainment industry, Lawson was sentenced to a year in prison for contempt of Congress and blacklisted by the studios.

mark's A. P. Moller Group—the largest container operation in the world and left the seventy-five-year-old Farrell Lines as the only U.S. shipping company still engaged in international container trade. By the end of 2000 it, too, had been snapped up, by P&O Nedlloyd. These two transactions were only the latest in the march of mergers that has left the top twenty liner companies—which, as noted, control some 85 percent of the global container shipping market—in the hands of foreign companies or governments. The box boats passing the *Colombo Bay* on the open ocean or docking near us in port are P&O Nedlloyd sister ships, or Maersk Sealand vessels, or bear company names such as Evergreen (Taiwan), COSCO (China), Hanjin (South Korea), NYK (Japan), Hapag-Lloyd (Germany), and APL (Singapore)—until 1997 the U.S.-owned American President Lines.

The reasons for the American shipping industry's decline are spelled out with admirable clarity and not a little anger in *The Abandoned Ocean,* a history of U.S. maritime policy by Andrew Gibson, the assistant secretary of commerce for maritime affairs in the Nixon administration, and Arthur Donovan, a professor of maritime history at the U.S. Merchant Marine Academy at Kings Point, New York. They trace the slide in considerable detail, in essence, arguing that the U.S. maritime enterprise was ultimately done in by a steady and rich diet of federal subsidies and protectionism that lasted for most of the twentieth century. The authors credit the government for recognizing that these props were needed during both world wars and the Cold War, because U.S. shipbuilders, liner companies, and the country's merchant marine was critical to creating and maintaining the substantial U.S.-flag fleet needed for national security. But they decry the unintended and ultimately fatal consequences of the wartime policies, which was the formation of a government-military-industry-labor coalition that became addicted to the subsidies and protectionist legislation, which accreted like barnacles over many decades.

When this corporate welfare began drying up during the first

Reagan administration, the long-coddled industry and its sailors found themselves unable to compete on the world's oceans. Moreover, the Department of Defense by now had developed its own substantial sea-lift capabilities, which could always be, and were during the 1991 and 2003 gulf wars, augmented by vessels leased from foreign companies. "It would be difficult to overstate," Gibson and Donovan write, "the extent to which American maritime policies . . . have fallen out of step with the policies of leading maritime nations. In the second half of the twentieth century only former colonies that gained their independence following World War II and the former Soviet Union adopted maritime policies as backward-looking as the United States. . . . Today many nations are carriers in international trade, and the thoroughly invigorated global maritime industry is highly competitive. Yet in the United States the industry's fundamental dependence on the federal government remains basically unaltered."

Their conclusion seems reasoned and just, and steeped as they are in the long tradition of the merchant service, it is understandable that they should convey a certain nostalgia for the days when its sailors had a high profile manning whalers, clippers, and Liberty Ships. It was a brave universe of hard work and occasional high drama, inspiration not only for Melville but for many other American writers, among them Cooper, Hawthorne, Poe, Crane, London, Bellow, and Eugene O'Neill, a merchant seaman himself before he etched his experiences into *Bound East for Cardiff, The Long Voyage Home, The Hairy Ape,* and other plays. But as my mates on the *Colombo Bay* would be the first to say (and Conrad to lament), there is not much romance left in the technologized, just-in-time world of twenty-first-century merchant shipping, and even if there were, the collapse of the U.S. shipping industry doesn't seem a particular tragedy.

Perhaps I am overidentifying, but I suspect my "foreign" shipmates are no less capable of bringing home the boxes than my countrymen once were. Nor are Federico, Artemio, and the rest of the Filipino crew, and Peter, Shakeel, and the *Colombo Bay*'s other British officers, less deserving of the work, though die-hard American chauvinists obsessed with giant sucking sounds doubtless feel otherwise. P&O Nedlloyd and the other top twenty container operations have been rewarded for their efficiency in the marketplace, the sort of triumph U.S. capitalism is forever saluting. What has occurred here is just the kind of Darwinian selection America's mainstream politicians and their corporate backers seek when at every opportunity they urge that globalization be allowed to work its market magic unrestrained.

■ ■ ■

We have begun our six-day crossing of the Atlantic. Both Simon and Shakeel had assured me that we would pass through the Strait of Gibraltar around 0800, but when I arrive on the bridge just before 0700, Andy Lewington, the new first mate, reports that we slipped through the thirty-six-mile long passage in the dark two hours ago. So much for catching a glimpse of the Rock of Gibraltar and Mount Acho, which stand guard on either side of the strait's eastern end, where fourteen miles of water separate Europe from Africa. These Pillars of Hercules marked the end of the known world for the Mediterranean sailors of antiquity, who filled the void beyond with tales of mythical islands like Atlantis, which was believed to have risen from the sea after being engulfed by a tidal wave. The Phoenicians braved the Gibraltar pinhole first, in the first century BC, and exploration of the Atlantic began; but the myth persisted, with Atlantis showing up on many charts as in the Horse Latitudes, about equidistant between the Canary Islands and Florida—44°48' N, 26°10' W, to be exact, a specificity not dispatched until a detailed survey in the mid-nineteenth century demonstrated that no island existed there. It is chilly—outside—for the first time since Hong Kong, proper October weather; moderate swells splash against the hull under a cloudless sky. All that's left of the Old World is a bit of Spain, caught astern in the just risen sun.

Andy predicts good weather for the next two days, as far as the Azores. He is dressed in sweatpants and a sweater, an informality prompted in part by the departure of the only woman aboard and by a master less concerned with dress than Peter was. Andy is forty-one and trim, and exudes a quiet confidence, much as Matt did; he has been a merchant seaman for more than two decades, starting when a teenager with the usual combination of sea time and nautical courses, then rising through the ranks. Home when he is ashore is Nottingham, where his wife of two years, Corby, is in the process of changing jobs, enabling her to join him for a few weeks when the *Colombo Bay* calls at Malta November 2 on her eastbound run. Andy was promoted to first mate in 1993, two years after obtaining his master's ticket, the extra level of competency P&O Nedlloyd requires for the officers who are second in command. Many other companies are not so stringent, and he could have signed on as a captain with several of them; but he decided to stay with P&O Nedlloyd, which he joined in 1989, when it was P&O Containers, because British officers would be serving with him.

This homogeneity, and the red duster tradition it represents, are slowly disappearing, just as British crews did, and for the same reason. To cut costs P&O Nedlloyd is beginning to staff its ships with a British or Dutch "top two" (master and first mate) and fill the junior officer ranks with Filipinos, Russians, Poles, Hungarians, and other nationalities. "I have not sailed in such a situation," Andy says, "but I know from talks with fellow mariners that it has produced a catalog of problems, from officers with poor qualifications and seamanship to tension between the different nationalities." He does not like what he hears and speaks of leaving P&O Nedlloyd for more congenial employment—"pilotage, maybe; something to do with the sea, because it's all I know."

As the BBC delivers the latest reports on the air strikes in

Afghanistan, Andy offers his sympathies for the 9/11 attacks, then introduces a topic that seems like a non sequitur—mountaineering. It is one of his passions, and he has done a lot of it around the world. In 1991 he and six countrymen went to Skardu, in Kashmir, to try a peak ten miles south of K2 that had never been climbed before. They started their main ascent at a small village where Westerners had rarely been seen, where there were no newspapers or television and the natives lived by a barter economy. "We made friends with our porters, a wonderful bunch of people, and when we all returned to the village three weeks after our climb, we were invited to the head-man's house for tea," Andy says. "On the wall of his mud hut he had pictures of Thatcher and Reagan, with writing underneath. We asked what it said. He replied, 'Death to Margaret Thatcher, Death to Ronald Reagan, Death to the Capitalist West.' Yet these people had been totally friendly, because climbers bring in the only money that they see for the whole year. This shows the power of the mul-lahs. Anyone with the power of a mullah can prime someone to go to America and do what the suicide pilots did on September 11. Be-cause these people have nothing. They have nothing to lose."

This hopelessness doubtless radicalizes some and moves them to terrorism, but it turns thousands more people into desperate refugees who will try almost anything to get to what the Chinese call *gum shan,* the mountain of gold in North America and the rest of the developed world. The UN's International Maritime Organiza-tion reported that, in 2000, more than 1,200 people stowed away aboard ships in 385 separate incidents, totals widely regarded as conservative because, like piracy attacks, so many cases go unre-ported. Since the early nineties those that have made headlines are the grim stories of stowaways in containers. In China these smug-gling operations are run by gangsters called Snakeheads, who typi-cally will make a booking to transport a piece of machinery that requires a container with a tarpaulin on top because the machinery is so heavy it must be lowered into the box from above. The Snakeheads pick up the container, haul it to some out-of-the-way place, stash it with human cargo instead of the machinery, and truck it to Hong Kong or some other busy port, where it is loaded on a ship. That there is a tarp on top of this portable dungeon is no guarantee that other containers won't be stacked above it or that it won't wind up deep in the vessel's hold.

In April 2001 the *Pretty River* and *Maple River,* both owned by the Chinese liner company COSCO, arrived on the West Coast. In mid-Pacific a crew member on the *Pretty River* told his captain that he had heard voices coming from inside one of the boxes on deck; when the ship arrived at the Port of Vancouver, British Columbia, thirty men and six women stumbled out of two forty-footers, the walls and floors of each covered with urine and excrement that had spilled from a makeshift toilet as the vessel rolled during her passage from northern China. The *Pretty River* was headed for Long Beach, California, where only a few days before a stowaway had tried to escape to shore by jumping from a container on the *Maple River;* he broke an ankle and was nabbed, leading port officials to twenty-two other souls hiding in two containers that, like those aboard the *Pretty River,* had been crudely fitted with mattresses, blankets, and minimal food and water, and were equally foul.

The stowaways on both vessels were malnourished and dehydrated, but all had managed to survive more than two weeks in their dark, stinking prisons—not always the case. In January 2000 the Japanese-owned NYK *Cape May* was eastbound across the Pacific when stowaways were discovered locked in a container buried in the hold. At the Port of Seattle, crane operators frantically lifted thirty-five boxes to get at the entombed migrants; when longshoremen finally opened the steel doors, fifteen barefoot refugees emerged, barely able to walk. Inside, three others lay dead. A fourth died later from injuries suffered during the ordeal, which had taken almost three weeks because the stowaways sat in the container in Hong Kong for five days before it was loaded aboard the *Cape May.*

Five months later sixty Chinese refugees who had made it by various, sometimes clandestine routes to the Netherlands huddled in a decrepit container hidden in a warehouse on the Rotterdam docks. They were about to embark on the final leg of their journeys, which would bring them at last to England and the abundant new life they had imagined for months if not years. Near the doors of the container, boxes of tomatoes had been stacked to block any view of the jammed in migrants, who had been supplied with four large bottles of water and plastic bags for excrement. On the afternoon of June 18, one of the hottest days of that summer in Europe, the container rolled out of the warehouse, pulled by a white Mercedes truck driven by Perry Wacker, a thirty-two-year-old teamster and petty criminal working for the Snakeheads behind the operation. Three hours later he arrived at the Belgian port of Zeebrugge and drove aboard the *European Pathway,* a P&O freight-only ferry bound for Dover.

Silence now was crucial, so Wacker closed the sole vent that let light and air into the container; he then sat down to a dinner of roast lamb and watched two videos while the ferry pushed through the Strait of Dover. Inside the container, *The Guardian* would report, "the fifty-six men and four women baked. They discarded layers of clothes, finished the water, and desperately sucked on the tomatoes for moisture. Within two hours, many of them were near collapse. The stagnant, fetid air . . . was slowly turning to carbon dioxide; every breath added poison to the atmosphere. . . . Resigned to their fate, the sixty settled down, held hands, and ate some of the tomatoes. In China it is believed you should not leave a hungry ghost." By the time the *European Pathway* docked at Dover, just before midnight, all but two of the sixty refugees were dead.

One of the survivors was Ke Su Di, a twenty-year-old who eleven days before had fled his crimped future as a delivery boy in Fujian Province, the area of China opposite Taiwan, where the Snakeheads are especially active. He had flown from Beijing to Belgrade, the gateway for illegal immigration into Europe, made his way into and

through Hungary to Austria, flew to Paris, then went on to Rotterdam by train. "In China, life was not so good . . . and the snakehead
told me there would be no risk," Ke Su Di told the *Guardian*. "We
want to come to Britain because you can earn good money. Life is
good there."

His parents had paid the gang $5,700 as the first installment of a
$28,000 fee—the equivalent of ten years' wages—to smuggle their
son out of China and into the British world of his dreams. The
Snakeheads demand that the remainder be paid off either by the
family or over many years by Ke Su Di himself, out of whatever he
manages to earn working the few menial jobs open to him in England, likely including delivery boy. If he refuses to pay, or simply
cannot, the gang makes it clear that unless he comes through soon
his family back in Fujian will suffer. By one estimate, 100,000 people
are smuggled out of China annually; in 2001 Europol, the European
Union's cross-border police force, estimated that the Snakeheads
and other criminal outfits make as much money from people trafficking as they do from drug smuggling; the BND, the German intelligence service, reported that smuggling people into the European
Union had become a $4 billion a year enterprise. Perry Wacker, who
literally sealed his human cargo's fate, stood to make at least
$44,000 for his turn at the wheel.

What he received instead was fourteen years in prison, six years
for each of the fifty-eight victims (to run concurrently) plus eight
years for conspiracy. At the trial's conclusion, in April 2001, the
British court also sentenced Ying Guo, a thirty-year-old woman
from Essex who was to be the migrants' contact and translator in
Britain, to six years for conspiracy. At the time several other smugglers were in custody awaiting trial in the Netherlands, seven of
them on manslaughter charges related to the container deaths. Earlier in the year authorities in Fujian Province had arrested Chen Xiakong, the Snakehead leader who had promised Ke Su Di and his
less fortunate companions an easy passage to *gum shan*.

Despite such crackdowns, the gangs keep operating and the waves of asylum seekers keep coming. Eight months after Wacker's conviction, another container came aboard a ferry at Zeebrugge. The vessel encountered a Force 10 gale as it moved through the English Channel on a two-and-a-half-day passage to the port of Belview, on the southeast coast of Ireland. The container was then trucked to a business park near Wexford, where thirteen Turkish refugees were found inside. Eight had suffocated during their hundred hours in the steel box: three adult males, an adult female, boys four, nine, and seventeen, and a ten-year-old girl. A mother lay motionless, her dead son in her arms.

Not long after we left Malta, I asked Christian if he had ever had to deal with stowaways. He said he had never discovered any in a container, but in the early nineties, when he was first mate on P&O Nedlloyd's *Tolaga Bay,* four Chinese men posing as a repair gang snuck aboard at Hong Kong. "They had been told by the gang that had arranged for them to be smuggled into Hong Kong from Shanghai that in four days they would be in Japan and could get off," he said. "Unfortunately for them, we weren't going to Japan. Four days later we were in Pusan, South Korea; the Koreans hate the Chinese, so we had to lock them up to protect them from the dockworkers, who would have attacked them for trying to get into their country. The four stayed with the ship for four weeks, doing easy painting and cleaning work; we kept them under lock and key whenever we were in sight of land so they couldn't do anything silly, like steal a lifeboat. When we called at Algeciras, the Spanish port next to Gibraltar, quite out of the blue an official from the Chinese consulate came down to the ship and said they would handle the matter and see to it that the four strays got back home to undergo a year of reeducation at a suitable center, so they would know why they didn't want to leave China." Their apprehension cannot have pleased the would-be migrants, but for P&O Nedlloyd it was a rare instance of the problem being resolved smoothly.

Far more often the "disembarkation" of stowaways becomes a major headache for a vessel's master and his home office. The United States and most other developed countries see stowaways as just one more dimension of the growing illegal immigration they are trying hard to stem. Normally, port officials refuse to allow stowaways to come ashore, thus requiring the liner company to feed and clothe their guests and provide them with accommodations. If they prove disorderly, the officers and crew must guard them as well, not an easy task for seamen with no police or military training or weapons. In 2000, the IMO reported, there were two incidents of stowaways having to stay aboard vessels for between 100 and 150 days. In another case, a company put a stowaway in the hands of European authorities, only to be told later that the officials had changed their minds and the refugee must be put back to sea the next time one of the firm's vessels called at the port. When a stowaway escapes from a ship, the liner company can be hit with hefty fines, in Spain as high as $130,000. If a stowaway merely seeks refugee status in Canada, the company can be fined more than $9,000; should the migrant's application be rejected, Canadian law permits an appeal, the cost of which also must be paid by the company, or its agent. Often, too, companies wind up paying for repatriating the stowaways. In 1997 the IMO promulgated guidelines laying out the varying responsibilities of master, owner, flag state, and other parties in dealing with stowaways. The hope was that the regulations would produce more and better cooperation between companies and shoreside authorities. Stephen Bligh, P&O Nedlloyd's fleet marine manager, calls the regulations "reasonable and practical," but they are also voluntary and, as the number and determination of stowaways have increased, have more often than not proved unenforceable.

The collision between a nation's immigration policies and the desperate plight of asylum seekers was making headlines all over the world in the days before I flew to Hong Kong to join the *Colombo*

Bay. On August 26, Australia's Rescue Coordination Centre asked the Norwegian container ship *Tampa,* en route from Fremantle to Singapore, to come to the aid of some 430 migrants crammed onto the KM *Palapa 1,* a dilapidated, sixty-five-foot wooden fishing boat foundering in the Indian Ocean. The migrants, most of them Afghans who had paid people smugglers thousands of dollars to escape the Taliban regime, had made it from their homeland through Pakistan to Karachi, flown from there to Jakarta, then traveled overnight by truck from the Indonesian capital to the west coast of Java, where the *Palapa 1* waited to take them, most hoped, to Christmas Island, an Australian territory some 200 miles to the south that had become a magnet for Muslims fleeing Afghanistan's and other dictatorial regimes. On the second day at sea, the engine failed and the vessel began to drift. On the night of the third day, a storm blew up with seas so violent that some of the forty-three children aboard had to be tied to the mast to keep them from washing overboard. By the fourth morning, August 26, the stern had begun to collapse and the leaking boat was slowly sinking when an Australian air patrol plane spotted the SOS one of the refugees had written on a woman's scarf. Soon the orange hull of the *Tampa* was in sight, and before the day was out all refugees had been brought up her ladder and were safely aboard.

The *Tampa* is roughly the same size as the *Colombo Bay* and like her is designed to accommodate a maximum of about three dozen people. Arne Rinnan, the Norwegian master, turned five empty containers into dormitories and converted another into a makeshift toilet, and the crew distributed chicken soup at dinner and bread and boiled eggs for breakfast, from a larder that would last only a few days with so many mouths to feed. Two women, seven months pregnant, huddled under blankets in the hold; one refugee had suffered an apparent heart attack, another a broken leg; many others were sick with fatigue, dysentery, scabies and dehydration. Captain Rinnan planned to take the rescuees back to Indonesia, the port of

Merak in Sunda Strait being only about 220 miles to the north; but when the migrants learned that was to be their fate, many began a hunger strike and some threatened to jump overboard. The captain told Australian radio that the refugees had thanked him for their deliverance but insisted on being taken to Christmas Island, which was only a few hours away; several of the migrants became aggressive during a discussion on the bridge, pointing out that they had left everything behind in Afghanistan and now had nothing to lose. Captain Rinnan began to fear that the people he had rescued, who outnumbered the *Tampa*'s twenty-seven hands by sixteen to one, might even try to take over the vessel. Concerned for the safety of his ship and men, he ordered the accommodation locked down and headed for Christmas Island.

On August 29, the *Tampa* came within four nautical miles of the island and was greeted by some fifty of Australia's elite Special Air Service troops, who raced through the surf in high-speed boats and boarded the vessel to make sure none of the refugees were put ashore. In Canberra, Prime Minister John Howard, running for reelection, told a cheering parliament that he had ordered the ship seized because he was determined to slam the gates on asylum seekers; he planned to introduce new bills to justify his action retroactively and, if necessary, force the legislators to sit until they had passed. Philip Ruddock, the nation's immigration minister, said Captain Rinnan had, by allowing the refugees' threats to jump overboard to move him, acted "under duress."

Human rights advocates in Australia and around the world decried the government's lack of compassion, more than one pointing out that the "fatal shore" was founded as a penal colony and had grown and prospered primarily because of immigration. But a TV station's telephone poll of 45,000 people suggested that almost 90 percent of Australians backed the government's hard line. Nor had the Indonesian government proved any more welcoming when the *Tampa* was considering that option. The refugees "are under the full protection of a ship which belongs to a very rich country. Why should they transfer the problem to us?" said the foreign minister, Hasan Wirayuda. "They were on their way to Australia. Let them deal with it."

The Howard government supplied the *Tampa* with water, food, and medical help but remained determined not to let a single migrant set foot on Australian soil. With Christmas Island in view night and day, the rescuees waited in limbo while a court challenge to the government's decision played out. It ultimately failed, but a compromise of sorts was worked out when, after intense negotiations, Australia reached agreements with New Zealand and the microscopic republic of Nauru to accept the refugees. After eight days aboard the *Tampa*, all—save the four Indonesian crewmen of the KM *Palapa 1*, who were arrested—were transferred to the HMAS *Manoora*, an Australian navy troopship, which took the migrants on a week-long passage east to Port Moresby, the capital of Papua, New Guinea. From there about 150 of the rescuees flew to New Zealand, and the rest went to a refugee camp on Nauru, an eight-and-a-half-square-mile island in the Pacific that is arguably the definition of the middle of nowhere. The Howard government paid this smallest of the world's independent nations (population 12,000) $10 million to take the *Tampa* contingent and several hundred others who had beaten on Australia's door. "This is not the way to handle a refugee situation," Kofi Annan, the UN secretary-general, said, echoing worldwide criticism of the cash-for-dumping expedient. It nonetheless proved good politics at home. Before the *Tampa* case, Howard was trailing in the polls; three months after the incident he easily won reelection.

The Norwegian government honored Captain Rinnan for his compassion, as did the UN High Commission on Refugees, which gave him, his crew, and the ship's owners its Nansen Refugee Award, an annual recognition of humanitarian service that bestows $100,000 on a refugee project of the recipient's choice. Captain Rinnan also received, as a tribute of respect, a badge from the Special Air Service troops who had stormed the *Tampa*, and as his ship sailed away from Christmas Island, fireworks shot skyward onshore, a salute to the rescuers and perhaps also an explosion of relief that the transferred refugees were heading elsewhere.

Captain Rinnan had done what the Australian government asked him to do, what both the tradition and codified laws of the sea required him to do, what any humane master would have done: come to the aid of a vessel in distress, saving more than 430 lives. For his pains he did not expect to be becalmed off Christmas Island for more than a week, with undelivered cargo, financial losses mounting, and a ship full of sick, angry, and sometimes menacing refugees, while a long-standing democracy of only 20 million people on a huge continent bolted the latch. Yet such standoffs are likely to increase as people smugglers move more and more hope-filled asylum seekers into broken-down vessels all over the globe. Both the maritime community and refugee agencies fear that some captains, faced with the growing prospect of unsympathetic governments, will simply sail away from their responsibility and leave the boat people to the sharks.*

Two months after the migrants took temporary refuge in the *Tampa*'s empty containers, hundreds of fighters of the Taliban regime they had fled also found themselves crammed into such steel boxes. They had surrendered to soldiers of the northern Afghan-

---

*Business continued during the *Tampa* affair. Peter Stone, a P&O Nedlloyd vice president in Hong Kong, told me that Wallenius Wilhelmsen Lines, the ship's owner, asked P&O Nedlloyd and two or three other carriers to take on some of the cargo it was having to forgo because of the delay at Christmas Island. P&O was agreeable but while working out the arrangements discovered that WWL had underbid them on one of the accounts the Norwegians now wanted help with. The Norwegians had offered a lower rate to the shipper, which had then gone to P&O and said, Either reduce your rate significantly or we go with WWL. P&O had declined to do so and now abandoned its offer of aid.

istan warlord Abdul Rashid Dostum, who was in league with U.S. Special Forces as the six-year Taliban rule began to crumble after seven weeks of bombardment by the U.S. and British warplanes. In late November trucks began pulling the containers to Sheberghan, where Dostum had his headquarters. Luke Harding, who covered the war for the *Guardian,* described the convoy in a report for *Granta:*

> Nobody knew how many had perished on this journey—some estimates suggested about 900—but that many had died seemed beyond any doubt. Shiberghan prison still contained about 1,200 Taliban soldiers [when Harding returned to the town in January] and I managed to talk to several of them through the bars of their cells. The conditions inside the containers had been terrible. A Pakistani, Irfan Ali, said: "There was no air and it was very hot. There were 300 of us in my container. By the time we arrived in Shiberghan only ten of us were still alive." The eighty-three-mile journey should have taken only a couple of hours; Irfan Ali had survived nineteen hours in his container. . . . [The drivers] had given a grim account of the prisoners' final moments. Most had suffocated, though many also seem to have died when Dostum's guards shot into several of the containers while they were parked. . . . The dead, and a few who were merely unconscious, were loaded into lorries and taken into the desert, where Dostum's soldiers raked them with bullets to make sure there were no survivors. Then they buried them.

The mass grave discovered near Sheberghan in the spring of 2002 confirmed that Harding's report, and those of other correspondents on the scene, had not exaggerated the slaughter, a war crime instigated by a warlord who had been on the U.S. payroll for a year. In August 2002 the Pentagon insisted no evidence showed that American troops had been involved in the massacre, a statement few who were there credit, given the close cooperation between Dostum and the Special Forces operatives.

At the time of the transport, some eighty-five survivors of a bloody uprising by Taliban and Al Qaeda captives at Dostum's prison fortress outside Mazar-i-Sharif also wound up in containers, among them John Walker Lindh, the twenty-year-old Californian who would eventually plead guilty to aiding the Taliban and be sentenced to twenty years in prison. On November 25, Lindh had just been interrogated at the fortress by Johnny Michael Spann, a young CIA officer, when the revolt broke out; the Taliban prisoners overpowered and killed Spann, then raided a cache of weapons. A murderous weeklong siege followed, which Lindh managed to survive in the basement of the fortress with no food and a bullet wound in the thigh. When the prisoners finally surrendered, Lindh emerged to international headlines as the "American Taliban" and, after receiving medical treatment, was taken to Camp Rhino, a U.S. Marine base thirty-five miles south of Kandahar. During the first days of his renewed interrogation, he was, despite his leg wound and deteriorated condition, kept in a container, sometimes naked, blindfolded, and tied to a stretcher with duct tape. On December 9 he signed a waiver of his right to counsel. "He thought it was the only way he was ever going to get out of that box," a member of his legal team said later.

The container soon became the U.S. government's coop of choice for Taliban and Al Qaeda captives. At Bagram Air Base, twenty-seven miles north of Kabul, a cluster of the forty-foot makeshift slammers surrounded by a triple layer of concertina wire constituted the main detention center in Afghanistan. The military eventually transferred most of the detainees there to the U.S. Naval Base at Guantánamo, Cuba, where along with other captives denied due process in the Bush administration's war on terror, they would soon again be caged in containers. This new compound, called Camp Delta, was constructed in early 2002 by Brown & Root Services, a subsidiary of Halliburton Co., the Dallas-based corporation where

Dick Cheney had been chairman and CEO until becoming George W. Bush's vice presidential running mate.

Brown & Root flew in some 200 Filipino welders, fabricators, carpenters, and other skilled workers, who for about $900 a month, worked twelve hours a day to get the job done posthaste. They removed one side and each end of the boxes, substituting plastic-covered steel fencing mesh; left the roof, floor, and one steel wall, to which they attached metal shelf bunks; and cut floor-level squat toilets, installing plumbing underneath the containers, which sat four feet off the ground. The Filipinos divided each container into five cells, about eight feet deep, eight feet high, and seven feet wide, dimensions that moved the journalist Joseph Lelyveld to observe after a visit that "each cell is only slightly smaller than the cells on Death Row in Brown & Root's home state of Texas." When this book went to press, more than two years after the attacks on the World Trade Center and the Pentagon, some 650 prisoners, almost all still not charged with a crime or permitted counsel, remained in these pens, like potatoes rotting in an unclaimed container on a dock.

The government will never run out of forty-footers in which to stash alleged terrorists. The world is awash in empties, from boxes rusting by the sides of roads in developing nations to those neatly stacked at dozens of U.S. ports, testifying to the country's negative balance of trade. Around the Port of Newark alone they sit by the thousands in eight-high stacks flanking the New Jersey Turnpike, waiting in vain for cargo at a harbor that in 2001 saw almost twice as many containers arrive with foreign goods as depart with products made in the USA. In their abundance, empties come for as little as $1,000 for all manner of purposes besides lockups. "Shipping containers are design's material du jour," the *New York Times* declared in 2003, citing as one example the home of Los Angeles developer Richard Carlson, a 3,000-square-foot structure created out of four containers, with a fifth sunk in the garden as a lap pool. In Germany, after the wall came down in 1989, the government used containers as frames with which to create comfortable apartments to house the influx of ethnic Germans arriving from the former Soviet Union. In shantytowns all over the globe empties also wind up as makeshift homes, though rarely with heat, running water, or sanitation. They are turned into storage bins by hardware stores, marinas, trailer parks, garden centers, and farms; fitted and buried as survival bunkers; set ablaze inside to train firefighters; filled with low-level nuclear waste and other hazardous material. In South Africa the merchant navy donates its used containers to a Cape Town company called Creative Solutions, which has turned more than 4,000 of them into shops, hairdressing parlors, nursery schools, and community centers.

In the summer of 1995, Walt Disney Studios leased 180 containers and stacked them in Central Park to hold up four 85- by-120-foot movie screens for the world premiere of *Pocahontas*. The Vatican liked the idea so much it used the same concept a few weeks later to carry the Pope's mass in the park. In April 2002 the NBC television show *Fear Factor*—which challenges contestants to risk their necks for the amusement of viewers safe on their couches—featured four containers suspended sixty feet above the ground. Each one had cones at either end, one with a flag stuck into it; while the containers swayed, the competitors had to move the flag from one cone to the other, then jump to the next container and repeat the process until all four flags had been moved. The winner was one Larry Kane, with an elapsed time of thirty-eight seconds, facts likely to be of only marginal interest to the shade of Malcom McLean.

■ ■ ■

By midday on October 10, mutiny is in the air. Nothing indecorous, like the *Bounty* unpleasantness; perhaps just a polite petition to Christian that he remain in his quarters for the next forty-eight hours or so, catching up on desk work, doing some reading, and watching a few videos while we pause in our headlong rush to Halifax. The trigger for this fantasy insurrection, which I'm indulging in on the bridge with Simon and the cadet, is Pico, now poking through an aureole of clouds only seven miles to starboard. This volcanic peak, rising 7,700 feet from the middle of the ocean almost 1,000 miles due west of Lisbon, looks more like a misplaced alp than a preening upstart of the Mid-Atlantic Ridge, the submerged mountain range that stretches from southwest of Cape Town to the west of Ireland.

Pico slopes gently down to the coast, the entire island of the same name a beckoning Shangri-la—or, better, an earthly outpost of Fiddler's Green, the sailors' paradise, where the grog always flows and the ladies are ever accommodating. If we dropped one of the orange pods from its davits, we could motor ashore in less than an hour. And if we didn't find utopia, so be it; the worldly attractions of this dot, one of ten in the Azores archipelago, would do: the houses built from blocks of black lava, the frescoes of vegetation and vineyards on the hillsides, the snug harbors where fishing boats squeak against the docks and lunch is alfresco, the chance to go whale watching where the *Pequod* had been before. "No small number of . . . whaling seamen," Ishmael reminds us, "belong to the Azores, where the outward bound Nantucket whalers frequently touch to augment their crews from the hardy peasants of those rocky shores."

I settle for the fo'c'sle. The bow waves that slid by without much fuss when we were in the Mediterranean and before now explode against the hull in a swirl of angry suds as we seesaw west. Spray rains onto the deck, already a pointillist canvas of dried salt whose sparkle belies its caustic vandalism. Powdery clouds sit just above the horizon, a bench of bewigged British judges, lenient jurists ready to dismiss any charge against the men of the *Colombo Bay*. The sun's reflection on the water is hypnotic, atavistic. Was that a whale? Two? Three? A pod? No, alas, just the plump swells, which undulating all about us constantly deceive the eye and tempt the cry, "Thar she blows!" I do spot a white plastic carton, which bobs by on our port and is soon out of sight astern, a pip-squeak insult that fails to sully the pristine blue-green here in the middle of the Atlantic.

Like the rest of us, ships litter, which properly appalls environmentalists but from time to time delights scientists and their troops of flotsam-hunting shore sleuths. In May 1990 the *Hansa Carrier* hit a storm north of Japan and lost twenty-one containers, four of which opened and spilled more than 60,000 pairs of Nikes into the sea. This was a bonanza for Curtis C. Ebbesmeyer, a Seattle oceanographer who charts currents with the help of a worldwide network of devoted beachcombers. By the time a year or so had passed, some 1,600 of the sneakers—identified by the serial numbers on their tongues—had been recovered along the Oregon coast, on the Queen Charlotte Islands near Alaska, and other shores. Based on these wash-ups, W. James Ingraham Jr., who worked in the Seattle office of U.S. National Oceanic and Atmospheric Administration, used an Ocean Surface Current Simulator to estimate the running shoes' long-distance float, leading to a refined understanding of the surface variability of Pacific currents.

Twenty months after the *Hansa Carrier* spill, another ship ran into a violent storm southeast of the Aleutians while en route from Hong Kong to Tacoma, Washington. This time some dozen forty-footers washed overboard, including one with 29,000 bathtub toys— blue turtles, yellow ducks, red beavers, and green frogs made in China that had been bound for Kiddie Products, Inc., their U.S. distributor. By November 1992, ten months after the spill, the plastic toys began washing up near Sitka, Alaska, and Ebbesmeyer set about plotting the drift. He told me it took him a year of negotiation to persuade the shipping company to divulge the longitude, latitude, and date of the spill, which it ultimately did only if he agreed not to name the ship.

Eventually his network of beachcombers turned up some 400 more bathtub toys along 520 miles of Alaska coastline between Cordova and Coronation Island. Two years after the spill, some of the toys spent the winter trapped in Bering Sea ice, then continued their odyssey with the thaw. Summing up their research in 1994, Ebbesmeyer and his friend Ingraham predicted that "by the year 2000 a few toys will have been transported to many oceanic locations in the Northern Hemisphere." Subsequent reports proved them right, as the hardy ducks and their companions continued to wash up into the twenty-first century and the trackings produced by Ingraham's Ocean Surface Current Simulator widened and grew ever more intertwined, on the map a tangled ball of wool blotting out almost all of the northern Pacific, with a lone strand dangling as far south as Hawaii.

When I return from the fo'c'sle, an email from Diane awaits on the bridge. I expect it to mention anthrax, and when it does not I take it as confirmation of my own view: that the death on October 4 of a Florida man who inhaled the spores is nothing to worry about. Even after the afternoon BBC broadcast reports that two people who worked with the deceased have tested positive for the bacterium, I dismiss the development as just a cruel coincidence. The victims worked at American Media, Inc., publisher of the *National Enquirer*, in Boca Raton, not likely a follow-up target for Al Qaeda. The BBC gives the story little play, concentrating instead on the ordnance now raining on Afghanistan.

The bombardment is a topic at dinner, which features potato and leek soup, lamb, cabbage, carrots, rice pudding, and for the first time since Hong Kong some frank confrontation. Christian, who has already assailed the U.S. Navy for arrogantly ruling the sea when it encounters merchant vessels, now attacks Bush's bombing policy and the willingness of Blair to go along. He argues that hard-line diplomacy already had the Taliban isolated and that bombing is not likely to produce Osama bin Laden but instead will infuriate the Muslim world, as BBC reports from Cairo, Jakarta, Palestine, and elsewhere already have made plain it was doing. "We all know that

America is the greatest military power on earth, there's no need to prove it," he says. "Bush's announcement that the U.S. is embarked on a global war against terrorism is nonsense. Is he going to bomb Northern Ireland, the Basque separatists, the Tamil Tigers? I don't think so."

He gets no argument from me, only an exculpatory bleat that I didn't vote for our commander in chief, and besides, he has the job only because of five Republican Supreme Court justices. I do wonder, if silently, what Christian's view would be if the suicide planes had crashed into Canary Wharf and Buckingham Palace, how this sea captain would be responding had Moby Dick taken off his leg instead of Ahab's. Mostly, I welcome the mini-lecture and hope a lively give-and-take will follow in the lounge. It does not. Instead, the talk turns to *Monty Python, Are You Being Served? Fawlty Towers,* and other programs on British TV's supreme comic menu. I assure the room that these shows are popular in the United States and proudly demonstrate my knowledge of the Ministry of Silly Walks, the stuffy Captain Peacock, and the thickheaded Manuel. There follows, amid much laughter, a kind of can-you-top-this quotation bee: "This is an-ex-parrot!" "Are you free, Mr. Humphries?" "Qué?"

All of us agree that, lamentably, such fare would never be written today because of the PC police, who it turned out would strike again only a few months after our jollity, this time at the very heart of mar-itime tradition. In March 2002, *Lloyd's List,* the world's most re-spected shipping newspaper, whose origins date back to the late seventeenth century, announced that it would hereafter refer to ves-sels as *it* instead of *she* and *her.* For centuries seafarers had regarded ships as nurturing, protective wombs; now, with the stroke of a press release, they had been desexed by shipping's official tablet. One who weighed in on this development was the British novelist Julian Barnes, who was mostly amused by all the fuss but suggested that unglamorous vessels like container ships probably "deserve no bet-ter than neuterdom," which struck me as no way to speak of a lady, especially one who—or *that,* if you insist—had cradled me safely over several thousand miles.

The next evening at dinner we pass thirty-eight miles south of 41°46' N and 50°14' W, the coordinates near the Grand Banks off Newfoundland where the *Titanic* struck the iceberg and sank almost ninety years ago. Icebergs remain a hazard in these waters, especially in the spring. Most float down from Disko Bay in Greenland, where huge sections of the ice cap break away from the mainland, creating up to 40,000 floating mountains that move south on the Labrador Current. Only 1 to 2 percent of them make it into the North Atlantic shipping lanes and fishing waters before melting, but even the "growlers" that split off of these surviving mother bergs still stave in ships occasionally. In March 2000 the shrimp trawler BCM *Atlantic* hit a small iceberg in a snowstorm east of Goose Bay; her crew soon took to the boats and was rescued three hours later by another vessel, but not before the trawler went to the bottom. Such collisions are now rare because ice patrols, headquartered in Halifax, keep track of all icebergs in the northwestern Atlantic, sending out charts and other communications indicating their position and likely drift to all ships in the area.

In the lounge after dinner, Shakeel reminds us that, once more, the clock will be retarded one hour overnight. I ask what it's like to be on a ship and lose instead of gain an hour's sleep most nights, and there follows a brief seminar on the bleary-eyed eastbound run from ports in Australia and New Zealand to Europe. All hands confirm Conrad's observation that "for a true expression of dishevelled wildness there is nothing like a gale in the bright moonlight of a high latitude." It is through these stormy waters, fifty-plus degrees south, that ships must plow for two weeks just to get from New Zealand to Cape Horn. "You're in the middle of nowhere and trapped inside the accommodation most of the time because you're constantly rolling in the high seas," says Christian to nods all around. "You're losing an hour of sleep day after day; the whole ship goes into a depression, tempers get short, fights sometimes break out." Morale begins to improve only when the ship sails around the Horn and into the warmth and sun of the South Atlantic, and still there are twelve days to go to reach Lisbon, which offers the first opportunity to get ashore in almost a month.

Even on the *Colombo Bay*'s westbound voyage, during which we've picked up a half day of bonus hours and so far been blessed with benign weather, fatigue sockets the eyes of many onboard, especially those who have stood the regular four on, eight off watches for weeks now. This system, which dates back to the sixteenth century, was conceived in part so that when the master was sleeping he had an experienced hand—either his first or second mate—on the bridge in the darkness hours. The third mate, newly qualified, stands the 0800-to-1200 and 2000-to-midnight watches when the captain is always available to give immediate assistance, as Christian did when Simon ran into the U.S. Navy in the Mediterranean.

Watch keepers try to grab what sleep they can during their eight-hour breaks, but they seldom get much. When Shakeel comes off his midnight-to-0400 watch, he can't always drop off right away, and even if he does he must get up by 0830 if he wants breakfast. He can slip back to bed thereafter but must rise again to stand his 1200-to-1600 watch, then doze for an hour before coming to the lounge at 1730 before dinner. Andy Lewington comes off watch at 0800 and, as Matt did, grabs a quick breakfast, makes rounds of the vessel to oversee the crew's maintenance work, and then, also as part of his first mate duties, deals with cargo matters. He catches some sleep from about 1300 to 1500, gets up to stand his 1600-to-2000 watch, then goes back to bed for two or three hours before the cycle begins anew at 0400. When the *Colombo Bay* is nearing, in, or leaving port, most watch standers have assignments whether they are between their watches or not, and if they are lucky enough to get some free time ashore that, too, often comes at the expense of sleep.

In 1998 the U.S. Coast Guard released a study of crew fatigue and performance on its cutters that found, among other conclusions, that the broken sleep demanded by traditional watch-keeping schedules like that on the *Colombo Bay* and those on thousands of other ships impair a seaman's vigilance. Sleep deprivation reduced his ability to focus on critical tasks, such as monitoring the radar, the radio, and the engine, and on maintaining a weather eye, especially in the kinds of boring situations that prevail when a vessel is on autopilot for hours in the middle of the ocean. The study recommended alternative watch-keeping rotations more in keeping with the human circadian rhythm, one of which, it turned out, Andy had tried on his previous voyage, aboard a P&O Nedlloyd ship making the same run as the *Colombo Bay*. For three months he worked on the bridge from 0600 to 0800, and again from 1200 to 1800. That permitted him to do all work that required him to be away from the bridge between 0800 and 1130. "Basically, I had from 1800 to 0600 off, save when the ship was docking or leaving port. I got eight uninterrupted hours of sleep a night, and I felt an awful lot better for it, and it's taken all these years for someone to think of this idea." The second and third mates worked more or less the same system, though because of their lower rank their long breaks didn't fall as normally as Andy's.

He made a pitch for the Coast Guard system when he joined us in Malta, but there were no takers. Simon didn't like the idea of six straight hours on the bridge, and he liked even less the prospect of being up there during the evening meal. Shakeel felt he couldn't get his chart work done at night, which would be six hours pretty much wasted. Andy, though, is a convert and plans to try again when the ship returns to Malta on November 2 and a new second and third come aboard.

In the morning the BBC reports that five more people at America Media, Inc., have tested positive for anthrax, as has an employee at NBC in New York. Despite the growing speculation that Al Qaeda is spreading the germs and the "full alert" officials have declared, I still resist the notion that this is the other terrorist shoe dropping. But if it is, I want to be with Diane and welcome the contours of Maine, Nova Scotia, and Newfoundland now spread out on the chart table, the reassuring pencil line dead-on straight toward Halifax. By evening we are moving through thick fog, a harbinger of rough weather to come. Iris and Jerry are history, but Tropical Storm Karen is heading our way; reports put her off Nova Scotia not long after we leave Halifax tomorrow afternoon. "This will make a good ending for your book," says Shakeel.

CHAPTER TEN

By 0600 the pilot is aboard and the lights of Halifax in the distance are fading against the dawn as Canadian and American voices echo across the bridge like greetings by old friends in the doorway of a familiar house. The sky is overcast, the water calm, the autumn chill a bracing change after five weeks of endless summer. I pull on my warm-up jacket for the first time and go out on the port wing as we pass a dozen frigates and destroyers of the Canadian navy, intrusive gray sentinels tied up to the downtown docks on this peaceful Sunday morning. The pilot explains that they will soon sail to join the armada supporting the action in Afghanistan. The Macdonald and MacKay Bridges span the harbor narrows, connecting Halifax with Dartmouth on our starboard; the traffic flowing across them stays right, another welcome home after five port cities where the legacy of British imperialism dictates left. After slipping beneath the bridges at a stately seven knots, we swing hard to port into the Bedford Basin and head for the Fairview Container Terminal. As required by Canadian law, the cadet has removed all pornographic videos from the library shelves and placed them in the bond locker, where they will remain while we are in port, so no entrepreneur among us will be tempted to sell them to debauched Nova Scotians.

Just before we berth, Christian takes me aside and warns that he expects some serious rolling when we depart. Karen is now swirling about 500 miles east of the New England coast, and reports indicate we will meet her soon after we leave the harbor this evening. "Don't worry," I tell Diane when I call her from the lobby of the Sheraton Halifax, as if Karen were a woman with whom I am about to have a one-night stand and expect my wife to understand because, after all, it's just a harmless fling. I might have viewed the coming encounter with more urgency had I known at the time that Karen's feisty sister Iris had hit southern Belize a week before with 145 mile per hour winds, leaving 13,000 people homeless and causing some thirty deaths, many of them passengers and crew of the dive vessel *Wave Dancer*, which capsized after the hurricane ripped the 120-foot vessel from her moorings.

I next call Amanda, with guilt aforethought rousing her from her Sunday slumber. In a voice thick with sleep she reports that Gustav, who is a Ph.D. candidate in anthropology at the University of Chicago, is in that city packing the rest of his things and closing his apartment to move in with her in Brooklyn while he finishes his dissertation. This is good news; he is smart and kind, with a quiet wit, and all interested parties have agreed for some time that they make a fine couple. He is also half Swedish, and Amanda says that after the terrorist attack they talked about moving to Stockholm. When she assures me they've abandoned the idea, I find myself saying that if they change their minds they have my blessing.

This pessimistic view of the future is only reinforced by John Le Carré, whose angry essay on recent events appears in the *Toronto Globe and Mail* that I pick up at the hotel newsstand. WE HAVE ALREADY LOST, decrees the headline, over his attack on international corporate greed run amok and the failure of the West to mount a Marshall Plan in the developing world after the Cold War ended. He sees the chase for bin Laden as "a horrible, necessary, humiliating police action to redress the failure of our intelligence services"—he would know—"and our blind stupidity in arming and exploiting fanatics to fight the Soviet invader, then abandoning them to a devastated, leaderless country." We may catch or destroy bin Laden, he writes, but the war on terrorism will leave us trapped in a "devil's cycle of despair, hatred and—yet again—revenge," in a world where the suicidal armies of destruction will only grow in size and determination. (Even the author of *The Little Drummer Girl* did not imagine, I suspect, that two years after 9/11 the devil's cycle would have ensnared the United States in Iraq as well as Afghanistan.)

With a certain perversity, I seek refuge from this gloomy prediction in Fairview Cemetery, which overlooks the *Colombo Bay* at her berth. One-hundred-and-twenty-one victims of the *Titanic* sinking are buried here, their bodies having been pulled from the sea and brought to Halifax, the closest major port, in the days after the disaster. The headstones, small identical blocks, curve through the grass like the hull of a ship, the line broken at one point to represent the area where the liner hit the iceberg that sent her to the bottom on April 15, 1912. That is the date on all the headstones, with numbers indicating the order in which the bodies were found, the last recovered by a vessel a month after the sinking.

Many of the headstones offer no names, though over the years a few identifications have been made by matching recovered clothing, jewelry, papers, and other personal effects. The letters *J H* sewn in an undergarment led to the identification of victim number 3, the only woman lost with those initials: Jenny Henriksson, of Stockholm. Her name was engraved on her headstone in a special ceremony in 1991, along with five others who recently had been identified. At the World Trade Center site, firefighters and hard hats are clawing in the rubble, coming upon a bracelet, a shoe, a pair of glasses, and by the time they finish, some 19,000 body parts. Almost all the victims are known by now, but day by day their friends and relatives have grown resigned to the fact that hundreds of bodies, like those hundreds that disappeared beneath the waves off Newfoundland, will never be found.

We depart Halifax at about 1630, a fine rain misting as the warm air pushed by Karen meets the colder Canadian atmosphere. By the time we emerge from the harbor, visibility is almost zero, the sea calm, the wind soft; Karen is still 400 miles away, though spinning directly toward us with winds of sixty-five miles per hour. To qualify as a hurricane, winds must exceed seventy-four miles per hour, so Karen has been downgraded to a tropical storm, which sounds more comforting than it is. In early June the season's alphabetical progression began with Tropical Storm Allison, which blew up in the Gulf of Mexico and before she was finished had dumped thirty-nine inches of rain, caused $5 billion in property damage, and killed forty-seven people in seven states.

Christian says I'm welcome on the bridge once the fun begins, then notices my clogs and politely urges more practical footwear. Be careful coming through the steel doors, he adds. "If you lose your balance, fall forward or backward, don't grab the door or you could lose a finger or two when it slams." He also reminds me to batten down the hatches in my cabin. I do so immediately, cushioning the ThinkPad in my shirt drawer, hooking and tightening chairs and table to their floor latches, clearing all surfaces, and locking the closet and medicine cabinet. I am not quite so conscientious at dinner, ingesting Sunday steak, chips, creamed cauliflower, and strawberry shortcake with ice cream on top of the lobster sandwich and chips I had for lunch in Halifax.

This gastronomic voracity begins to suggest payback at about 2030, as I lie in bed and watch my denim shirt swing on its wall hook like a stern finger. By the looks of it, we are rolling ten to fifteen degrees, enough to make me abandon Conrad so I can grab the sides of the bed to keep from sliding. In the hope of countering growing queasiness, I reach for the pack of CDs, slip on *Sondheim at the Movies,* and turn out the light as the boxes outside the port hole strain against their lashing bars, sounding as if they will tear free and tumble overboard at any moment. With each roll the ship seems certain not to right herself; then, like a crying child after an endless, blue-faced pause between sobs, she catches her nautical breath and rolls back.

"I am, perhaps, unduly sensitive," Conrad writes, "but I confess that the idea of being suddenly spilt into an infuriated ocean in the midst of darkness and uproar affected me always with a sensation of shrinking distaste." This drollery should be memorized by New York's TV weather sages, who forever issue reassuring reports that the latest northbound storm, before getting anywhere near the city, will "head out to sea," a phrase that suggests they think of the Atlantic, when they do so at all, as an unpopulated meteorological dumping ground where blows just dance about harmlessly until they poop out. The hour-long parade of Sondheim songs proves a healing lullaby, as if he were rewarding me for my years of devotion; by the last cut—"Goodbye for Now," from the film *Reds*—no hint of seasickness remains. I try to get some sleep, tossing and turning less of my own volition than of Karen's. When next I check the alarm clock it is almost 0200; I retard the hands for the last time, pull on my sweats, and go up to the bridge on eastern daylight time.

It's Shakeel's watch but, no surprise, Christian is on hand. He explains that Karen was supposed to track north-northeast, passing behind us as we headed southwest down the coast of Nova Scotia; instead, the storm turned north-northwest, so after reaching Cape Sable at the southwestern end of the island, we took avoidance action and pointed west toward the Gulf of Maine. Christian judges that had we kept to our original southerly course, which would have taken us just east of the Georges Bank, we would have headed right into Karen, which would have smacked us from behind because of her counterclockwise winds. Waves breaking over the stern of a heavily laden vessel like the *Colombo Bay* can be extremely hazardous, especially when the speed of the ship is about the same as that of the following sea, a condition that can lift the rudder out of the water, leaving the helmsman unable to steer; this is called pooping and can leave a ship broadside to the waves and in danger of rolling over.

Karen is now about 100 miles due east of the Georges Bank, at least 300 miles from our position as we move into the gulf with visibility low and windshield wipers agitating, the heavy rain and wave motion creating yellowish Rorschachs on the radar screen. By 0400 we are 145 miles due east of Cape Ann and angle southeast toward our next way point, 50 miles off Cape Cod. At 0700 the cadet appears on the bridge breakfasting from a large bag of Lay's potato chips that he and Simon acquired in Halifax along with other personal stores. He asks how I enjoyed the night; I say it had its moments and salute the captain for his thoughtful detour. The cadet dismisses Karen as "tiddlywinks," adding between munches that he fears this voyage will never produce weather that will make him feel like a salty sea dog.

The cadet's bravado would have been tested had he still been aboard the *Colombo Bay* three months later, when she made her next westbound crossing of the Atlantic. Peter Davies had resumed command and beginning January 22 encountered a midocean storm that permitted no end run like the one we had just made into Gulf of Maine. Nor could the *Colombo Bay* turn tail; coming about would have risked capsizing by exposing the port or starboard side to waves that by the morning of the twenty-sixth had reached heights of up to sixty feet, pushed by wind gusts of eighty miles per hour. These conditions produced several "greenies," enormous surges that break over the bow and send a mass of green water over the ranks of containers all the way to the bridge. The ship was making only four or five knots pitching through these aqueous mountains, sometimes rolling as much as thirty degrees.

No containers tumbled off, but the waves pouring over the bow stove in three boxes just behind the fo'c'sle, and two containers above the poop deck also were breached, one full of rubber gloves, the other a reefer of canned crabmeat. By the twenty-seventh, as the storm diminished, dozens of the gloves hung on the protective mesh covering the poop deck like so many soaked birds. The spill of tins from the reefer looked like a slot machine jackpot, and did prove a score for hands inclined to augment their daily diet with crabmeat variations as the *Colombo Bay* pushed toward Nova Scotia.

"Had a few heart murmurs and . . . haven't mentally recovered yet," Peter wrote in an email sent a few hours before the ship arrived at Halifax on January 29. He hadn't lost his sense of humor, reporting that Elizabeth had emailed him saying "she didn't fancy the crabmeat but the rubber gloves would come in handy!!!!—Get it!" Two days later I visited him when the ship berthed in New York, two days behind schedule. He had been up for twenty-four hours straight during the height of the storm and had risen this morning at 0300, when the Coast Guard came aboard for its security inspection. He looked exhausted as we sat in his dayroom over a lunch of salmon sandwiches and salad and he described the events of the last week, which he illustrated with digital photographs of the damaged containers. I asked him if the lifeboats could have survived in the weather he had just encountered. He said the problem was less their survival than of launching them in the first place, given the degree of rolling and the size of the seas. He had faced worse storms in his four decades as a mariner but not many. "I'm not sure how many lives I have left," he said with a weary smile.

In 1998, the men on the APL *China* likely indulged in similar speculation when they found themselves trapped in an intense tropical storm labeled Super Typhoon Babs, which devastated parts of China's southeastern Fujian Province, flooded many towns and villages on Taiwan, and tore through the Philippines, killing at least 189 people, injuring some 400, and damaging almost 150,000 buildings. On October 26 the container ship, about the same size as the *Colombo Bay,* was crossing the Pacific from Kao-hsiung to Seattle. At the International Date Line, between the Midway Islands and the Aleutians, she was about 4,000 miles northwest of Babs's path, but the fallout from this "meteorological bomb" was battering the vessel and her 4,800 TEUs with winds of up to one hundred knots and seas of sixty feet, causing rolls of forty-five to fifty degrees. Many hands feared that the ship would founder, especially after water breached air vents and entered the emergency generating room, leaving her to wallow powerless for an hour in the dark. More than 400 containers spilled overboard, and a like number were damaged by the force of the waves, which flooded the Number 1 hold with sixteen feet of water.

The APL *China* managed to ride out the storm, but when she arrived in Seattle, two days late, her decks looked as if kindergartners had thrown a tantrum with their blocks; scores of once neatly stacked boxes now tilted topsy-turvy, many of them smashed open and a few hanging precariously over the sides. Both port and starboard gangways had been ripped away by the water and winds, and had gone to the bottom with the cargo, the majority of which was due on U.S. shelves for the Christmas season. By most estimates the lost and damaged payload was worth well over $100 million, making the APL *China*'s encounter with Babs the worst single-ship financial setback caused by a storm in the history of containerization. Still, like the *Colombo Bay,* the vessel would sail again, not the case for 167 other ships that, between 1994 and 2000, sank or were otherwise made total losses by nature's wrath, a number that represents 28 percent of all merchant shipping losses during the period.

■ ■ ■

Dodging the brunt of Karen has taken the *Colombo Bay* into the right whale sanctuary off Cape Cod. Melville ties a right whale and sperm whale to opposite sides of the *Pequod* and has quite a good time comparing their heads, noting that "there is a certain mathematical symmetry to the Sperm Whale's that the Right Whale's sadly lacks." The right whale's hanging lower lip offers a "huge sulk and pout," and its head reveals "an enormous practical resolution in facing death." The sperm whale's broad brow suggests "a prairie-like placidity, born of a speculative indifference as to death." The sperm whale is "a Platonian, who might have taken up Spinoza in his latter years"; the right whale Melville takes "to have been a Stoic."

This philosophic anthropomorphizing takes me back again to Chicago's Frolic Theater in the mid-forties; there I first sighted Willie, a whale who wanted to sing at the Met. He was the star of a Disney pastiche called *Make Mine Music,* a chipper fellow who could stand on his flukes and, with the assistance of Nelson Eddy tucked somewhere behind his tonsils, toss off arias from *The Barber of Seville, I Pagliacci,* and *Tristan und Isolde.* These turns charmed sailors, seals, a seagull named Wiley, and me but not an impresario named Tetti Tatti, who with the waving hands and rolling *r*'s of a caricature Italian sets sail to rescue the opera singer he is convinced Willie has swallowed. His pursuit only grows hotter after Willie—who is not just a baritone but a tenor and bass as well—begins singing a trio. Certain that he now has three opera singers to liberate, and a publicity bonanza, Tetti Tatti wrests the ship's harpoon gun from his enchanted crew and slays his talented prey. Willie rises to a pastel Disney heaven, where his disembodied voice echoes in the clouds with more operatic strains, a finale that failed utterly to assuage my sense of the cruel injustice just done.

The right whale may be coming to an equally unhappy end. Despite sixty years of protection, it is one of the most endangered creatures on the planet; the National Oceanic and Atmospheric Administration estimates that there are only 300 right whales left in the North Atlantic and that ship strikes account for about 50 percent of their known deaths. One of the most widely reported occurred in April 1999, when a frequently observed forty-five-foot, sixty-ton right whale nicknamed Staccato was found floating in Cape Cod Bay. She was towed to a beach in Wellfleet, Massachusetts, where a team of scientists concluded that she had been hit by at

least one ship after a three-day necropsy revealed she had a broken
jaw and five broken vertebrae. The Coast Guard requires that all
large vessels report in if they seek to pass through the sanctuary; if
right whales have been sighted, vessels are sometimes asked to post
a watch, slow down, or alter direction. Christian sends our position
to the Coast Guard by radio but receives no response and keeps the
Colombo Bay on course. This is my best and probably last chance on
this voyage to spot a whale, Stoic or not, and I keep a protective eye
out as we move through patchy fog under a ceiling of gray. The
swells look more than ever like the backs of the rolling mammals,
but no real ones appear; after an hour I give up and by noon we have
left the sanctuary.

By midafternoon we have skirted the Nantucket Shoals and are
heading west past the familiar landmarks of my extended neighborhood—Martha's Vineyard, Block Island, Montauk, Southampton,
Fire Island, and Robert Moses State Park, where on a lucky July
day at the beach in 1980 friends introduced me to Diane. On the
bridge I have tea and BBC with Shakeel for the last time. The dis-
passionate voices report that Tom Daschle, the Senate majority
leader, has received an anthrax-laced letter; that the seven-month-
old son of a freelance television producer working for ABC has been
hospitalized with the infection; that President Bush has said this
bioterrorism may be linked to bin Laden. We shake our heads again,
in what by now has become a daily minimalist pas de deux. In the
lounge before dinner there is speculation about the coming Coast
Guard inspection and irritation over being confined to the ship in
port. The consensus is that given Tony Blair's cheerleading for
Bush's antiterrorism campaign, his willingness to send British
troops to Afghanistan, and the much-touted special relationship between Uncle Sam and John Bull, several hours' leave in New York
doesn't seem too much for a few sea-weary British officers to ask.

The restriction is particularly frustrating for several of the crew,
who had counted on calling home from New York, where the rates

are cheaper than in Asian or European ports. They have even less chance of getting ashore than the officers. Not only do they lack the leverage of the Anglo-Saxon bond but they are now under scrutiny by the Coast Guard because of the Abu Sayyaf, the separatist guerrillas in the southern Philippines, who still hold American missionaries they kidnapped. By the end of the month, two dozen U.S. military advisers will arrive there, the vanguard of support for Filipino troops in their search for these Muslim terrorists, who may be just ruthless bandits, as much of the crew believes, or may have links to Al Qaeda, as the Pentagon insists. In the galley after dinner I thank Artemio for keeping me so well fed. "Are you glad to be home, are you eager to see your family?" he asks, with the resigned smile of a man who has been at sea now for five and a half months and still has three and a half to go before he can return to Consorcia and his three boys. I'm tempted to lie, to hide my sheepishness over the easy escape my U.S. passport guarantees by insisting that I'd like to continue on to Norfolk and Savannah, as originally planned. But I am more than glad to be home and, looking away, say so.

At around 2000 we drop anchor near the Ambrose Light. We are about six miles off Long Beach, in an outer harbor where ships wait to move to their berths, an aquatic holding pen that has been more crowded than ever since September 11. This is where the Coast Guard is likely to come aboard for its inspection, but Christian has not yet heard at what hour and anticipates a long night. I ask him to let me know when he does hear and go to the cabin and pack. By 2300 no word has come and I drift off to sleep until 0400, then go up to the bridge, where Christian reports that the Coast Guard has decided to pass the *Colombo Bay* to its berth without an inspection. No reason was given, but the speculation is that lack of manpower makes it impossible to board every vessel and that our red duster also may have figured in the decision. Whatever the reasons, Christian is a happy master. At 0418, Shakeel radios from the fo'c'sle that the anchor is up, and we start toward the inner harbor, moving slowly through calm waters under a navy sky studded with stars. Planes slip smoothly in and out of JFK, LaGuardia, and Newark, their wing lights winking with an innocence that belies the fact that hijackers had turned four such aircraft into kamikazes just five weeks ago.

Our pilot, Tom Keating, comes aboard just after 0500, accompanied by Bob Jones, another pilot, who is hitching a ride back to Staten Island after ending his shift. Jones, who is sixty-seven, has worked the harbor for forty-three years and claims to be the oldest active pilot in the port, a history I probe without success; what consumes him at the moment is the "absolute miracle" of the Yankees' 5–3 victory over Oakland just a few hours ago. The home team had lost the first two games of the best-of-five playoffs, and the miracle had capped a three-game comeback to win the series, something no team had ever done. Keating is no less impressed, especially by a deft play at the plate that the Yankee shortstop Derek Jeter had made to head off a run and save the third game, a rescue also discussed in tones of disbelief by a pair of anonymous radio voices, an aside to their putatively more urgent concern with harbor traffic. This enthusiastic baseball talk continues for ten minutes as the *Colombo Bay* slides by Brooklyn, a zipper of lights flashing along the highway rimming the borough.

As we approach the Verrazano-Narrows Bridge, Keating softly issues small course and speed adjustments to the helmsman. His father and uncle were pilots, and he seems to relish the work, which he has done since becoming an apprentice in 1988. He is thirty-nine, militarily erect, and dressed in a white shirt and dark tie that remain neat despite his climb up the ladder from the pilot boat. I ask him about September 11. "In the immediate aftermath," he says, "the Coast Guard was inspecting every vessel. They were living with us on the pilot boats, would board the ships with us. They would pat down anyone standing at the top of the gangway, then muster officers and crew in the wheelhouse or on the mess deck. They would check every passport, then go through every space on the ship, every room, every locker. They found some pretty interesting things, such as pictures of Bush with a bull's-eye on his head and the date September 11." For two weeks following the attack, Keating and many other pilots helped coordinate rescue operations by a fleet of more than one hundred ferries, tour boats, yachts, and other small vessels. They evacuated some 500,000 people from Lower Manhattan and brought water, gas masks, acetylene torches, and other emergency supplies to the area from Weehawken and Jersey City across the Hudson.

Keating's cousin Paul Keating was a firefighter who lived near the World Trade Center. He phoned his sister, saying he was going to help his comrades, and dashed to the scene; his body was not recovered for five months. Paul's brother, Neil, was to be married ten days after the attack; the wedding was postponed while the family grieved and Neil coped with this latest devastating blow. He, too, is a pilot and in 1997 was on a ship's ladder when successive swells lifted the pilot boat, which crushed him three times against the hull he was climbing before a mate could pull him to safety on the boat's deck. His broken bones and other injuries required a year and a half of physical therapy. Tom Keating finds it painful to revisit the death and destruction he witnessed daily in the wake of the attack. "It's not the world you want your kids to grow up in," he says, fighting back tears.

His emotion is contagious. I picture Amanda asleep in Fort Greene, then Diane stamping to keep warm waiting at dawn on the bridge, after weeks of carbo loading, to begin the New York Marathon in 1980, the year we met. In two weeks thousands of runners will gather again on this 4,200-foot-long starting block, now an arching finish line sparkling with traffic. Two tugs appear on our flanks, sent to deflect the ship should one of us grab the wheel and try to ram the bridge. We pass under at 0635, the Stars and Stripes flying from the monkey island as the Statue of Liberty comes into view just off the port bow. Her guiding torch triggers a rush of frank patriotism, of an intensity I haven't felt since I collected newspapers and tinfoil and yanked carrots out of our postage-stamp-size backyard Victory garden to help defeat Hitler, Tojo, and Mussolini.

I feel awkward holding this star-spangled sentiment but, once Lower Manhattan appears in the distance, pugnacious in rejecting Dr. Johnson's notion that I am somehow a scoundrel. The shadowy skyscrapers of the financial district are backlit by the stark, almost white light that floods Ground Zero, where digging continues around the clock. When I hold up the binoculars my hands shake, making the light dance like the flames into which the Commendatore pulls Don Giovanni. The scene is riveting, but not Mozart and Da Ponte. They gave their opera an upbeat ending, the don's victims cheerfully singing that his howling descent into hell proves that sinners always meet their just rewards. Le Carré's libretto seems far more likely this time.

The sun is up by the time we've crossed the harbor and slipped into the Kill Van Kull, where we pass the Blue Circle Cement barge tied up on our port. So *that's* where she goes. As we inch toward the Bayonne Bridge, the monkey island seems about to be sheared off even if Christian orders full speed astern immediately. He smiles and holds up six fingers. Meters? I ask. Feet, he replies, as we slide under with seventy-two inches to spare, an air draft made possible by ballast taken on en route from Halifax that makes the *Colombo Bay* sit low enough for the squeeze. I go down to the galley to say a final good-bye to Artemio and his sous-chefs, and they insist on making me a special breakfast, anything I want. Scrambled eggs and onions? Artemio throws a handful of chopped onions on the griddle, sautés them until they darken, and with perfect timing as they begin to caramelize breaks two eggs over them and swirls up a firm and delicious plateful, which he serves with whole wheat toast and a juicy South African grapefruit. I want to offer him anything *he* wants—a gastronomic tour of Manhattan, perhaps, or just the use of our phone to talk to his family for as long as he wishes. But though the *Colombo Bay* somehow escaped inspection in the harbor, the Coast Guard has made it clear that neither crew nor officers will be permitted off the ship.

I return to the bridge as we move hard to port into the Arthur Kill, which runs between New Jersey and Staten Island just south of Newark airport, from which I flew to Hong Kong five weeks ago to embark on this unexpected voyage. We berth smoothly at the Howland Hook container terminal, and the gantries start plucking off boxes only minutes after we tie up. The good-byes are quick, because everyone is busy with port duties. As I wrestle my gear to the top of the gangway, Shakeel appears. He is in his boiler suit and looks pressed for time, but we manage to affirm the bond formed after so many afternoons listening to the BBC together. We promise to keep in touch, and he disappears through the upper deck door as I tread down the wobbly stairway for the last time.

On the dock, Vladimir Tocaj, the ship's agent, calls a car service on his cell phone. The driver is Jean Elto, a Haitian who has been in New York for seven years. "I love America," he says, as we head for the New Jersey Turnpike. He, too, talks of Derek Jeter's throw to the plate and earnestly explains that the Yankees won the playoffs because they wanted to reward the city after its terrible tragedy. The Holland Tunnel is still closed, and cars using the Lincoln Tunnel risk inspection and long delays, so we push north toward the George Washington Bridge. "God Bless America," reads a Shop Rite billboard with a big American flag. I strain to see the void in the Lower Manhattan skyline, but the palisades along the Hudson keep blocking the view; only when we cross the bridge does the enormity of the assault finally become invisibly clear.

Jean points down the river. "That's where they were."

"Yes, I know."

"The observation deck was really something. Were you ever up there?"

"Yes, with my daughter. She thought it was scary because it was so high."

As we move downtown we pass an even bigger flag, this one hanging from the sewage treatment plant on the West Side Highway. At Broadway and 125th Street, yet another flag and "United We Stand" appear on the white hard hat of a construction worker. Otherwise, everything appears the same. The students walking near the Columbia University campus look as purposeful or as distracted as before; two M104 buses travel down Broadway, maddeningly bunched together as always, and the bakery at 113th Street, a block from our apartment, is still called Nussbaum and Wu, a name I remain convinced is made up. The reds and browns in Riverside Park are right on schedule, and as I look into this welcoming foliage it is almost possible to imagine that nothing has changed.

EPILOGUE

By the time the *Colombo Bay* headed back across the Atlantic, she had left more than 3,000 containers on the docks at Halifax, New York, Norfolk, and Savannah. Hundreds of these boxes soon moved inland by train or truck: the tobacco loaded at Laem Chabang to Owensboro, Kentucky; carpets that started out in Cochin, India, to Calhoun, Georgia; toys and games that began their journey in New Delhi to Bolingbrook, Illinois; baby garments from the Philippines to South Brunswick, New Jersey; tapioca from Thailand to Hurlock, Maryland. As Malcom McLean had predicted, this movement of goods had become routine, an inexpensive supply chain that since the sixties had operated with few impediments beyond weather and now had given globalization an efficient, synchronous flow.

From the start, concern over security had been a distant second to making sure this rush of commerce remained smooth and uninterrupted. Despite theft and the use of containers to smuggle drugs, contraband, and people, the doors on the vast majority of boxes were still "sealed" with simple lead strips and bolts that cost about fifty cents apiece. Thousands of containers regularly traveled with their contents labeled merely FAK (freight of all kinds) and STC (said to contain). Even when manifests were more specific, they were often still vague. Many boxes on the *Colombo Bay* contained "basic shapes of metal" or "ferrous iron/ore and spongy products" or "foodstuffs NOS" (not otherwise specified). Nor did U.S. Customs have any way of knowing, unless inspectors opened and unloaded each container, whether more precise information was true, whether the tapioca was in fact inside the boxes as claimed. After 9/11, Americans woke up to the realization that the shipping container—until then something most citizens seldom thought of, if they knew anything about it at all—could be the vehicle of choice for sneaking a weapon of mass destruction into a country where every year more than 6 million of the boxes arrive by ship from all over the world.

In the months following 9/11, the media repeatedly reported that roughly 2 percent of these containers ever faced inspection, a figure that, however alarming, may well have been optimistic. Whatever the percentage, inspectors rarely opened any of these 120,000 containers to examine what was inside; there were just too many of them, and the pressure from shippers, liner companies, and consignees not to hold up the forward march was too great. Most often U.S. Customs and terminal officials "inspected" boxes by giving extra scrutiny to the relevant bills of lading and other paperwork and by making sure that the seals had not been tampered with. Even these steps were of dubious value since shipping documents were often inaccurate or incomplete and containers could be breached without breaking the seals, in some cases by removing the door hinges.

At a few major ports like New York, customs employed the Vehicle and Cargo Inspection System, a truck with a twenty-two-foot arm able to reach over a container and send through its walls gamma rays that produced a shadowy image of the box's innards on a computer screen inside the truck's cab. In theory, VACIS allowed inspectors to spot anything that was not supposed to be within, from stowaways and drugs to a dirty bomb. In practice, the technology and trained operators were in such short supply because of budgetary constraints that they examined only a small fraction of containers deemed suspect; moreover, the machine is an imperfect tool at best, able to "see" little more than shapes that look suspicious. At the Red Hook cargo terminal in Brooklyn, inspectors opened one container after the VACIS screen showed a solid, cylindrical form that looked out of place in a box supposedly filled with household goods; it turned out to be an industrial stove. "I wouldn't want to rely on them; they don't tell me too much," James Pond told me when I visited Activities New York, the Coast Guard facility on Staten Island, a few weeks after coming off the *Colombo Bay*.

Pond was a forty-one-year-old petty officer second class with twenty-two years in the Coast Guard, since 1994 as a container inspector. Shortly before we spoke, in January 2002, he had led an inspection team that boarded a medium-size container ship flying a Liberian flag of convenience, captained by a Yemeni master, and carrying thirty warheads for Sea Sparrow surface-to-air missiles. The vessel, which the Coast Guard would not name, already had sent crew and cargo information to the National Vessel Movement Center, which had been set up in the hills of West Virginia less than a month after 9/11 to track all ships headed for U.S. ports. Before the terrorist attacks, incoming ships had reported to the Coast Guard twenty-four hours prior to arrival, a long-standing routine established primarily to facilitate marine safety, not security; the cargo manifests and passports of a ship's company were not checked until she docked, and occasionally not even then. Now the Coast Guard required that all inbound ships email or fax cargo data and the passport information ninety-six hours in advance of arrival. The Liberian-flagged vessel was singled out not just because the warheads had shown up on her list of dangerous cargo but also because one or more hands fit the Coast Guard's "high risk matrix," the specifics of which the service also would not reveal.

Pond said that the seal on the container holding the warheads had been altered and that the six-digit number on it did not match the number on the shipping papers provided by the vessel's first mate. At this point the Coast Guard took full operational control of the ship, which was anchored off Brooklyn in a bay inauspiciously called Gravesend. When the first mate asked if he could take a look at the seal, Pond said the container was now off-limits to all hands and posted two members of his inspection team, both armed, near the box; he then photographed it from several angles. Checks determined that the warheads were bound for a Raytheon Corp. plant in the United States to have guidance systems installed. They had been manufactured in Germany, shipped by rail in the container to a French port, where it turned out concerned authorities had broken the container's seal to inspect the contents, then placed a makeshift lock on the box and made no annotation on the shipping papers.

Though this explanation for the appearance of tampering seemed plausible, Pond opted for extra caution and called in an Explosive Ordnance Detachment team from the U.S. Navy. He removed the seal from the container, which sat atop a stack just aft of the fo'c'sle, then withdrew to the bridge while the EOD team climbed up to and entered the box. Each of the thirty warheads was inside its own sealed canister, the canisters packed in a sectional wooden crate to keep them stabilized at sea. Once the EOD team concluded nothing appeared amiss, Pond returned to check each canister's seal and found them all intact. The container was then resealed with a Coast Guard seal and the ship allowed to proceed to its berth. "It was a little hairy, but it turned out to be safe," Pond recalled.

The inspection of this one container took two days and involved not only Pond's six-man boarding party but Coast Guard personnel onshore and the EOD team as well. "We are stretched thin," Lieutenant Commander Christopher Nichols, chief of the Vessel Traffic Service Branch at Activities New York, told me, echoing a lament I heard from every Coast Guard officer I spoke with. The *Colombo Bay* was not boarded before berthing because Activities New York had enough manpower to inspect only five of the forty or so tankers and container ships that arrive in New York Harbor each day, and even those examinations were necessarily cursory; it would take many hours to effectively scrutinize the cargoes and ships' companies and thoroughly explore the holds, machinery spaces, and accommodations of these mammoth vessels.

Not only did the Coast Guard lack sufficient personnel to pursue its post–9/11 mission but most of its equipment was ancient. The majority of its cutters were built in the fifties and sixties; some of its buoy tenders were commissioned during World War II; most of its helicopters were twenty years old or more. "A lot of our computers and communications systems are a good generation behind, say, the U.S. Navy's," Nichols said, in a tone less of complaint than of resignation. Under the new ninety-six-hour rule, the service was receiving thousands of names a day from inbound ships, but its computers couldn't communicate with those at the CIA, FBI, and INS to check the names against those agencies' databases of criminals and illegal immigrants.

In 2002 the Coast Guard became part of the new Department of Homeland Security and by 2003 its budget had jumped by $800 million, to $6.2 billion. The extra money was welcome, but neither it nor the bureaucratic reshuffle is likely to produce dramatic change soon in a service now charged with protecting more than 350 ports and 95,000 miles of coastline from terrorists while interdicting Cuban asylum seekers off the Florida Keys, finding smuggled drugs, rescuing Sunday boaters in distress, checking that ships that call at U.S. ports are safe and nonpolluting, and performing its myriad other routine duties.

In part to take some pressure off the Coast Guard, U.S. Customs, now renamed Customs and Border Protection and also enfolded into the Department of Homeland Security, pushed the country's borders back. Beginning on February 2, 2003, a Container Security Initiative (CSI) went into effect that required shipping lines to submit cargo manifests electronically for all vessels bound for the United States or Puerto Rico twenty-four hours before the boxes were loaded at their port of origin. In turn, exporters had to get their information to liner companies at least twenty-four hours before that, and in specific terms. Cargo could no longer be labeled FAK or STC, or carry some other generalized description; the names, addresses, and other contact information of both the shipper and the consignee now had to be exact; numbers and quantities in each shipment had to be broken down to the lowest possible level: for instance, 300 cases of perfume. The goal was to identify high-risk containers and prescreen them before they got anywhere near U.S. ports. By spring 2003 eighteen of the largest foreign ports had signed on to CSI, and the initiative was operational in ten, including Montreal, Halifax, Vancouver, Rotterdam, and Singapore.

In tandem with CSI, which requires compliance, officials developed a voluntary program called Customs-Trade Partnership Against Terrorism (C-TPAT). Importers and carriers (rail and air, as well as sea) must apply to participate in this government-business initiative, agree to conduct a comprehensive self-assessment of their supply chain's security, and then enhance it using guidelines formulated by customs and the trade community. As of mid-2003, some 3,600 companies, including P&O Nedlloyd, had signed on, lured in part by promised benefits such as a reduced number of port inspections if they met the higher security standards the partnership had instituted.

On March 20, 2003, Stephen Flynn, testifying on the fragile state of container security before the U.S. Senate Governmental Affairs Committee, commended the impulses behind both CSI and C-TPAT but warned that enforcement was woefully lacking. A retired Coast Guard commander, Flynn had been project director of an independent task force sponsored by the Council on Foreign Relations that six months earlier had released a report titled "America Still Unprepared—America Still in Danger." Not surprisingly, it had nothing reassuring to say about port security in the United States, and now Flynn was telling the committee that to date there was "nearly a complete absence" of customs personnel to monitor compliance by

C-TPAT participants and that only twenty inspectors had been assigned overseas to support CSI when what was required "was the equivalent of a diplomatic service."

Nor was weak enforcement the only problem. For large liner companies, like P&O Nedlloyd, CSI was something of a headache, but their highly computerized operations could handle it—*if* their customers supplied the data on time. Yet hundreds of small manufacturers did not have the sophisticated information technology required to generate the rigorous manifests customs now demanded, and many of them—especially those in China's Pearl River Delta region and elsewhere in East Asia—were long used to rushing shipments to the docks at the last minute, often with slapdash paperwork. The Container Security Initiative also touched off squabbling in Europe, over customs' decision initially to seek cooperation from individual countries—France, Germany, Belgium, and the Netherlands among them—instead of pursuing its antiterrorism effort through the European Union. Customs argued that it needed to get the program up and running as soon as possible in huge ports like Rotterdam, which in 2001 processed some 6 million TEUs. European ports not yet included in the CSI operation complained that it gave Rotterdam and other big ports a leg up, making them more attractive to shippers and liner companies because boxes passing through the favored ports were more likely to clear customs quickly once they arrived in the United States.

The Container Security Initiative and C-TPAT depend on not only the recruitment and training of hundreds more inspectors to work with their foreign counterparts at ports worldwide but on the efficacy of the technology they utilize. A variety of mobile X-ray machines that are an improvement on VACIS have come into use, and inspectors now employ hand-held radiation detectors and vapor tracers for sniffing out explosives. There are also proposals to replace the primitive, tamper-prone strip-and-bolt seals on container doors with electronic seals that, using GPS, would permit continuous monitoring of a box from its departure in Dongguan city to its arrival in Iowa City. Such monitoring might well guarantee the integrity of the container once it was en route but could not ensure that a lethal weapon had not been placed in it before it began its journey. Techno-fixes are never foolproof and are almost always expensive. The truck-mounted VACIS system costs $1.3 million each; a newly developed radiation-detection portal through which container-bearing trucks will pass, like passengers at an airport metal sensor, comes for $80,000 a piece. By the spring of 2003, customs had provided its field agents with 6,000 radiation detectors and was planning to buy 15,000 more, at $1,400 each.

Washington paid considerable lip service to the need for more and better technology, and for more inspectors at both foreign and domestic ports; but like their constituents, politicians spend far more time in airports and aloft than they do at container terminals and on box boats. Once Congress had committed $8 billion to airport security and the hiring of thousands of federal employees to screen passengers, it was in no mood to come anywhere near that amount for port security, even though a radiological, biological, or chemical weapon secreted in a container could take far more lives than did the suicide planes at the World Trade Center and Pentagon, and could paralyze world commerce as well. In his testimony before the Senate committee, Stephen Flynn warned that "should a container be used as a 'poor man's missile,' the shipment of all containerized cargo into our ports and across our borders would be halted. As a consequence, a modest investment by a terrorist could yield billions of dollars in losses to the U.S. economy."

In April 2003, Senator Ernest Hollings, coauthor of the Maritime Transportation Security Act, attempted to add $1 billion for port security to the Bush administration's request for almost $80 billion to fight the war in Iraq. A majority of his Senate colleagues rejected the proposal. Nor were importers and exporters, terminal operators and insurers any more enthusiastic about bearing the increased costs.

And liner companies remained squeezed by overcapacity, depressed freight rates, and a world economy weakened not only by the attacks of 9/11 and the wars and reconstruction efforts in Afghanistan and Iraq but by the sudden outbreak in China in 2003 of severe acute respiratory syndrome (SARS). P&O Nedlloyd had made a profit of $102 million in 2001, but by the end of 2002 was reporting an operating loss of $206 million in an industry whose prospects were anything but bright for the immediate future.

A year after I left the *Colombo Bay,* I received an email from Peter Davies saying that the company was asking for the voluntary retirements of 135 officers in all ranks, including twenty-one chief engineers and nineteen masters. "After much deliberation and checking of pensions earned," he wrote, "I decided to take the money and 'retire' early." Others, like James Blewman, who had showed me the company's operation in Colombo with such enthusiasm, were simply laid off—made redundant, as the British put it. Shakeel Azim, with whom I spent so many pleasant afternoons on the bridge learning about modern seafaring and listening to the BBC, still had his job as of this writing but the United States summarily yanked his visa after 9/11. This kind and gentle sailor, a British citizen, was instantly suspect because he is a Muslim who grew up in Pakistan. Like the thousands of other foreign sailors who spend long, lonely months at sea delivering the good life to American consumers, he was arbitrarily profiled and thus denied even the few hours ashore occasionally available to him at U.S. ports. Only after almost two years was his visa restored.

■ ■ ■

I have written this epilogue with mixed emotions. I felt obligated to give some sense of how the events of September 11 have affected world commerce in general and container ships and their seamen in particular. But for all the shadows of terrorism that now darken the sea, my five weeks aboard the *Colombo Bay* were mostly sunny, the adventure always compelling, the good fellowship constant. It was a voyage that does not call for a somber ending and shall not have one.

In the summer of 2003, Diane and I visited Peter and Elizabeth at their home in Whitby, the seaside town south of Newcastle where Captain James Cook grew up and learned the seafaring skills that took him to the South Seas in the eighteenth century. I had warned Diane that Peter might prove a gloomy host. He had told me in recent emails that retiring had been, as Elizabeth had warned, a mistake, that after four decades at sea he longed for another command; he had applied to several liner companies, but none seemed interested in hiring a fifty-eight-year-old master. When he came to fetch us in Newcastle, though, he was in high good humor, and he grew more and more expansive as we drove through the Yorkshire countryside toward Whitby. After about a half hour, he announced that only the day before he had been hired by Leonhardt and Blumberg, a German company, and in just a few weeks would be taking over a container ship called the *Direct Jabiru*, on a run from the West Coast of the United States to Australia and back. He was beaming, a man overboard who had just been pulled back on deck.

"How big is she?" I asked. "I have no idea," he replied, in a voice that suggested it wouldn't matter if the *Direct Jabiru* were no larger than the owl and the pussycat's pea green boat.

ACKNOWLEDGMENTS

Jeremy Nixon launched this book—by infecting me with tales of his seafaring days, by introducing me to the world and importance of container shipping, and by arranging my passage on the *Colombo Bay*. I thank him for setting me on this course, and for taking time from his bruising schedule as a senior vice president at P&O Nedlloyd to read the entire manuscript, and for making corrections and suggestions that more than once saved me from seeming even more of a landlubber than I am. His shoreside colleagues at the company were at every turn as generous as he was with their help, among them Peter Stone in Hong Kong, Yap Han Liang in Singapore, James Blewman in Colombo, and Alan Hicks, Tom Ericsson, Harold Cavagnaro, Christopher O'B. Harding, Ray Venturino, and Al Gebhardt Jr. in the New Jersey office. I thank them all.

I cannot imagine having sailed with a better master than Peter Davies. Despite the demands of commanding the *Colombo Bay,* he always made time to answer my questions, and did so with unfailing patience and good humor. I thank him and his wife, Elizabeth, for being such genial hosts and companions, and especially for the laughter they prompted nightly in the dining room and lounge. Like Peter, the ship's other hands welcomed me as a mate from the moment I came aboard in Hong Kong, and over five weeks also put up with my waves of queries with great tolerance. Most of them are named in the preceding pages; I thank them for their cooperation and friendship, and for the sympathy they showed to a shaken New York at sea during those first days after September 11.

Arthur Donovan, professor emeritus of maritime history at the U.S. Merchant Marine Academy and coauthor (with Andrew Gibson) of *The Abandoned Ocean,* provided consistently wise counsel. He talked with me at some length about the collapse of U.S. merchant shipping in the second half of the twentieth century, helped me clarify my murky understanding of hydrostatics, and caught several mistakes after reading the entire book in galleys. Aaron Asher also read the galleys and his editor's eye spotted a number of other errors. Benjamin Barber read the passage on globalization and suggested modifications that, for the most part, I incorporated. I am grateful to all three for their insights and support.

As propellers are to ships, librarians are to authors; we would be becalmed without them. The reference staff at Columbia University's Butler Library came to my assistance again and again during the two years I worked on this book, as did their counterparts at the remarkable Science, Industry and Business Library of the New York Public Library. Donald Gill, of the Bland Memorial Library at the U.S. Merchant Marine Academy in Kings Point, New York, also threw me a lifeline on more than one occasion. I salute and thank them all.

Of the books listed in the bibliography, I am particularly indebted to *The Oxford Companion to Ships and the Sea,* edited by Peter Kemp, and to *Poor Jack: The Perilous History of the Merchant Seaman,* by Ronald Hope. They provided a vivid picture of the maritime world, past and present, one illuminated daily by the literary mastery of my singular cabinmates, Herman Melville and Joseph Conrad.

Members of the U.S. Coast Guard at Activities New York on Staten Island were unfailingly responsive when I came seeking help, among them Lt. Cmdr. Christopher Nichols, Lt. Rudolph Russo, Lt.

Kenneth Moser, Petty Officer 2nd Class James Pond, Chief Brandon Brewer, and Petty Officer Frank Bari. Joe Duddy and Dr. Carlos Comperatore, of the Coast Guard's Research and Development Center in Groton, Connecticut, also came to my aid. For explaining the workings of the Port Newark Container Terminal, I am grateful to its president, Joe Assante. I thank Mario Zucchi and Stefano Negrini for giving me a ride on the Fantuzzi gantry there, and bow to James Brown, Hayward Davis, and Catfish Lewis for cheering me on when I was in the driver's seat. At KB Toys, John Reilly, Andrea Pignatelli, Michael Strubing, Heather Freeman, and Bob Alarie stepped me through the process that brought the company's military action figures from China to the United States aboard the *Colombo Bay*.

Others who came to my aid in various important ways were Nicholas Baines, Steven Bernstein, David Brickman, Robert Brown, Ed Burtynsky, Michael Bush, Simon Camilleri, Charles Edwards, Eugene Drucker, Erin Fuchs, Rob Howard, Leslie Jones, Tom Keating, Erich Kranz, Dick Laing, Tony McComb, Jenny McPhee, Richard Noble, Robert Pape, Irene Patner, Gustav Peebles, David Robinson, Louise Robinson, John Rosenthal, Petros Sabatacakis, Mariam Said, Will Stoker, Baylis Thomas, Eric Tirschwell, Vladimir Tocaj, Tissa Wickramasinghe, Charles Williams, and Nancy Williams. Thanks, too, to my young friend Warren Shingleton, who when I finished this book rewarded me with a model of the *Colombo Bay*.

Lynn Nesbit, my agent, and Alice Mayhew, my editor at Simon & Schuster, saw the possibilities in my initial proposal and buoyed me with their support from the start. This is the second book of mine Alice has edited and I am grateful once again for her belief in my work and for her encouragement and enthusiasm. Her sharp-eyed colleague, Isolde Sauer, oversaw the copy editing and proofreading by Susan Brown and Betty Harris; their close attention to detail made this a better book. Roger Labrie shepherded the manuscript toward publication with patience and consummate skill and was always a pleasure to work with, as were Victoria Meyer and Elizabeth Hayes in the Simon & Schuster publicity department. I thank them all for their care.

My wife, Diane, and daughter, Amanda, literally rescued this project. I was inclined to abandon it in the days after September 11, to jump ship in Singapore, and fly home. Their loving emails and phone calls urged me not to be so faint-hearted. I am a lucky man to have the support of two such wise and strong women, and I hug them again for urging me to sailor on.

NOTES

PROLOGUE

1   "there is *nothing*": Grahame, *Wind in the Willows,* p. 7.

2   "unhooped oceans": Melville, *Moby-Dick,* p. 216.

2   cherish the ocean: Ibid., p. 3.

3   For the scope of P&O Nedlloyd's container ship operation see the company's website, www.ponl.com.

4   more than 7 million: *Containerisation International Yearbook 2003* (London: Informa UK Ltd), p. 6.

4   Some 90 percent: *The Economist,* Apr. 6–12, 2002, p. 59.

5   "took waves over her decks": Junger, *The Perfect Storm,* pp. 114–15.

8   Ishmael also gave no quarter: Melville, *Moby-Dick,* p. 3.

CHAPTER ONE

12   "Merchant ships": Melville, *Moby-Dick,* p. 70.

13   "Dost know nothing": Ibid., p. 79.

13   He writes of: Conrad, *A Personal Record* and *The Mirror of the Sea,* p. 165.

13   "The machinery": Ibid., p. 196.

15   comprehensive pilot guide: Kemp, *Oxford Companion to Ships and the Sea,* p. 642.

16   6,000 containers a day: *The New York Times,* Jan. 26, 2003.

16    $100 billion: U.S. Census Bureau.

16   20 percent: *The New York Times,* September 3, 2003.

16   bridge-tunnel: *The New York Times,* Jan. 26, 2003.

23   "pure air of the forecastle deck": Melville, *Moby-Dick,* p. 7.

CHAPTER TWO

32   "It struck me": *American Shipper,* July 2001, p. 22.

32   This concept: De la Pedraja, *Dictionary of the U.S. Merchant Marine,*
      pp. 149–52.

33   "an utter folly": Gibson and Donovan, *Abandoned Ocean,* p. 210.

34   The following year: See year 1967 at www.horizon-lines.com/his-
      tory.asp#1970.

34   "It just won't work": Transcript of interview with Paul Richardson,
      Containerization Oral History Collection 1995–1998, Lemelson
      Center for the Study of Invention and Innovation, Archives Center,
      National Museum of American History, Washington, D.C.

34    $160 million in stock: *American Shipper,* July 2001, p. 24.

34   First Colony Farms: Ibid.

34   4,400 TEUs: *Forbes,* Mar. 23, 1987.

35   just over 10,000: *The Nation,* Oct. 28, 2002, p. 24.

35   330 million TEUs: UNCTAD, *Review of Maritime Transport, 2002,*
      p. 69.

35   1 trillion less: *The Economist,* Apr. 6–12, 2002, p. 59.

35   "Wal-Marts possible": *American Shipping,* July 2001, p. 26.

39   Venetian maritime statutes: *Encyclopaedia Britannica,* 15th ed.,
      vol. 28, p. 788.

39   Captain Bildad offers him: Melville, *Moby-Dick,* p. 86.

40   14,000 reefers: *Containerisation International,* Nov. 2001, p. 23.

40   "clearly underperformed the S&P 500 index:" Ibid., Dec. 2001, p. 45.

40   26 percent: *Journal of Economic Issues,* vol. 34, no. 4 (Dec. 2000),
      p. 933.

40   an estimated 83 percent: *Containerisation International,* Nov. 2001, p. 63.

41    $75 million each: Ibid., Dec. 2001, p. 36.

41   Designs now exist: Ibid., Feb. 2002, pp. 52–53.

42   Parthenope, Ligeia, and Leucosia: Kemp, *Oxford Companion to Ships and the Sea,* p. 805.

CHAPTER THREE

43   flew over more tonnage: Kemp, *Oxford Companion to Ships and the Sea,* p. 695.

48   "My whole being": Conrad, *A Personal Record* and *The Mirror of the Sea,* p. 75.

49   "beware of fornication": Melville, *Moby-Dick,* p. 115.

49   one-third of the "sex workers": *The New York Times,* Dec. 8, 2001.

56   manning capital: http://www.dole.gov.ph/news/pressreleases2001/october2001/385.htm; www.ufs.ph/tinig/sepoct02.

56   twelve times the average income: *The New York Times,* Apr. 4, 2003.

57   sixty-five-year-old company: www.cfsharp.com/shipping.

60   By the middle of 2003: For international shipping statistics, see the statistics link at the U.S. Maritime Administration's website, www.marad.dot.gov.

60   fake seafaring licenses: *The Sunday Times* (London), March 12, 2001.

60   FOC dodge: *Ships, Slaves and Competition,* report of the International Commission on Shipping (ICONS), 2001, p. 248.

60   "poverty that drives men": Hope, *Poor Jack,* pp. 351–52.

61   266-page report: *Ships, Slaves and Competition,* p. 57.

62   represent only a fraction: Flags of convenience link at International Transport Workers' Federation website, www.itf.org.uk.

62   The 50 percent: Ibid.

62   Panama topped the list: *Lloyd's Shipping and Nautical Yearbook 2000.* London: LLP Professional Publishing, p. 118.

62   The day before: http://www.ndtcabin.com/articles/flare/flare7.php:
       www.geocities.com/~sandusky99/98jan17.htm.

63   "One of our men": Hope, *Poor Jack,* pp. 203–4.

64   "The death rate": Ibid., p. 109.

64   "Drugs and spices": Ibid., p. 150.

65   some 7,000 persons: ICONS Report, p. 255.

66   National Research Council: *International Herald Tribune,* May 24,
       2002.

CHAPTER FOUR

69   Tankers, container ships: Lloyd's Maritime Information Services,
       Vessel Movements, as reported by the U.S. Department of Trans-
       portation at www.marad.dot.gov/Marad_Statistics/World-Port-Calls-
       00.htm.

72   "Right now no one": *International Herald Tribune,* Sept. 21, 2001.

73   the sailing ship *Tilkhurst:* Karl, *Joseph Conrad,* p. 223.

74   What is best here: Amnesty International Report 2002, Singapore.

74   at least thirteen Singaporeans arrested: *The New York Times,* Jan.
       14, 2002.

74   more than 17 million TEUs: *Containerisation International Year-
       book 2003,* p. 9.

75   At Global Gateway South: *The Wall Street Journal,* July 10, 2001.

75   these ports handled: *The New York Times,* Sept. 28, 2002.

75   to almost 30 million TEUs: *Containerisation International,* Apr.
       2002, p. 37.

76   up to 120,000 a year: Ibid., p. 39.

76   upward of $100,000: *The New York Times,* Nov. 25, 2002.

76   By October 3: Ibid., Oct. 5, 2002.

76   On October 8: Ibid., Oct. 9, 2002.

77   "We now have a new dock boss": Ibid.

77   27 percent below normal: Ibid., Oct. 24, 2002.

78   six-year contract: Ibid., Nov. 25, 2002.

80   "bowed to the blast": Melville, *Moby-Dick*, p. 255.

80   Crossing the Line rite: A. B. Campbell, *Customs and Traditions in the Royal Navy* (Aldershot: Gale & Polden, 1956), p. 38, as cited in "Crossing the Line: Tradition, Ceremony, Initiation," an unpublished research paper by C. Swartz.

80   "On Tuesday, 11th May": Hope, *Poor Jack,* pp. 52–53.

83   "Ships do want humoring": Conrad, *A Personal Record* and *The Mirror of the Sea,* p. 178.

83   shipped out on the *Highland Forest:* Karl, *Joseph Conrad,* p. 237.

83   "Neither before nor since": Conrad, *A Personal Record* and *The Mirror of the Sea,* pp. 180–81.

84   "poetic justice": Ibid., p. 181.

84   "at an Eastern port": Conrad, *Lord Jim,* p. 51.

89   "with clatter and hurry": Conrad, *A Personal Record* and *The Mirror of the Sea,* pp. 174–75.

CHAPTER FIVE

92   "rascally Asiatics": Melville, *Moby-Dick,* p. 418.

92   "The shores of the straits": Ibid., pp. 415–16.

93   In the mid-nineteenth century: Gottschalk and Flanagan, *Jolly Roger,* p. 2.

93   to a peak of more than 460: *The Economist,* July 21, 2001, p. 32.

94   *Matsumi Maru No. 7:* www.iccwbo.org/home/news_archives/2002/ excerpt_%20one.asp.

95   ten times the number: *Containerisation International,* March 2001, p. 3.

95   six warships: International Chamber of Commerce report, Feb. 12, 2002, www.iccwbo.org/home/news_archives/2002/piracy.asp.

95   Sir Peter Blake: *The New York Times,* Dec. 7–8, 2001; Dec. 28, 2002.

96   "Chinese police claimed": *The Economist,* Dec. 18, 1999, p. 87.

97   "the *Tenyu* case involved": *The Washington Post,* July 5, 1999.

97   using forged documents: *The Economist,* Dec. 18, 1999, p. 87; *Newsweek,* July 5, 1999, p. 46.

97     $45 million in cargo: *The Straits Times,* June 27, 2001.

97   tanker *Global Mars: Lloyd's List,* March, 13–14, 2000; see also www.geocities.com/glen_crippen/00-04/PIR-hijacked_ship.html.

99   tanker *Petchem:* www.maritimesecurity.org/asa2000.htm.

99   In late August: www.iccwbo.org/home/news_archives/2002/excerpt_ trends.asp; www.geocities.com/glen_crippen/01-09/PIR-acehattack. html.

100   Sir Francis Drake: Kemp, *Oxford Companion to Ships and the Sea,* pp. 263, 670.

101   maximum load: Kendall, p. 163.

102   Some two-thirds of . . . LNG trade: *Journal of Commerce,* June 3, 2002.

103   French supertanker *Limburg:* Associated Press, Oct. 8, 9, 10, 2002.

104   shock wire: Secure-Ship White Paper, at www.secure-marine.com.

105   some $1 billion was lost: *Jane's Intelligence Review,* Aug. 2002, p. 50.

105   more than $6.2 trillion: World Trade Organization news release, Oct. 19, 2001, www.wto.org/english/news_e/pres01_e/pr249_e.htm.

112   Beckingham Palace: *The New York Times,* Nov. 4, 2002.

114   In late July: *The Guardian,* July 24, 2001; BBC News, July 21, 2001.

115   electronic charts: Kendall, p. 381.

119   Poseidon himself dallies: Summers, *Gay and Lesbian Literary Heritage,* "Myth," p. 509.

119   "in the most loving": Melville, *Moby-Dick,* p. 28.

119   "a cosy, loving pair": Ibid., pp. 57–58.

119   "musky meadow": Ibid., p. 455.

119   "Squeeze!": Ibid., p. 456.

119   may have been gay: Summers, *Gay and Lesbian Literary Heritage,* "Herman Melville," p. 475.

120   "like pears closely packed": Melville, *White-Jacket,* pp. 375–76.

120   "Handsome Sailor": Melville, *Billy Budd,* p. 302.

120   "the mate and his boy": Hope, *Poor Jack,* p. 142.

121   the poet Hart Crane: Summers, *Gay and Lesbian Literary Heritage,*
       p. 178.

CHAPTER SIX

126   totaled 188: For statistics on suicide bombings, see Robert A. Pape,
       "The Strategic Logic of Suicide Terrorism," *American Political Sci-
       ence Review* (August 2003, vol. 97, no. 3), pp. 1–19.

127   "arbitrary arrest": Amnesty International Report 2002, Sri Lanka.

127   Kumar Ponnambalam: Human Rights Watch Report 2001, Sri
       Lanka.

129   truck bomb: "Sri Lanka: How Ethnic Tension Grew," BBC News re-
       port, Jan 28, 1998.

129   almost 300: World Trade Center Association Internet site, iserve.
       wtca.org/awtc/about.html.

129   "that swoon in the air": As quoted in Wright, Gillian, *Odyssey Guide
       to Sri Lanka* (Hong Kong: The Guidebook Company Ltd.), p. 68.

132   "The war has become an institution": *The New York Times,* Aug. 17,
       2001.

CHAPTER SEVEN

139   increased 12 percent: *The Economist,* Apr. 6, 2002, p. 62.

142   "can't live everlastingly": Conrad, *Youth/Heart of Darkness/The End
       of the Tether,* pp. 98–99.

142   "It is a curious fact": Hope, *Poor Jack,* pp. 286–87.

143   "The Captain," he wrote: Ibid., p. 287.

146   "only to see the judge": *The New York Times,* Dec. 15, 2002.

148   chromated copper arsenic: "Face the Facts," BBC Radio 4, July 19,
       2002; see also "Situation Report No. 1: Djibouti, Toxic Pollution,"
       UN Office for the Co-ordination of Humanitarian Affairs, Mar. 8,
       2002.

149 *Hanjin Pennsylvania:* For a brief account and photos of the fire, see www.geocities.com/uksteve.geo/form1.html; also see hazworld.com news accounts dated Nov. 18 and 22, 2002, at www.existec.com/index.asp?np=news_26 newstop and 27 newstop.

150 "I seemed somehow": Conrad, *Youth/Heart of Darkness/The End of the Tether,* p. 26; also, Karl, *Joseph Conrad,* pp. 207 ff.

151 "smoke kept coming": Ibid., p. 23.

155 "sentimental sap": Hart, Lorenz, "You Took Advantage of Me" (1928), in *The Complete Lyrics of Lorenz Hart, Expanded Edition,* Dorothy Hart and Robert Kimball, eds. (New York: Da Capo, 1995), p. 118.

155 *Carnatic:* For this account I am indebted to Ned Middleton; see touregypt.net/vdc/Carnatic.htm.

157 *Karine A:* The New York Times, Jan. 12, 2002.

CHAPTER EIGHT

159 "Your journalist": Conrad, *A Personal Record* and *The Mirror of the Sea,* pp. 145–46.

163 total of 267 million tons: *Encyclopaedia Britannica,* 15th ed., vol. 17, p. 767.

163 totaling 374 million tons: *Shipping Statistics Yearbook 2001* (Bremen: Institute of Shipping Economics and Logistics), p. 439.

163 some $2 billion annually: *The Financial Times,* March 9, 2001.

163 $250,000 per transit: Email from Jeremy Nixon, Feb. 19, 2003.

166 Mubarak-Peace Bridge: See www.sis.gov.eg/suez/suez12.htm.

167 half . . . are box boats: *Shipping Statistics Yearbook 2001,* p. 439.

169 more than 300 million people: *The New York Times Magazine,* Aug. 18, 2002, p. 30.

169 foreign aid: *The New York Times,* Nov. 1, 2001.

171 "It has sheltered the infancy": Conrad, *A Personal Record* and *The Mirror of the Sea,* p. 260.

171   an inch or so: Kemp, *Oxford Companion to Ships and the Sea*, p. 536.

171   "sacked the city": Fagles, *Odyssey*, p. 212.

172   by one report: Kemp, *Oxford Companion to Ships and the Sea*, p. 58.

172   "has not stained": Conrad, *A Personal Record* and *The Mirror of the Sea*, p. 261.

174   "is being in a jail": James Boswell, *Life of Samuel Johnson* (London: Oxford University Press, 1998), p. 247.

CHAPTER NINE

178   "a fragment detached": Conrad, *The Nigger of the "Narcissus,"* p. 21.

179   Admiral Robert Fitzroy: Kemp, *Oxford Companion to Ships and the Sea*, p. 546.

180   "what trances of torments": Melville, *Moby-Dick*, p. 219.

182   represented 36 percent: *Lloyd's Register of Shipping*, World Fleet Statistics, cited at www.coltoncompany.com/shipping/statistics/wld-flt.htm.

182   remained below 6,000: Ibid.

184   "It would be difficult": Gibson and Donovan, *Abandoned Ocean*, pp. 294–95.

185   no island existed there: Kemp, *Oxford Companion to Ships and the Sea*, pp. 46–47.

187   *gum shan: The Christian Science Monitor,* Jan. 25, 2001.

187   more than 1,200 people: *Containerisation International,* Apr. 2002, p. 54.

188   The discovery of stowaways aboard the *Pretty River, Maple River,* and *Cape May* was widely reported; see, e.g., *Seattle Post-Intelligencer,* Jan. 11–12, 2000, and July 11, 2001; *The New York Times,* Jan. 4, 2000, and *Los Angeles Times,* April 3–4, 2001.

189   "the fifty-six men and four women": The deaths of the 58 Chinese refugees discovered in the container at Dover were widely covered; see, e.g., *The Guardian,* April 6–7, 2001.

190   By one estimate, 100,000 people: *Containerisation International,* Apr. 2002, p. 54.

190    $4 billion a year enterprise: Report from the International Chamber of Commerce Commercial Crime Services, July 16, 2001; see www.iccwbo.org/ccs/news_archives/2001/smugglingrise.asp.

191   Eight had suffocated: *The Irish Times,* Dec. 10, 2001; *The New York Times,* Dec. 9–10, 2001.

192   In another case: *Containerisation International,* Apr. 2002, p. 54.

192   "reasonable and practical": *Containerisation International,* Apr. 2002 pp. 54 ff.

194   headed for Christmas Island: *The Sydney Morning Herald,* Aug. 28, 2001.

194   "under duress": *The New York Times,* Aug. 30, 2001.

194   telephone poll: *The Guardian,* Aug. 29, 2001.

194   "under the full protection": Ibid.

195   "This is not the way": Associated Press, Sept. 3, 2001.

195   easily won reelection: BBC World Service analysis of asylum seekers in Australia, Mar. 22, 2002.

195   Captain Rinnan also received: *New Zealand Herald,* Oct. 18, 2002.

196   fireworks shot skyward: *The Age* (Australia), Sept. 4, 2001.

197   Nobody knew how many: *Granta,* Winter 2002, pp. 145–46.

197   other correspondents: see, e.g., Carlotta Gall, *The New York Times,* Dec. 11, 2001.

197   U.S. payroll for a year: *The Guardian,* Sept. 14, 2002.

197   Pentagon insisted: *The New York Times,* Aug. 29, 2002.

198   "He thought it was the only way": *The New Yorker,* Mar. 10, 2003, p. 57.

199   "each cell is only slightly smaller": *The New York Review of Books,* Nov. 7, 2002, p. 64.

199   almost twice as many: *The New York Times,* Aug. 8, 2001.

199   "material du jour": *The New York Times,* July 17, 2003.

200   more than 4,000: For an account of container conversion by the

South African company Creative Solutions, see www.tve.org/ho/ doc.cfm?aid=343&lang=English.

200   *Fear Factor:* NBC; viewed by author.

201   "No small number": Melville, *Moby-Dick,* p. 131.

203   Subsequent reports proved: *Smithsonian,* July 2001, pp. 36–47; see also the American Geophysical Union, at www.agu.org/sci_soc/ ducks.html.

204   "deserve no better": *The New Yorker,* Apr. 8, 2002, p. 32.

205   Most float down from Disko Bay: Kemp, *Oxford Companion to Ships and the Sea,* p. 413; see also www.wordplay.com/tourism/icebergs.

205   "for a true expression": Conrad, *A Personal Record* and *The Mirror of the Sea,* Conrad, p. 201.

207   impair a seaman's vigilance: *Crew Fatigue and Performance on U.S. Coast Guard Cutters, Final Report,* October 1998 (Groton, Conn.: U.S. Coast Guard Research and Development Center), pp. 27–31.

CHAPTER TEN

210   feisty sister Iris: www.disasterrelief.org./Disasters/011206storm- wrapup;www.global-travel.co.uk/wavedancer.htm;www.sptimes. com/news/weather/george/shtml.

210   "WE HAVE ALREADY LOST": *The Globe and Mail* (Toronto), Oct. 15, 2001.

211   19,000 body parts: *The New Yorker,* May 20, 2002, p. 71.

212   Tropical Storm Allison: www.disasterrelief.org/Disasters/011206- stormwrapup.

213   "I am, perhaps, unduly sensitive": Conrad, *A Personal Record* and *The Mirror of the Sea,* p. 162.

216   worst single-ship financial setback: *Marine Digest and Transporta- tion News,* Dec. 1998, p. 10.

216   not the case for 167 other ships: *Shipping Statistics Yearbook 2001* (Bremen: Institute of Shipping Economics and Logistics), p. 53.

216   comparing their heads: Melville, *Moby-Dick,* pp. 359–67.

217   50 percent of their known deaths:www.rightwhale.noaa.gov/right_
whale/about_whale.html.

EPILOGUE

226   6 million of the boxes: Fact Sheet: U.S. Customs Service's Container
Security Initiative, Feb. 22, 2002.

227   an industrial stove: *The New York Times,* Mar. 20, 2003.

229   to $6.2 billion: U.S. Coast Guard.

230   eighteen of the largest foreign ports: U.S. Customs and Border Protection news release, Apr. 2, 2003.

230   "nearly a complete absence": "The Fragile State of Container Security," testimony by Stephen E. Flynn before the U.S. Senate Governmental Affairs Committee, Mar. 20, 2003.

231   some 6 million TEUs: UNCTAD, *Review of Maritime Transport,
2002,* p. 72.

231   European ports . . . complained: *The New York Times,* Nov. 6, 2002,
and Jan. 28, 2003.

232   The truck-mounted VACIS system: *The New York Times,* Mar. 20,
2003.

232   "Should a container be used": "The Fragile State of Container Security."

232   rejected the proposal: *The Wall Street Journal,* Apr. 21, 2003.

233   Prospects for the immediate future: *Containerisation International,*
Apr. 2003, p. 22.

BIBLIOGRAPHY

Branch, Alan E. *Elements of Shipping,* 7th ed. London: Chapman & Hall, 1996.

Buckley, James J., and Lane C. Kendall. *The Business of Shipping,* 7th ed. Centreville, Md.: Cornell Maritime Press, 2001.

Conrad, Joseph. *Lord Jim.* New York: Penguin Books, 1989.

————. *The Nigger of the "Narcissus."* New York: Penguin Books, 1989.

————. *A Personal Record* and *The Mirror of the Sea.* New York: Penguin Books, 1998.

————. *Youth/Heart of Darkness/The End of the Tether.* New York: Penguin Books, 1995.

Cordingly, David. *Under the Black Flag: The Romance and the Reality of Life Among the Pirates.* New York: Random House, 1995.

De la Pedraja, René. *A Historical Dictionary of the U.S. Merchant Marine and Shipping Industry Since the Introduction of Steam.* Westport, Conn.: Greenwood Press, 1994.

————. *The Rise and Decline of U.S. Merchant Shipping in the Twentieth Century.* New York: Twayne Publishers, 1992.

Fagles, Robert, trans. *The Odyssey.* New York: Penguin Books, 1996.

Gibson, Andrew, and Arthur Donovan. *The Abandoned Ocean: A History of United States Maritime Policy.* Columbia, S.C.: University of South Carolina Press, 2001.

Gottschalk, J. A., and B. P. Flanagan. *Jolly Roger with an Uzi: The Rise and Threat of Modern Piracy.* Annapolis, Md.: Naval Institute Press, 2000.

Grahame, Kenneth. *The Wind in the Willows.* New York: Aladdin Paperbacks, 1989.

Haws, Duncan, and Alex A. Hurst. *Maritime History of the World: A Chronological Survey of Maritime Events from 5,000 BC Until the Present Day, Supplemented by Commentaries.* Brighton, U.K.: Teredo Books, 1985.

Hope, Ronald. *Poor Jack: The Perilous History of the Merchant Seaman.* London: Chatham Publishing, 2001.

Junger, Sebastian. *The Perfect Storm.* New York: HarperPerennial, 1999.

Karl, Frederick R. *Joseph Conrad: The Three Lives.* New York: Farrar, Straus & Giroux, 1979.

Kemp, Peter, ed. *The Oxford Companion to Ships and the Sea.* New York: Oxford University Press, 1988.

Melville, Herman. *Moby-Dick, or The Whale.* New York: Penguin Books, 1992.

———. *Billy Budd and Other Stories.* New York: Penguin Books, 1986.

———. *White-Jacket, or The World in a Man-of-War.* In *The Writings of Herman Melville,* vol. 5. Evanston, Ill.: Northwestern University Press, 1970.

Mueller, G. O. W., and F. Adler. *Outlaws of the Ocean.* New York: Hearst Marine Books, 1985.

Muller, Gerhardt. *Intermodal Freight Transportation,* 4th ed. Washington, D.C.: Eno Transportation Foundation, 1999.

Summers, Claude J., ed. *The Gay and Lesbian Literary Heritage: A Reader's Companion to the Writers and Their Works, from Antiquity to the Present.* New York: Henry Holt, 1995.

UNCTAD Secretariat. *Review of Maritime Transport,* 2002. Geneva: United Nations Conference on Trade and Development, 2002.

Woodman, Richard. *The History of the Ship: The Comprehensive Story of Seafaring from the Earliest Times to the Present Day.* New York: Lyons Press, 1997.

INDEX

Abandoned Ocean, The (Gibson and
 Donovan), 183–84
Action in the North Atlantic, 181–82
Activities New York, 227, 228
Afghanistan, 18, 21, 113, 114, 135,
 145, 165, 172, 178, 179, 186–87,
 193–98, 203, 209, 211, 218,
 233
Alarie, Bob, 36
Algiers, 171–72
Al Qaeda, 18, 74, 103, 126, 145, 198,
 203, 207, 219
Al Salamah, 161
American Media, Inc., 203
American President Lines (APL),
 41, 78
"America Still Unprepared—America
 Still in Danger," 230
Amnesty International, 127
Andrea Gail, 5
Annan, Kofi, 195
anthrax, 203, 207, 218
A. P. Moller, 41, 183
Archimedes' Principle, 84
Atlantic Ocean, 178–79, 185
Australia, 192–96
Azim, Shakeel, 13–14, 18–21, 25, 54,
 69, 79, 95, 106–7, 111, 115, 133,

138, 152, 154, 159, 175, 178, 185,
 205, 208, 218, 219, 223, 233
Azores, 178, 186, 201

Ball, Alex, 51
Barbary pirates, 171–72
Barnes, Julian, 204
BBC, 18, 21, 53, 111, 139, 157, 172,
 178, 186, 203, 207, 218, 223,
 233
Beagle, 179
Beaufort scale, 137, 179
Billy Budd (Melville), 120
bin Laden, Osama, 126, 136, 165, 172,
 179, 203, 210, 218
Bisset, Sir James, 143
Blair, Tony, 111, 203, 218
Blake, Sir Peter, 95–96
Blewman, James, 128–36, 233
Bligh, Stephen, 192
BND (Bundesnachrichtendienst), 190
Boag, Danny, 65–66
boiler suits, 24, 38, 54, 55, 147, 223
Bonds, Barry, 9, 136, 172, 177
bribery, 133–34, 170
British India Steam Navigation Co.
 Ltd., 20, 28
British Merchant Service, 38, 43

Brown & Root Services, 198–99
Bush, George W., 76–77, 126, 135, 199, 203, 218, 221
Bush, Mike, 137–38
Bush administration, 146, 198–99, 232

Cam Rahn Bay, 21, 34
Canada, 16, 28, 62, 192, 209
canal pilots, 161, 164–65, 166
Carlson, Richard, 199
Carnatic, 155–56
Castrojas, Federico, 57–59
Central Intelligence Agency (CIA), 165, 198
Cervantes, Miguel de, 171–72
C. F. Sharp, 57, 110
charts, 114–16
Cheney, Dick, 199
Chen Xiakong, 190
China, People's Republic of, 26, 28–29, 169, 231, 233
    exports from, 11, 15–16, 36–37
    manufacturing in, 11, 16, 36, 72
    piracy and hijackings and, 96–97
    smuggling and stowaway operations and, 4, 187–90
China, 215–16
Christmas Island, 194–96
CNN, 6, 8, 135, 141
Coast Guard, U.S., 33, 52, 63, 206–7, 215, 218–19, 220, 223, 227–29
Cold War, 182*n*, 183
Collecte Localisation Satellites, 104
Colombo, 114, 125–36, 138
Colombo Bay:
    adjusting clock of, 18, 205
    anchors of, 23, 159–60
    author's cabin on, 10
    bond locker of, 39, 209
    bridge of, 17, 117–18, 212
    cargo capacity of, 9, 21–22, 36
    decks of, 14, 22–23
    description of, 9–10, 11, 14, 21–22
    engine of, 24–26
    forecastle deck of, 22–23
    fuel consumption of, 11, 26
    holds of, 147
    incinerator of, 26–27
    insects captured on, 106–7
    lifeboats of, 11, 54, 215
    maximum speed of, 18, 26
    meals on, 108–10, 152–55
    officers and crew of, 11, 14
    operating costs of, 26, 40, 78
    poop deck of, 23
    propeller of, 23–24
    route of (maps), 44–45, 168–69
    rudder of, 15, 27
    upper deck of, 22
    video library of, 113
    voyage event recorder of, 117–18, 122*n*
Comino, 174
Congress, U.S., 232
Conrad, Joseph, 13, 20, 48, 65, 73, 83–84, 89, 142, 150–51, 159–60, 172, 178, 184, 205, 212–13
Containerisation International, 40
containers:
    for Dangerous Goods, 148–50
    history of, 31–36
    Hong Kong's daily handling of, 16
    as housing, 199–200
    military and wartime use of, 196–99
    ship stability and, 85–89
    size and types of, 4, 37
    stacking of, 21–22
    unknown contents of, 147–48, 225–26, 229–30
    U.S. yearly handling of, 4, 16

Container Security Initiative (CSI), 229–31

container ships:
  cargo capacity of, 4, 9, 34, 41–42
  globalization role of, 3, 11–12, 35–36
  inspections of, 53, 215, 219–21, 225–32
  number of, 4
  stowaways on, *see* stowaways
  see also merchant vessels and service

Contship Holland, 5

Cooke, Alistair, 111

COSCO, 188

Council on Foreign Relations, 230

Coward, Noël, 155

Crane, Hart, 121

Creative Solutions, 200

CSX Lines, 182

Cuba, 198–99

Customs and Border Protection, U.S., 225–26, 229

Customs-Trade Partnership Against Terrorism (C-TPAT), 230–32

Dangerous Goods (DG) containers, 148–50

Darwin, Sir Charles, 179

Daschle, Tom, 218

David, Romesh, 131

Davies, Elizabeth, 11, 14, 18, 27, 28–29, 48, 50–51, 59, 69, 80, 84, 108–9, 110, 111, 114, 127–28, 135, 153–54, 165, 173, 176, 215, 233–34

Davies, Peter, 14, 15, 16, 17–18, 24, 27–29, 39, 43, 48, 50–51, 53, 54–55, 59, 72, 78, 79–80, 83, 84, 93, 106–11, 112–13, 116*n*,

127–28, 135, 136, 142, 146, 147, 159–62, 170, 173, 176, 177, 186, 214–15, 233–34

Defense Department, U.S., 116, 184, 197, 219

Donovan, Arthur, 183–84

Dostum, Abdul Rashid, 197–98

draft, 41–42, 159, 163

Drake, Sir Francis, 100

Ebbesmeyer, Curtis C., 202–3

Economist, The, 96

Econoships, 34–35

Egypt, 103, 161–70

Emam, Ashraf, 164–65, 166, 170

Europol,190

Fahd, King of Saudi Arabia, 161

Farrell Lines, 183

Fear Factor, 200

Filipinos, 14, 55–56, 185

fires, 150–151

Fitzroy, Sir Robert, 179

flags of convenience (FOC) vessels, 60–63, 106, 182, 227

Flynn, Stephen, 230–31, 232

foreign aid, 169–70

freeboard, 22, 24, 94

gantry cranes, 9, 41, 43, 45–48

Germany, 199–200

Gibraltar, Strait of, 177, 185

Gibson, Andrew, 183–84

Gill, Alexander, 37–39, 51, 53, 70, 80, 107–8, 118, 123, 153, 173

globalization, 3, 11–12, 35–36, 167–70, 225

Global Positioning System (GPS), 116, 231

Good Hope, Cape of, 79–80, 84, 128, 136

Gozo, 174

Grand Alliance, 88

Granta, 197

gravity, center of, 83–85

Great Britain, 19, 20–21, 27, 72, 174, 179, 189

Green, Gordon, 61

Green Friday, 36, 76

"greenies," 214

Guantánamo, 198–99

Guardian, The, 189–90, 197

gum sham, 187, 190

Halifax, 208, 209–11, 230

Halliburton, 198–99

Hanjin Pennsylvania, 149–50, 152

harbor pilots, 15, 43, 125, 161, 164, 170, 175, 209, 220–21

Harding, Luke, 197

hawsepipes, 160–61

Henriksson, Jenny, 211

hijacking, 96–102

Ho Chi Minh City, 21

Holland America Line, 121

Hollings, Ernest, 232

Hollywood Ten, 182*n*

Holmes, J. W., 142–43

Homeland Security Department, U.S., 229

homosexuality, 119–24

Hong Kong, 6, 8, 14–17, 36, 62, 69, 75, 188, 191, 192

Hope, Ronald, 63, 80–81

House Un-American Activities Committee, 182*n*

Howard, John, 194–95

Hudson, 116*n*

Ibarrola, Nemesio, 56–57

icebergs, 205, 211

Ideal X, 33

India, 19, 169

Indonesia, 193–95

Ingraham, W. James, Jr., 202–3

insurance, 131, 139, 163

International Commission on Shipping, 61

International Labor Organization, 63

International Longshore and Warehouse Union (ILWU), 35, 75–78

International Maritime Bureau (IMB), 93, 97, 100, 104, 106

International Maritime Dangerous Goods (IMDG) Code, 148–49

International Maritime Organization, 63, 148, 187, 192

International Transportation Workers' Federation (ITF), 61–62

Iraq, 76, 211, 232–33

Iris, Hurricane, 178, 210

Ishikawajima-Harima Heavy Industries Co., Ltd., 11, 40

Islamic fundamentalists, 19, 74, 99, 102–3, 126

Japan, 11, 12, 29, 60, 97, 102

John Paul II, Pope, 200

Johnson, Samuel, 174, 222

Jones, Bob, 220

Jones, Philip Buton, 156

JTI, 64–65

Junger, Sebastian, 5

Kane, Larry, 200

Karen, Tropical Storm, 208, 209–10, 211–15, 216

KB Toys, 36–37

Keating, Tom, 220–21

Ke Su Di, 189–90

Kingdon, Steve, 24–27, 50, 53–55, 79, 108, 111, 113, 135, 136, 142, 154, 176
Knights of St. John, 174–75
knots, definition of, 114*n*
Koran, 19
Kumaratunga, Chandrika, 127, 135

Laem Chabang, 18, 22, 24, 37, 43, 55, 62, 64, 93, 102
Lawson, John Howard, 182*n*
Le Carré, John, 210–11, 222
lechón barbecue, 152–55
Lelyveld, Joseph, 199
Lesseps, Ferdinand de, 166
Lewington, Andy, 185, 186, 206–7
Liberty Ships, 181–82, 184
Liekens, Veronique, 135, 136
Lindh, John Walker, 198
Lin Zexu, 15
liquified natural gas (LNG), 101–2, 103
Litton Marine Systems, 116
Lloyd's List, 66, 204
Lord Jim (Conrad), 84

McAlees, Frank, 25, 26, 65, 108, 113, 135, 141–42, 153, 154
McGwire, Mark, 136, 172, 177
McLean, Malcom, 32–36, 64, 182, 200, 225
McLean Trucking, 32–33, 34
McVeigh, Timothy, 6, 102
Maersk Sealand, 182–83
Malta, 38, 80, 164, 173–76, 186
Marine Observer, The, 106–7
Marine Society, 64
Marlow, Chris, 25, 65–66, 153
master's tickets, 186

Mead, Richard, 77
medical emergencies, 142–45
Mediterranean Sea, 15, 170–72, 201
Meltsner, Michael, 141
Melville, Herman, 119–20, 184
    see also Moby-Dick
merchant vessels and service, 3, 38
    corporate conferences and, 88–89
    corporate mergers and, 40, 182–83
    economic cycles and, 40
    evolution of, 31
    national origin and, 14, 55–56, 184–85
    salaries in, 56, 57, 59
    separation from home and family in, 20, 58–61, 69–70, 109
    technology and labor issues in, 75–78
    tours of duty in, 56
    U.S. decline in, 181–85
    see also container ships; officers
Mexico, 16
Mirror of the Sea, The (Conrad), 13, 172
Moby-Dick (Melville), 1, 2, 8, 12–13, 23, 39–40, 49, 80, 92–93, 119, 179–80, 201, 216–17
Modelo, Prudencio, 154
Mubarak, Hosni, 166
Mubarak-Peace Bridge, 166
Mullins, Matt, 9–10, 21, 53, 54–55, 69, 80, 88, 89, 106, 113, 133, 142–44, 147, 152, 155, 156, 173, 186
Musharraf, Pervez, 19, 172
Muslims, 14, 19, 20–21, 99, 161, 165
    see also Islamic fundamentalists

Nansen Refugee Award, 195
Narcissus, 178

Nasser, Gamal Abdel, 162
National Oceanic and Atmospheric Administration (NOAA), 217
National Research Council, 66
National Vessel Movement Center, 227
Nauru, 195
nautical miles, length of, 114n
Navy, U.S., 181, 203, 228
NBC, 207
Neptune Orient Lines (NOL), 41
New York, N.Y., 2, 6, 14, 41, 52, 177, 200, 207, 218–24, 226, 228–29
  see also September 11 attacks
New York Times, The, 7, 76, 77, 101n, 132, 199
New Zealand, 195
Nichols, Christopher, 228–29
Nicol, John, 63–64
Nixon, Jeremy, 3, 4, 5, 8, 12, 20, 38, 75, 81–82, 91, 121, 130, 139, 145
Norway, 193, 195

ocean currents, 202–3
officers, 59
  length of tours of, 20
  national origin and, 14, 55, 185, 186
  salaries of, 38
  shore leave of, 25, 38, 177–78
oil, oil spills, 33, 66–67, 157
Oklahoma City bombing, 6, 102
Onassis, Aristotle, 60–61
opium wars, 15–16

Pacific Maritime Association (PMA), 75–78
Pacific Ocean, 9
Pakistan, 19, 20, 172, 178
Panama Canal, 28–29, 34, 41
Panama Maritime Authority, 60
P&O Nedlloyd, 3, 4, 6, 8, 18, 20, 25, 39, 40–41, 43, 51, 56, 57, 63, 78, 82, 86, 95, 105, 109, 113, 116n, 118, 121, 125, 127, 129, 130, 131, 132, 164, 168, 183, 185, 186, 189, 191, 196n, 207, 231, 233
P&O Ports, 132
Pangilinan, Artemio, 109, 153, 219, 222
Pattaya, 48–50
Pearl River Delta, 15–16, 231
Peck, Gregory, 12
Peninsular & Oriental, 155
Pentagon, attack on, 6
Perfect Storm, The (Junger), 5
Periplous of Scylax of Caryanda, The, 15
Personal Record, A (Conrad), 13
Philippines, 56
Pico, 201
piracy, 3, 4, 91–106, 171–72
Piracy Reporting Centre (PRC), 93–94, 104–5
Pocahontas, 200
polliwogs, 80–82
Pond, James, 227–28
pooping, 213–14
Poor Jack (Hope), 63–64, 80–81
Portugal, 171
Poseidon, 26, 119
Powell, Colin, 135

Qarouh'-Kuwaiti, 28–29

radar, 117
Raffles, Thomas Stamford, 69, 72
Reagan administration, 184
Red Sea, 146–47, 155, 156, 164
reefers, 37, 40, 133, 147–48
refugees, 191–98
Richardson, Paul, 34

Rinnan, Captain, 193–96
R. J. Reynolds Tobacco Company, 34, 64, 182
Robis, Ernesto, 152–53
rolling, 83–84, 113–14, 180, 209, 212–14
Rotterdam, 28, 51, 56, 189, 230, 231
Ruddock, Philip, 194

Sadat, Anwar el, 161, 162
Sahara, 182*n*
Sail Ho! (Bisset), 143
Schweitzer, Christopher, 120–21
Sea-Land Service, 34, 35, 64, 182–83
seasickness, 137–38
Seatrain, 32–33
Seattle, Wash., 5, 9, 22, 37, 59, 77–78, 144–45, 188
SecureShip, 104
Senate Governmental Affairs Committee, U.S., 230–31, 232
September 11 attacks, 6–8, 14, 17, 18, 41, 50, 53, 72, 73, 80, 102, 107, 111, 115, 126, 139–41, 161, 165, 187, 211, 220, 223, 226, 227, 232–33
Ship Captain's Medical Guide, 143, 145
SHIPLOC, 104–5
Singapore, 8, 41, 51, 55, 59, 69–75, 78–79, 82, 102–3, 109, 130, 133, 230
slavery, 64, 171–72
smuggling, 4, 52, 187–90
Snakeheads, 4, 187–90
South Africa, Republic of, 200
South China Sea, 17, 23
South Shields, nautical college at, 20, 25, 38, 118
Soviet Union, 165, 184
Spain, 171, 192

Spann, Johnny Michael, 198
Special Forces, U.S., 197–98
Sri Lanka, 113–14, 115, 125–36, 168
Stoker, Will, 77–78
Stone, Peter, 196*n*
storms, 5–6, 78, 137–38, 178–79, 208, 209–10, 211–16
stowaways, 4, 187–92
Suez Canal, 3, 6, 69, 79, 103, 114, 139, 155–67, 170, 172
Suez Canal Authority, 159, 163, 170
supertankers, 9
Sweden, 173

Taipei, 5
Taiwan, 9, 36, 76
Taliban, 18, 172, 193, 196–98
Tamil Tigers, 114, 125–27, 129, 131, 135
Tampa, 193–96
Task Force 150, 145
terrorism, 102–6, 114, 125–27, 129, 131, 135, 141–42, 172, 203–4, 207–8, 210–11, 218–24, 225–33
see also September 11 attacks
TEU (twenty equivalent units), 4
Texas, 173–74
Thailand, 18, 43, 48–50
thatkodai, 126
Titanic, 105, 211
Tolaga Bay, 191
Toronto Globe and Mail, The, 210–11
trades, 16, 167–70, 199
Twain, Mark, 129

United Nations, 162
  Convention on the Law of the Sea, 63
  High Commission of Refugees, 195
United States Lines, 34–35

Urwin, Christian, 177, 180–81, 186, 191, 200–201, 203–6, 209, 212, 213, 218, 219

Valletta, 174–76
Valmonte, Primo, 110
Vehicle and Cargo Inspection System (VACIS), 226–27, 231–32
Ventura, Jesse, 49–50
Verrazano-Narrows Bridge, 2, 52, 220
Vietnam War, 21, 34, 48
Villarta, Johnny, 53
Volendam, 121, 124

Wacker, Perry, 189, 190
Wallenius Wilhelmsen Lines, 196*n*
Walt Disney Studios, 200
War Shipping Administration (WSA), 32–33
Washington Post, The, 97
watch duty, 57, 95, 115, 206–7
weather charts, 178–79

Westall, Simon, 82, 101, 107–8, 117–24, 146, 152, 159–60, 173, 180–81, 185, 201, 206, 214
whales, 3, 40, 216–18
"wharfies," 133, 168
White-Jacket (Melville), 120
Wickramasinghe, Tissa, 132, 133–34
Windsor-Price, Christopher, 107, 123, 138, 144–45, 173–74
Wirayuda, Hasan, 195
World Trade Center Association, 129
World Trade Centers:
  in New York, *see* September 11 attacks
  number of, 129
  in Singapore, 73
  in Sri Lanka, 126, 128–29
World War II, 181–82

Yemen, 146
Ying Guo, 190
Youth (Conrad), 150–51

ABOUT THE AUTHOR

Richard Pollak is a contributing editor of *The Nation,* where he previously served as literary editor and executive editor. He is the author of *The Episode,* a novel, and of *The Creation of Dr. B: A Biography of Bruno Bettelheim.* He lives in New York with his wife, the pianist Diane Walsh. He may be reached through his website: www.richardpollak.com.